Praise for
Strategic Navigation: A Systems Approach to Business Strategy

"Getting strategy right isn't a matter of luck. Bill Dettmer shows us a way to apply logical, systems thinking to develop a living strategy."

—David Kaser
Raytheon Six Sigma Master Expert

"Von Clausewitz once said strategy is an evolution of a central idea through continually changing circumstances. If Von Clausewitz were alive today he would use the tools in this book to identify, track and react to those changing circumstances."

—Dr. William Woehr,
Board member Ikusi S.A.
Retired director—Hewlett Packard
Engineering & Manufacturing Solutions

"The shortcomings of the strategic plans of old are well known. Yet the strategist in us all still strives for a way to develop, communicate, and execute the high-level concepts that drive our enterprises forward. Bill Dettmer has shown how to do this by synthesizing the essence of the various strategy schools, American military planning, and a healthy dose of quick-response tactics from John Boyd. But the key remains Goldratt's 'thinking process' tools to rigorously develop, debug, and execute these strategies in a form that is easily understood and disseminated throughout the whole organization."

—Kelvyn Youngman, PhD
TOC practitioner
New Zealand/Japan

"Strategic Navigation *raises the bar for strategic management professionals. Anyone who practices what this book teaches will have a decided advantage over their competition."*

—Tim Sellan, President
Sellan Consulting

Strategic Navigation

A Systems Approach
to Business Strategy

Also available from ASQ Quality Press:

Goldratt's Theory of Constraints: A Systems Approach to Continuous Improvement
H. William Dettmer

Breaking the Constraints to World-Class Performance
H. William Dettmer

From Quality to Business Excellence: A Systems Approach to Management
Charles Cobb

The Change Agent's Guide to Radical Improvement
Ken Miller

The Change Agent's Handbook: A Survival Guide for Quality Improvement Champions
David W. Hutton

Principles and Practices of Organizational Performance Excellence
Thomas J. Cartin

Customer Centered Six Sigma: Linking Customers, Process Improvement, and Financial Results
Earl Naumann and Steven H. Hoisington

The Certified Quality Manager Handbook, Second Edition
Duke Okes and Russell T. Westcott, editors

To request a complimentary catalog of ASQ Quality Press publications,
call 800-248-1946, or visit our Web site at http://qualitypress.asq.org.

Strategic Navigation

A Systems Approach
to Business Strategy

H. William Dettmer

ASQ Quality Press
Milwaukee, Wisconsin

American Society for Quality, Quality Press, Milwaukee 53203
© 2003 by H. William Dettmer
All rights reserved. Published 2003
Printed in the United States of America

12 11 10 09 08 07 06 05 04 03   5 4 3 2 1

Library of Congress Cataloging-in-Publication Data

Dettmer, H. William.
   Strategic navigation : a systems approach to business strategy / H. William Dettmer.
      p. cm.
   Includes bibliographical references and index.
   ISBN 0-87389-603-3 (case binding : alk. paper)
   1. Theory of constraints (Management). 2. Business planning. 3. Strategic
planning. I. Title.

HD69.T46D487 2003
658.4'012—dc21   2003012994

ISBN 0-87389-603-3

Cover photo: USS New Jersey, 25 Sep 1982, Department of Defense Visual Information Center—PH2. Photographer: Shayna Brennan.

Publisher: William A. Tony
Acquisitions Editor: Annemieke Hytinen
Project Editor: Paul O'Mara
Production Administrator: Gretchen Trautman
Special Marketing Representative: David Luth

ASQ Mission: The American Society for Quality advances individual, organizational, and community excellence worldwide through learning, quality improvement, and knowledge exchange.

Attention Bookstores, Wholesalers, Schools and Corporations: ASQ Quality Press books, videotapes, audiotapes, and software are available at quantity discounts with bulk purchases for business, educational, or instructional use. For information, please contact ASQ Quality Press at 800-248-1946, or write to ASQ Quality Press, P.O. Box 3005, Milwaukee, WI 53201-3005.

To place orders or to request a free copy of the ASQ Quality Press Publications Catalog, including ASQ membership information, call 800-248-1946. Visit our Web site at www.asq.org or http://qualitypress.asq.org.

 Printed on acid-free paper

American Society for Quality
ASQ®

Quality Press
600 N. Plankinton Avenue
Milwaukee, Wisconsin 53203
Call toll free 800-248-1946
Fax 414-272-1734
www.asq.org
http://qualitypress.asq.org
http://standardsgroup.asq.org
E-mail: authors@asq.org

For Melissa and Amanda Dettmer

Nothing I have ever achieved in my life, or ever will achieve, can hope to give me the pride I feel in having helped shape your lives and character. I can truly claim to have left the world a better place because of you. A hundred years from now, no other things that I have done will matter, but the world may be different because I was important in the lives of my children. If I die tomorrow, I will leave this world fulfilled.

Blessed indeed is the man who hears gentle voices call him father!

—Lydia M. Child

Children are love made visible.

—Unknown

By profession I am a soldier and take pride in that fact.
But I am prouder—infinitely prouder—to be a father.

—General Douglas MacArthur (1880–1964)

Table of Contents

List of Illustrations

Acknowledgments

Even though only the author's name goes on the cover, a book like this is always a team effort. I'm indebted to a number of people for their assistance in writing this book.

First and foremost, this book couldn't have been written without the contributions of Dr. Eliyahu M. Goldratt, who provided the theoretical foundation and the tools to apply what I have called, in this book, the constraint management model for strategy development. Dr. Goldratt also gave permission to use ideas from his *Necessary and Sufficient* seminar in chapter 4.

I'm grateful, too, for the kind permission of Mrs. Efrat Goldratt-Ashlag to use the timeless *Efrat's cloud,* which she conceived, in chapter 8.

Dr. Ellen Domb was kind enough to grant permission to use a diagram from her book in chapter 3 on *hoshin* planning.

When it comes to translating ideas from the brain to paper, any author can tell you that "it seemed right when I wrote it," but it can often come out incomprehensibly to the readers for whom it was intended. Fortunately, I had the generous contribution of time and advice from several colleagues in making this book make sense.

Dr. Kelvyn Youngman provided invaluable suggestions for organizing material and ensuring that "all the bases were covered." Kelvyn's patience with me knows no bounds. Tim Sellan gave me the information technology viewpoint and provided thought-provoking articles about strategy in that environment. He, too, was patient with me beyond reasonable expectation. David Lymburner and Dave Kaser gave me the benefit of the practitioner's viewpoint. All four of them helped me purge the typographical and syntactical errors, not to mention grammatical oversights.

Dr. Paul Selden was generous with both his time to review the manuscript and his conscientious effort to offer detailed suggestions, many of which I was able to use to productively improve the book. I would also be remiss if I didn't acknowledge Paul's contribution to the thinking process symbology: the use of a "stop sign" (octagon) symbol to represent obstacles in the Prerequisite Tree.

Leo Slaninko, a consummate graphic artist and life-long friend, provided invaluable assistance with several key illustrations in this book. It's impossible to fail with people like Leo behind you.

Dr. Dick Biery generously provided professional guidance on critical success factors in not-for-profit organizations.

And finally, I can't fail to recognize the superlative work on editing, production, and publication done by the ASQ Quality Press team. This is my third book with Quality Press, and each one looks better than the one before.

Introduction

Plans get you into things, but you got to work your own way out.

—Will Rogers

Strategic planning is a relatively new thing. Nobody really did it before 1965, and it didn't show up on the radar screens of many companies for several years thereafter. By the mid-1980s, everybody was doing it. The Japanese added a few terms, such as *hoshin kanri* and *kaizen*. In the mid-1980s, Michael Porter's seminal work on positioning was the biggest thing in strategic thinking. More contemporary schools of thought that valued learning, organizational culture, and emergent strategy gained visibility. By the late 1990s, strategic planning, and terms such as *mission, vision,* and *values,* had evolved into buzzwords.

The reality, however, is that strategic planning hasn't lived up to the expectations of most companies that have embraced it. It's been primarily a "feel good" effort. Managers and executives feel good about having sweated through the development of a traditional strategic plan, and they have nice, thick, doorstop-sized documents to show for it. But the ultimate effects of strategic planning on the bottom line have been mixed at best, and questionable at worst.

Does this mean that organizations shouldn't bother doing strategic planning? Maybe so, at least as it has traditionally been done. But is there another way to realize the purported benefits of strategic planning without the typical "baggage" and ineffectiveness that seem to go along with it? The short answer is "yes," and this book will suggest a way to make that happen.

The interdependent nature of complex systems and meta-systems was never more clearly exemplified than in September 2001. Until the morning of September 11, the world was generally at peace, except for a few trouble spots such as Israel and the occupied territories. The world economy was steady, if somewhat stagnant. In the space of about an hour, four coordinated acts of terrorism, years in the planning, sent shock waves throughout the world. America and many of the European industrialized nations went onto a wartime footing. Priorities changed overnight in economic, political, social, and cultural spheres. It became clear that the world would never be quite the same again. Chaos and uncertainty became the rule rather than the exception.

In the economic arena alone, the entire environmental landscape changed. What had been uncertainty about whether America would slide into economic recession turned into certainty in a flash. The bottom fell out of both the stock market and the airline industry, each so heavily intertwined in all kinds of other industries that the repercussions were almost instantaneous. Businesses dependent on air travel—hotels, car rental agencies, entertainment, and travel agencies—took immediate and devastating hits, and they began grasping for any possible way to offset the certain crash in profits.

Seeing the eventuality of its backlog of airplane orders drying up, Boeing immediately announced its intention to lay off 30,000 employees. The airlines, combined, laid off another 100,000. Within two weeks, the job loss resulting from the terror attack was variously estimated at 300,000 in the United States alone, with more likely to come. Consumers stopped buying. Investors selling off stocks precipitated the single largest plunge in market averages since the Great Depression. Any hope of a quick recovery in the struggling technology sector, severely battered in 1999 and early 2000 by the "dot-bomb" explosion, evaporated. Because economies are no longer purely national, businesses throughout the world were affected.

If *ever* there were a time when a rational, structured, agile method of creating new strategies was needed, *this* was certainly it. Yet few companies anywhere looked for one. Instead, they reacted by short-term "gut" instinct: slash costs and play it by ear to figure out how to survive. Few executives exhibited the presence of mind to do more than wonder what the longer-term future might hold and how their competitive business environment might change.* Yet a reasoned, deliberate adjustment in strategy is precisely what the situation demanded.

Strategy and planning in a military context date back well over 2,000 years. Between the fifth and third centuries B.C., a compilation of strategic military thought called *The Art of War* was created in China by a general named Sun Tzu. His writings were later read and interpreted by 11 other Chinese military thinkers between the second and twelfth centuries A.D. Many of the principles originally articulated by Sun Tzu, expanded and explained by the later thinkers, have application far beyond the battlefield. In fact, *The Art of War* is required reading at a number of business schools today. In an attempt to put some of what is recommended in this book into context, you'll see occasional quotations from *The Art of War* located where their content is germane to the subjects discussed in this book.

---

* Take the athletic apparel manufacturers, for instance. Most of their products are made in Indonesia. And not only does Indonesia have the largest Muslim population in the world, it also has one of those Muslim populations most sympathetic to Osama bin Laden and his cause. What long-term effect might this have on Nike's source of inexpensive labor?

But the "military experience" is much more applicable to nonmilitary enterprises—commercial business, government agencies, and not-for-profit organizations—than most people realize. And there's considerably more substance to it than the ancient maxims of Sun Tzu. In fact, any organization can adopt major aspects of the military planning model to its operations and realize considerable benefits in coherence and focus.

As I circulated a draft of this book to colleagues for review, one posed a question: "Your writing seems to focus on 'fighting the enemy' and 'competition.' That makes sense for a military mission, but isn't business success today built more on 'satisfying the customer?'"

This is an excellent observation, and one that points out the need to know where various critical success factors such as customer satisfaction fit in the scheme of things—something this book is intended to do. But my emphasis on competition is deliberate. In a capitalistic society, business *is* competition, whether we pay attention to that fact or not. The mom-and-pop store in the heartland (or even in a big city) may not see it as competition, because no apparent competitor is obviously trying to take its customers away. But "stuff happens" that confirms the existence of competition, even if we don't really pay attention to it.

Sometimes competition is obvious—Wal-Mart opens a new store nearby. Sometimes it isn't—local business is gradually lost to e-commerce companies that market and sell nationwide (or worldwide) through the Internet. How many small bookstores has Amazon.com put out of business, probably without even knowing it? How many small or medium-sized businesses aren't even a blip on the radar screen of larger ones? Yet, can the small business afford to ignore the presence of the giant, even though confrontation might not be direct?

As long as there's someone out there who might take your customers away, or introduce a new product that renders whatever you're offering irrelevant, or in some other way consciously or unconsciously hurts your business, you're in competition—even if you don't recognize it as such. You're better off seeing the business world that way, even if your opponent is not obvious at the moment. As George Washington once observed, the safest way to secure peace is to be ready at all times for war. And is not war the ultimate competition? So, I suggest that satisfying customers is certainly essential to "being ready for war" in business. But it's not sufficient alone. Other critical success factors play a part, as well. This book is designed to help ensure that you don't overlook any of them. It takes a military tone to emphasize the competitive nature of business.

A few words about the content and structure of this book are in order. There's a seductive tendency to try to write a book that would be all things to all people. That's not going to happen here. This book's purpose is twofold.

My first objective is to introduce readers to the conceptual framework of military strategy and maneuver warfare. I elected to do so because it has a rich history dating back 2,300 years, which makes it ripe for a longitudinal analysis. Moreover, most of the principles of war planning and executing military operations are generic enough to be eminently transferable to nonmilitary uses, both commercial for-profit and noncommercial or government agency. If this were not the case, you wouldn't see so many business schools teaching Sun Tzu.

My second objective is to introduce a logical, systematic tool set for translating the military strategy "template" into action—in whatever kind of domain you happen to operate. The tool set I describe satisfies several crucial, basic criteria for robustness. It's relatively quick to use (compared with traditional methods). It's flexible enough to facilitate quick-onset, short-notice changes in the external environment. It supports initiative and creativity on the parts of both the strategists and the executors. And, finally, its form of expression is "lean and mean"—it's visual and graphic, rather than a doorstop-sized document.

So, who is the target audience for this book? Senior executives, for sure, since they're the ones ultimately responsible for steering the corporate ship. There will be enough concepts and strategy-development guidance here to satisfy "big picture" thinkers of any organization, large or small.

But this book is for the subordinates of executives as well—those who will be charged with actually translating the strategic concepts into executable plans and changing course rapidly in midstream when the boss—or the external environment—mandates a destination change. The tool set contained in this book is designed to do just that.

The book is divided into two major parts, the chapters that describe strategy formation and tools, and appendixes that provide more detail on methods as well as some real-world examples. The chapters include a synthesis of existing concepts and principles, nonmilitary as well as military, with relatively new ideas, such as Boyd's OODA loop (chapters 2 and 4). So, if you find yourself thinking, "This is a lot like [fill in the blank]," you might well be right. What's new about this book is less the new ideas presented than it is the synthesis of existing ideas and new ones in—I hope—more useful ways.

The first chapter starts with a quick review of strategic planning the way it has traditionally been done and contemporary developments in the art. It examines the pitfalls associated with them. In chapter 3, we'll take a closer look at the military model of strategic planning, one that has worked surprisingly well for the last 50 years, notwithstanding unfavorable press in other areas, such as the defense budget and systems acquisition.

Then, in chapter 4, we'll consider a new model for charting the future, which I've called the *constraint management model*. This new model has its roots in military strategic and operational planning, but it uses some aspects of *hoshin kanri* (chapter 2), the aforementioned OODA loop, and logical tools to translate the military template to nonmilitary uses. In other words, it applies to any kind of organization: commercial, not-for-profit, government agency, or spiritual.

Chapter 5 starts with a clean sheet of paper, leading strategists through the high-level question "Where are we going, and what must we do to get there?" It provides practitioners with a useful tool for converting mission and vision into discrete system-level milestones. Chapter 6 addresses the content or subject matter knowledge needed to build and execute an effective strategy. It covers some aspects of the creative process needed to form good strategy and introduces a tool for eliciting that creativity from the minds of those best positioned to provide it.

Chapters 7, 8, 10, and 11 explain the other components of the logical tool set. The first of these describes how to determine the size and scope of the gap between where the organization is now and where its ultimate goal lies. Chapter 8 addresses the most critical roadblock to the execution of any strategy: power conflicts, both internal and external. Starting with the output of chapters 7 and 8, chapter 10 describes how the actual strategy is logically constructed, and chapter 11 provides the beginning of the execution process. What about chapter 9? It explains how the principles of war can be applied to the strategy content of chapter 10 and the execution operations of chapter 11. Chapter 12 ties everything together.

This approach doesn't result in a doorstop-sized document that sits on a shelf gathering dust. Instead, it uses simple, logic-based cause-and-effect tools—a thinking process—to develop and deploy dynamic strategy: one capable of responding and adjusting effectively to short-notice changes in environmental conditions. It's equally valuable for evaluating *existing* operating and strategic plans, and highlighting the parts that need strengthening.

My goal for this book is to change the way people and organizations chart *and realize* their futures.

H. William Dettmer
Port Angeles, Washington
gsi@goalsys.com

1

Traditional Strategic Planning

Where am I going? I don't know.
When will I get there? I ain't certain.
All that I know is I am on my way.

—"Paint Your Wagon"
(Lerner and Lowe)

*S**trategic planning:* the term implies that strategy formulation and planning go hand-in-hand. And in fact, that's the way strategy has been treated for the past 35 years. The practitioners of strategic planning have founded their efforts on a basic assumption: that the largely creative task of conceiving and formulating strategy can be standardized into a pedagogical series of actions—planning—with the effect that the desired results are both achieved and repeatable. Does this really happen? Let's take a closer look.

PLANNING AND STRATEGY

Ask most people how they would define *strategy,* and they will usually give you the definition of a plan: "a direction, guide, or course of action into the future."[1] Russell Ackoff defined planning as "the design of a desired future and of effective ways of bringing it about."[2] But strategy is a pattern of behavior as well—the way things are done, but on a somewhat grander scale.

Planning is one of the five classical functions of management: *planning, organizing, staffing, leading,* and *controlling.*[3] So planning is one of those things that managers just *do*—"Fish gotta swim, birds gotta fly, managers gotta plan and plan till they die." But why bother planning at all? Why not just fly by the seat of your pants?

There are typically four reasons why organizations plan[4]:

1. To coordinate their activities

2. To ensure that the future is taken into account

3. To be "rational"

4. To control

Basically, it all boils down to "control." They want to be captains of their own ship, masters of their fate. They want to be sure that they swim, even if others sink, and to do so they can't depend on fate. As Elbert Hubbard once said, "Positive *anything* is better than negative nothing." Any executive who answers to a higher authority, such as a board of directors, feels an obligation to control his or her operation. The other four functions of management, of which planning is the first, serve to satisfy this need for control.

There's a uniquely American term—*Monday morning quarterbacking*—that explains control behavior. It means that the day after the game, there's no shortage of people willing to criticize what was done and how it really should have been done. The overriding characteristic of Monday morning quarterbacking is that it is always done through the comfort and safety of hindsight, knowing how things actually turned out, and ignoring the heat and pressure of the actual battle.

Consider the ultimate in Monday morning quarterbacking, the aircraft accident report: "Primary cause: Pilot error, in that the pilot failed to maintain control of the aircraft . . ." Virtually every accident report since Orville and Wilbur Wright first wrapped their airplane around a tree has zeroed in on loss of control. Never mind that contributing factors may have made that impossible to avoid. The captain is ultimately responsible for his ship, the aircraft commander for his airplane. And most managers feel that if they're going to be held responsible, they want to be in full control. Or as close to it as fate will allow.

So, to maximize the odds of success, they deliberately plan, and then they plan for contingencies (the high-risk, critical outcome times when the deliberate plan might break down). And the challenge of maintaining control of the ship into an uncertain future is even more compelling, so they want to do long-range planning. Long-range planning typically requires answering the questions "Where are we going, and how will we get there?" The alternative—just going along for the ride—is unacceptable, because it implies "no control." If you don't care what the destination is, then any path will do.

What about *strategy?* This is a somewhat elusive term. People are fond of distinguishing between strategy and tactics, where strategy refers to "important" things, and "tactics" to mere details. Unfortunately, things aren't intrinsically strategic or tactical. Where you stand on this depends on where you sit. One person's strategy is another person's tactics.[5] Strategy also encompasses elements of *position*—the determination of particular products and markets, and *perspective*—its concept of how business is done.

THE FAILURE OF STRATEGIC PLANNING

Let's go back a step, to the question of indeterminate results. What evidence is there to suggest that strategic planning—referred to in the early days as corporate planning—doesn't fulfill the expectations held for it? Mintzberg has observed that planners are notably reluctant to evaluate their own efforts, both what they *do* and what they *get done*.[6] Others, however, are not. Here are some typical conclusions by people who have studied strategic planning efforts with varying degrees of intensity (anecdotal evidence, surveys, and full-blown analyses):

- No study was found that has "assessed the consequences of adhering to or deviating from long-range plans."[7]

- One of the earliest studies indicated that while companies engaging in their activities in a "systematic planned" way achieved higher, more predictable performance on average, other companies that did not engage in planning surpassed the performance of the best planners.[8]

- Some studies in the 1970s, by Malik and Karger for example, found favorable results for planning, while others, by Sheehan, Grinyer, and Norburn, didn't.[9] Mintzberg cites even more such studies with contrary results. In fact, he concluded that "planning is not 'the one best way,' that it certainly does not pay in general, and that at best, it may have some suitability in particular contexts, such as larger organizations, those in mass production, and so on."[10]

- A well-known proponent of planning, after visiting a wide variety of European and American companies between 1967 and 1972, concluded: ". . . most companies find formal planning has not been the panacea or solution originally thought. Success in planning does not come easy . . ."[11]

- Igor Ansoff, one of the most renowned academics in this field, observed that "in spite of almost 20 years of existence of the strategic planning technology, a majority of firms today engage in the far less threatening and perturbing extrapolative long-range planning."[12]

- "The criticism of strategic planning was well deserved. Strategic planning in most companies has not contributed to strategic thinking."[13]

There's no shortage of literature on the subject of strategic planning. There's also no shortage of premature conclusions about it. Ansoff cited General Electric as a "leading practitioner of strategic planning, [having] tried and regressed twice before the currently successful process was established as part of the firm's general management."[14] But by the time Ansoff's pronouncement saw print, GE's "successful process" had also collapsed, with much publicity.

The CEO of General Motors, after three "unsuccessful tries" at establishing a headquarters planning system, was quoted as saying "we got these great plans together, put them on the shelf, and marched off to do what we would be doing anyway. It took us a while to realize that wasn't getting us anywhere."[15]

TO PLAN, PLANNING, AND PLANS

Why all these bad reviews for strategic planning? Mintzberg differentiates between *plan* (a verb), *planning* (a noun characterizing a formal process), and *plans* (another noun referring to documents that grow out of the process).[16] Just because you have a *plan* doesn't necessarily mean that you engaged in *planning,* or *planned.* (If you can keep all that straight, you're doing well!)

What Mintzberg is implying is that the need *to plan* (verb) isn't invalid—on the contrary, it's crucial for success. Neither is *the plan* (the noun, meaning a document) at fault. The results of the effort to plan (verb) must be communicated somehow to those who need to know about it. Rather, it's the *planning* (formal process) that has failed.

It's this element—the formal process of strategic planning—that this book is intended to repair.

STRATEGY FORMATION*: SCHOOLS OF THOUGHT

One thing is certain: there is no general agreement on how to create and implement strategy. Mintzberg et al., have identified 10 schools of strategic thought.[17] Each differs from the other in its assumptions, characteristics, and areas of emphasis. (See Figure 1.1.)

The first three of these schools are quite different from the remaining seven. The *design, planning,* and *positioning* schools of thought are prescriptive, deliberate, and largely objective. They're *prescriptive* in that the strategy they develop provides detailed guidance on what to do and how to do it. They're *deliberate,* in that for these schools strategy is the result of deliberate effort to create it—it doesn't just emerge. And these schools are *objective,* in that they depend on and employ large amounts of quantitative data. The underlying purpose of these three schools of thought is *control*—they seek to keep senior management firmly in control of the organization's direction.

These first three schools might be considered "traditional" schools of thought. They're the ones concerning which the largest body of strategic planning literature exists. Not coincidentally, these are also the schools that Mintzberg and others have criticized (in the preceding section, The Failure of Strategic Planning) as suffering from varying degrees of ineffectiveness.

Yet, if you accept Mintzberg's conclusions—and it's *very* hard not to—strategic *planning* (formal, detailed processes) doesn't really satisfy an organization's need to *plan* (verb) its future. It's slow, tedious, not flexible, unresponsive to rapid changes in the "rules of the game of business," and it doesn't do much to tie organizations together into a coherent, coordinated system with all parts aiming unerringly at a unified goal. If it doesn't do all these things, what does?

---

* Mintzberg differentiates between strategy *formation* and strategy *formulation.* He suggests that successful strategy often emerges (forms) as a pattern that was not expressly intended, rather than exclusively as the product of deliberate design (formulation). The formation of strategy might be likened to a "toe in the water" type of testing: "This worked. Let's try it again, in another way." Formulated strategy, on the other hand, is designed and intended from the very beginning.

For the first 20 years of mainstream interest in strategic planning, 1965–85, the three traditional schools dominated both the management literature and practice.[18] The *positioning* school is still influential, though its popularity has leveled off recently. In the last few years, seven other, more contemporary, schools of strategic thought have evolved and attracted substantially more attention from students of strategy. These seven are the *entrepreneurial, cognitive, learning, power, cultural, environmental,* and *configuration.* Figure 1.1a summarizes the traditional schools, Figure 1.1b the contemporary ones.

The latter seven schools might be characterized as descriptive, emergent, and subjective. They're *descriptive,* in that they describe what's happening in the environment and how strategy forms, rather than prescribing specifically what to do. They're *emergent,* in that they assume that potential strategies become obvious, or present themselves

Attributes	School of Strategic Thought (Sees strategy formation as:)	Assumptions
Prescriptive Deliberative Objective	**Design** (A process of conception)	1. Strategy should be a deliberate process of conscious thought. 2. The CEO is responsible for strategy formation. 3. The strategy formation model must be simple and informal. 4. Strategies should be individualized. 5. The process is complete when strategies are fully formed—a definite end. 6. Strategies should be simple and explicit. 7. Implementation should occur only after the strategy is completely formulated.
	Planning (A formal process)	1. Strategies result from a controlled, conscious process of formal planning, decomposed into distinct steps, each delineated by checklists, and supported by techniques. 2. The CEO is responsible for the overall process, but actual planning is done by staff planners. 3. Strategies appear full-blown from the process. They are made explicit through detailed attention to objectives, budgets, programs, and operating plans.
	Positioning (An analytical process)	Same as *design* and planning schools, except for two key additions: 1. There are only a few key strategies—positions in the marketplace—that are desirable in any given industry. These are ones that can be defended against existing and future competitors. 2. Strategy selection is based on analytical calculation. [Primary architect: Michael Porter]

Figure 1.1a Schools of strategic thought (traditional).
Summarized from Mintzberg, Ahlstrand, and Lampel, *Strategy Safari* (1998).

Attributes	School of Strategic Thought (Sees strategy formation as:)	Assumptions
Descriptive Emergent Subjective	**Entrepreneurial** (A visionary process)	1. Strategy comes from the mind of a leader as a sense of long-term direction, vision. 2. A semi-conscious process, at best. 3. Leader promotes vision single-mindedly, maintains close personal control 4. The strategic vision is malleable. 5. The organization is malleable. 6. Strategy is "niche" type.
	Cognitive (A mental process)	1. Strategy forms in the mind of the strategist. 2. Strategies emerge as perspectives—concepts, maps, schemes, frames. 3. Inputs are filtered, distorted, and interpreted before modeling. 4. Strategy is difficult to attain, less than optimal, difficult to change.
	Learning (An emergent process)	1. Complex, unpredictable environment and diffusion of knowledge preclude deliberate control. 2. Collective systems do the learning. 3. Learning is emergent. 4. Leadership doesn't preconceive strategy. 5. Strategies appear as patterns from the past.
	Power (A negotiation process)	1. Strategy formation is shaped by power and politics. 2. Strategies are emergent and are ploys and positions more than perspectives. 3. Internally, strategy-making is done through persuasion, bargaining, and confrontation. 4. Externally, strategy-making is done through controlling, or cooperating with, other organizations, or through alliances.
	Cultural (A collective process)	1. Strategy is a process of social interactions. 2. Acculturation/socialization is tacit and nonverbal. 3. Beliefs are hard to articulate. 4. Strategy is perspective and deliberate, if not conscious. 5. Culture and ideology perpetuate existing strategy, or shifts, but not strategic change.
	Environmental (A reactive process)	1. The environment is the central factor in the strategy-making process. 2. Organizations must respond to organizational forces or be "selected out." 3. Leadership is a passive element in the strategy-making process. 4. Organizations "cluster" together in distinct ecological-type niches or positions, where they remain until they die.
	Configuration (A transformation process)	1. Strategies emerge from organizational configuration. 2. Periods of stability are interrupted by some kind of transformation process. 3. A cycle of stability and transformation approximates the lifecycle of the organization. 4. The objective is to sustain stability, but periodically transform. 5. Strategy can be deliberate or emergent, as the situation warrants. 6. Strategies last until the next change cycle.

Figure 1.1b *Schools of strategic thought (contemporary).*
Summarized from Mintzberg, Ahlstrand, and Lampel, *Strategy Safari* (1998).

as opportunities that emerge from the environment. And they're *subjective,* in that they depend in large degree on people's vision, intuition, and personal experience—characteristics that are anything but quantifiable and objective. Because these schools are not locked into a control-oriented prescriptive process, as the traditional schools are, they're presumed to be more flexible and responsive, and adaptable to the uncertainty of an ever-changing external environment.

Proponents of the *control* schools place a high value on order, process, and repeatability. Proponents of the *flexibility* schools place a high premium on creativity, reaction, and uniqueness. Fans of the contemporary flexibility schools have a high tolerance for ambiguity, while those of the traditional control schools don't.

THE DELIBERATE (TRADITIONAL) SCHOOLS: PROS AND CONS

Each of the strategy schools of thought offers advantages—and each carries some "baggage" (disadvantages), too. The *design, planning,* and *positioning* schools offer the comfort of being in control of the strategy-making process (though not necessarily the reality that results from it). (See Figure 1.2.) These "deliberate" schools provide structured strategy processes, are generally objective and analytical in their approaches, and employ statistics and data liberally.

School of Strategic Thought	Advantages	Disadvantages
Design (A process of conception)	1. Applies best to an organization coming out of a period of changing circumstances, and into a period of stability. 2. Useful to new organizations that need a clear sense of direction to compete with more established rivals. 3. Provides a prescriptive approach 4. Assessment of strengths, weaknesses, opportunities, threats (SWOT).	1. How accurate/effective are assessments of SWOT? 2. Can't be sure in advance whether established competence is a strength or a weakness. 3. Strengths are often far narrower, weakness far broader than expected. 4. Structure follows strategy; promotes inflexibility. 5. Thinking often detached from acting.
Planning (A formal process)	1. Permits control over strategic planning process. 2. Provides the comfort of a pedagogical process: objectives setting; external audit; internal audit; strategy evaluation; strategy operationalizing; scheduling. 3. Enables scenario planning.	1. Inflexible, not responsive to changing environment. 2. Plans can be outdated before the ink is dry. 3. The course of the environment is not predictable. 4. Planners/strategists are usually detached from implementation. 5. Hard data is not always useful. 6. Formalization transfers the strategy process from individuals to the system. 7. Treats strategy as analysis, not synthesis.
Positioning (An analytical process)	1. Provides substance missing in *design* and *planning* schools. 2. Limits potential strategies to a "manageable" number. 3. Strategies need not be unique or tailor-made. 4. Statistics and analysis support strategy.	1. Not relevant to government agencies, nongovernment or noncommercial organizations. 2. Bias toward traditional big business. 3. Too dependent on analysis and calculation. 4. Ignores "soft" or nonquantifiable, noneconomic factors.

Figure 1.2   Traditional schools.

Summarized from Mintzberg, Ahlstrand, and Lampel, *Strategy Safari* (1998).

But they're not very flexible. The planners are usually not the same people who implement the strategy, meaning that thinking is often detached from acting. Moreover, the organization's environment can often change faster than a structured process can respond with an updated strategy. And many of the most critical issues concerning strategy are neither easily quantifiable nor do they lend themselves to analysis by "hard" data.

THE EMERGENT (CONTEMPORARY) SCHOOLS: PROS AND CONS

The other seven strategy schools of thought are more contemporary, meaning that the thinking and literature on these have evolved in the last decade or so. These schools are the *entrepreneurial, cognitive, learning, power, cultural, environmental,* and *configuration.* They're considered "emergent," and they incorporate consideration of nonquantifiable factors often missing in the traditional deliberate schools. They're less deterministic and more personalized, and they generally accommodate changes in the real-world environment far better than the deliberate schools do. In other words, they're as much outward-looking as inward. And they accommodate political and power realities, which the deliberate schools don't. (See Figure 1.3.)

But the emergent schools have their drawbacks, too. They are either so heavily dependent on a great visionary leader (entrepreneurial) or so reactive (learning, power, cultural) that they may produce no real strategy, "lose" strategy, or steer toward the wrong strategy. Some, like the environmental school, promote consistency and discourage changes in strategy.

There may be some correlation between a preference for a particular school and the personality of the leaders involved. Personalities with a predilection for order, process, and a need to control are more likely to be drawn to the deliberate strategy schools and not the emergent ones. Cultural experience is influential, too. Western leader-oriented management has had more of a difficult time coming to grips with the kind of decentralized influence and learning approaches commonly practiced in Japan.

A POSSIBLE SOLUTION: SYNTHESIS

With so many options to choose from—10 schools, emergent or deliberate, objective or subjective—how can we hope to have the best of both worlds? How can we realize the control inherent in the traditional schools, yet preserve the flexibility of the contemporary schools? Is it even possible to combine the advantages of the various schools while simultaneously mitigating or eliminating the disadvantages?

The premise of this book is that it *is* possible, but it will require a different approach: *synthesis,* rather than analysis. We'll have to synthesize elements of known forms into something new. That synthesis is laid out in chapter 4. But before we get to it, there are two other specific planning methodologies we must address: *hoshin kanri* and the military planning model.

School of Strategic Thought	Advantages	Disadvantages
Entrepreneurial (A visionary process)	1. Includes nonquantifiable factors often missing in traditional schools. 2. Unity of focus, inspiration. 3. Constant in ends, flexible in means. 4. Fast transition to "pursuit." 5. Small organization oriented.	1. Heavily dependent on "great leader." 2. Possible to be too tightly locked in one direction. 3. Heavy burden on the leader.
Cognitive (A mental process)	1. Accommodates cognitive psychology. 2. Less deterministic than *positioning*, more personalized than *planning* schools.	1. Characterized more by potential than by contribution. 2. Doesn't really address how strategy concepts form.
Learning (An emergent process)	1. Admits flexibility, acknowledges chaotic nature of the environment. 2. Advantageous for organizations facing a truly novel situation. 3. Has an acknowledgement of reality lacking in other schools.	1. May result in no strategy, lost strategy, or the wrong strategy. 2. Groupthink and distraction are possible. 3. Waiting for strategy to emerge may not be practical in a crisis.
Power (A negotiation process)	1. Accommodate the real world—an environment of power and politics. 2. Useful in complex, highly decntralized organizations of experts with power to further their own interests or work.	1. May miss emerging patterns because of overattention on divisiveness, fractioning. 2. Can be a source of waste and distortion. 3. Creates a risk of collusion in large organizations.
Cultural (A collective process)	1. Culture provides needed stable foundation in a time of constant change. 2. Integrated consensus on ideology, perspectives.	1. Promotes consistency, but discourages change in strategy. 2. Old logic must be "unlearned" before strategic learning can occur. 3. Can blind managers to changing external conditions
Environmental (A reactive process)	1. Recognition of the constraints that external environments place on strategy.	1. Organizations have no real strategic choice—they can only play the hand the environment deals them. 2. Emphasizes conformance to external conditions; reactive, not proactive.
Configuration (A transformation process)	1. Promotes continuity/stability between intervals of major change. 2. Accommodates key aspects of other schools.	1. May oversimplify structure, bureaucracy. 2. Narrow view of change: static or rapidly changing (no allowance for incremental changes) 3. Constructive configurations become destructive eventually.

Figure 1.3 Contemporary schools.
Summarized from Mintzberg, Ahlstrand, and Lampel, *Strategy Safari* (1998).

Therefore the victories of good warriors are not noted for cleverness or bravery. Therefore their victories in battle are not flukes. Their victories are not flukes because they position themselves where they will surely win, prevailing over those who have already lost.

—Master Sun
Sun Tzu and the Art of War

ENDNOTES

1. H. Mintzberg, *The Rise and Fall of Strategic Planning* (New York: The Free Press, 1994).
2. R. L. Ackoff, *A Concept of Corporate Planning* (New York: John Wiley & Sons, 1970): 1.
3. H. Weihrich and H. Koontz, *Management: A Global Persective*, 10th ed. (New York: McGraw-Hill, 1993).
4. Mintzberg, *Rise and Fall*, 16–20.
5. R. P. Rumelt, "Evaluation of Strategy: Theory and Models," in D. E. Schendel and C. W. Hofer, eds., *Strategic Management* (Boston: Little, Brown, and Co., 1979): 197.
6. Mintzberg, *Rise and Fall*, 91.
7. W. H. Starbuck, "Acting First and Thinking Later: Theory versus Reality in Strategic Change, " in J. M. Pennings et al., *Organizational Strategy and Change* (San Francisco: Jossey-Bass, 1985): 371.
8. H. I. Ansoff et al., "Does Planning Pay? The Effect of Planning on Success of Acquisitions in American Firms," *Long Range Planning* III, no. 2 (December 1970): 6.
9. See note 7.
10. Mintzberg, *Rise and Fall,* 21.
11. K. A. Ringbakk, "The Corporate Planning Life Cycle—An International Point of View," *Long Range Planning* (September 1972): 10.
12. H. I. Ansoff, "The State of Practice in Planning Systems," *Sloan Management Review* (winter 1977): 20.
13. M. E. Porter, "Corporate Strategy: The State of Strategic Thinking," *The Economist* 303, no. 7499 (23 May 1987): 17.
14. H. I. Ansoff, *Implanting Strategic Management* (Englewood Cliffs, NJ: Prentice Hall, 1984): 188.
15. "The New Breed of Strategic Planner," *Business Week* (17 September 1984): 62.
16. Mintzberg, *Rise and Fall*, 31–32.
17. H. Mintzberg, B. Ahlstrand, and J. Lampel, *Strategy Safari: A Guided Tour through the Wilds of Strategic Management* (New York: The Free Press, 1998).
18. Ibid.

2

The *Hoshin* Strategic Model

Defense is for times of insufficiency, attack is for times of surplus.

—Master Sun
Sun Tzu and the Art of War

We've seen that traditional approaches to strategic planning haven't worked very well. In most cases, they don't actually develop strategy, though they do become mired in detail, especially financial numbers.

In the 1960s, Japanese companies formulated a different approach known as policy deployment, or management by policy.[1] When it made the Pacific crossing to North America, it was referred to by its Japanese name: *hoshin kanri*. It has been promoted by its proponents as a means to do strategic planning, too.

PLANNING, DOING, AND REVIEW

For those with exposure to traditional strategic planning, *hoshin kanri* is a completely different way of thinking about it. It goes well beyond the traditional approach, which essentially begins with basic assumptions about the nature of the business a company is in, tries to develop strategies to achieve objectives related to those assumptions, then basically leaves it to management to figure out how to make those things happen.

Hoshin kanri, on the other hand, is considerably more "complete." It promotes "doing" and "review" as well as planning. It incorporates operational and project planning, as well as strategy formation.

PLANNING

At the strategic level, *hoshin* planning begins with a clean sheet of paper. It forces senior management to address three questions:

- What business are we in? (Mission)

- Where do we expect to go with this business? (Vision)

- What principles and concepts are important to us in doing so? (Values)

The answers to these questions are certainly strategic in nature. But there are other strategic issues as well[2*]:

- What are the long-term growth and profitability objectives of the business?

- What must be done to achieve these objectives?

- What is the nature of the environment in which the company will operate/compete?

DOING (PART 1)

Typically, operational planning addresses the tactical details of how a business will be run in the near term, perhaps no more than a year. An annual business plan is the equivalent of an operating plan. They include such details as revenue and profit forecasts, cash flow projections, required manpower levels, marketing and sales programs, manufacturing capacity planning, capital improvements, and so on.

Business plans are not the same as strategic plans, and though some companies' strategic plans have program elements in them, traditional strategic planning methods usually leave the detailed annual business planning to someone else. But *hoshin* planning includes operational planning as an integral part of the process. Operating plans are part of the "doing" needed to realize the strategy.

DOING (PART 2)

Actual implementation of plans invariably takes place at a project level. Even if a company doesn't actively engage in formal project management, the short-term objectives of a one-year business plan embody all the characteristics of projects. Even if the activities themselves are repetitive, such as manufacturing or sales, the quarterly, semiannual, and annual targets inherent in business plans introduce a "project atmosphere" to a company's activities.

---

* These issues assume that the organization is a commercial, for-profit company, but *hoshin kanri* can be applied to not-for-profit organizations and government agencies as well. Liberal interpretation or rewording of statements that specifically address profit generation or competition is essentially all that is required.

Many companies, however, acknowledge that they are involved in projects, such as new product development, capital expansion, or installation of new equipment. For companies that specialize in the rapid turnover of new generations of products, or whose business is producing one-time deliverables to a specified performance level, on time, and within a prescribed budget, projects are the core of their business.

Either way, if it isn't executed, a strategic plan is just a "doorstop" or a pile of paper sitting on a shelf. While most traditional strategic planning methods leave implementation to others, *hoshin* planning "drills down" to the levels of the organization that will make the plan happen. This is another way that *hoshin* planning includes "doing" as well as planning.

REVIEWING

Success in realizing any plan—strategic, operational, or project—depends on knowing how well the organization is progressing through the execution process. In chapter 4, I refer to this as *strategic navigation.* A plan tells you where you're going and how to get there. It should even tell you why you're making the trip. But it doesn't make the trip for you, and if you start to wander off course, it won't tell you where you are or what to do about it.

Most management teams are smart enough to know that they need to assess where they are in relation to where they plan to end up. Deviations from the plan can then be evaluated individually, and corrective actions taken to put the train back on the tracks when required. This typically happens through a review process of some kind—a formal effort to ask, "How are we doing in comparison to the plan?" *Hoshin* planning incorporates this kind of review and corrective action, too.

While the Japanese popularized the method characterized as "plan–do–check–act" (PDCA), they learned it from W. Edwards Deming and Joseph Juran in the 1950s. Deming himself credited Walter Shewhart at American Telephone and Telegraph (AT&T) with the technique in the 1920s,[3] but its origins go back even farther than that. This method, inherent in the "review" phase of *hoshin* planning, is simple:[4]

- *Plan.* Determine the goals to be achieved and methods to reach them.

- *Do.* Implement the methods.

- *Check.* Examine the results. Was the goal achieved? Was the improvement hypothesis validated?

- *Act.* If the goals were achieved, adopt the new methods permanently. If not, determine the cause of failure and return to "Plan." Continue this cycle until no more improvement or progress is required.

People familiar with total quality management and its derivatives (lean production, Six Sigma, and so on) readily recognize these steps. They form the basic prescription in all similar continuous improvement philosophies. Many managers, however, consider their application only at the process level, to improve discrete functions within

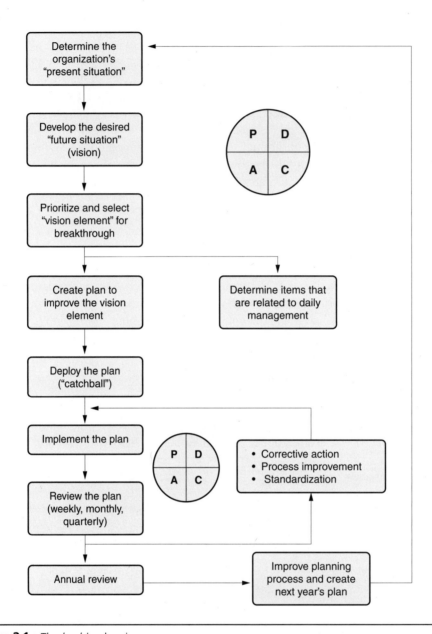

Figure 2.1 The *hoshin* planning process.

Adapted from Cowley and Domb, *Beyond Strategic Vision* (1997). Used with permission.

the organization. In a larger sense, the elimination of deviations between a strategic plan and actual system-level performance could be considered an improvement effort as well. *Hoshin* planning includes the PDCA cycle as an integral part of policy deployment.* Figure 2.1 depicts the *hoshin* planning process. Figure 2.2 shows how the elements of *hoshin kanri* compare with the traditional functions of strategic planning.

---

* Readers interested in learning more about hoshin planning should read *Beyond Strategic Vision: Effective Corporate Action with Hoshin Plannning,* by Michael Cowley and Ellen Domb. (ISBN 0-7506-9843-8) This is the most concise yet comprehensive book I have seen on hoshin planning.

Function	Hoshin Kanri Strategic Planning Model
Goals/ Objectives (What is the ultimate destination?)	**Analyze the Present Situation** • Mission • Organizational performance • Strategic vision • Customer needs and satisfaction • Values • Markets • Critical success measures • Performance versus last plan • Strengths, weaknesses, • More opportunities, threats

Strategies
 	
(How to get there?)
	Prioritize and Select Breakthrough Vision Element
	• Determine "breakthrough" objectives
	  • Select vision elements to emphasize
	  • Prioritize and select the 1–2 most important
	Create Improvement Plan
	• Develop first-level strategies
	  • Brainstorming, other creative techniques

Business Plans, Programs, and Projects
 	
(How to execute the strategy?)
	Deploy the Plan
	• Develop second-level strategies
	  • Continue developing subordinate strategies until they decompose
	    into clearly definable tasks
	Implement the Plan
	• Measure and document in detail
	Review the Plan
	• Weekly, monthly, quarterly, annually
	Corrective Action
	• Modify procedures, plans, etc., as required (PDCA)

Funding (How to finance strategy execution?)	**[Not Specifically Addressed]**

Figure 2.2   The *hoshin kanri* strategic planning model.
Adapted from Cowley and Domb, *Beyond Strategic Vision* (1997). Used with permission.

STRATEGY FORMATION

Henry Minztberg devotes considerable time and attention to the issue of *strategy formation*. He points out that traditional strategic planning decomposes into four hierarchies of elements and the activities that generate them[5]:

- Objectives
- Budgets
- Strategies
- Programs

Mintzberg makes a persuasive case for the fact that there isn't always a connection between these hierarchies. For example, in just looking at the names of these hierarchies themselves, you might assume that objectives drive the development of strategies to achieve them, that programs operationalize the strategies, and that budgets fund the programs. But in many cases, you'd be wrong.

As often as not, budgets drive the range of objectives. In some cases, programs originate within the organization (equipment technology upgrades, for example), with little consideration of what strategy or objective they support. And strategies sometimes emerge from either opportunities in the external environment or brainstorms from within the organization with little or no reference to preconceived objectives.

Consequently, Mintzberg concludes that strategy—deciding on the paths to take to reach a company's objectives—can spring from either a controlled process or it can emerge, unbidden and unanticipated. And owing to the fact that documented successes exist for both ways, an effective strategic planning methodology should be flexible enough to allow for either eventuality.

THE BUREAUCRACY PITFALL

Mintzberg also observes that the operationalizing of strategy—in other words, transitioning from ideas to action—is where most of the strategic planning models become very detailed.[6] *Hoshin* planning is no exception. In fact, the majority of the *hoshin* planning process is devoted to the details of operationalizing strategy: the PDCA cycle, at all levels throughout the organization.

This devotion to detail is obviously needed in many organizations. Without such a formal structure, many companies would fall victim to *entropy,* as applied to organizational systems.* But one CEO has observed, "*Hoshin* planning is custom-made for the anally retentive. It luxuriates in the details of record keeping, data collection, calendars, schedules, frequent and rigorous plan and progress reviews, and the roles and responsibilities associated with these activities." He was implying that a bureaucratic empire could easily result from the aggressive application of *hoshin kanri* without a reasonable effort to keep it in check. Clearly, this intensity is desirable in some organizations— maybe even necessary. But it's not in others, and distinguishing where the line is between "enough" and "too much" can be difficult.

---

* In thermodynamics, entropy is a measure of the energy unavailable for work during a process, a quantity that increases as a system undergoes spontaneous change. (*Webster's New Universal Unabridged Dictionary,* New York: Barnes and Noble, 1989). As applied to organizations, it's liberally interpreted to mean the tendency of a system to evolve toward confusion or disorganization, unless concerted efforts are made to hold it together.

TOO LITTLE DETAIL, OR TOO MUCH? A WAY OUT OF THE DILEMMA

Everybody makes value judgments—right versus wrong. I'm no exception. But where the application of methods is concerned, I suggest that there may be more than one "right" way. Further, I suggest that the determination of the "right way" is highly situational. What's right for one organization in one situation might not be right for another.

Forty years ago, two systems researchers concluded that management of organizations is either *mechanistic* or *organic*.[7] Mechanistic management systems are characterized by specialized differentiation of tasks, individuals viewing their tasks as being distinct from the whole, precisely defined rights and obligations, hierarchical structure, vertical interactions between superiors and subordinates, and top-down instructions. Organic management systems, on the other hand, emphasize individual performance based on knowledge of the whole system, continual redefinition of tasks through interaction with others, and much lateral interaction and consulting.[8] A mechanistic management approach is likely to be more suitable for relatively stable organization environments, while organizations that must cope with unstable, changing conditions are probably better suited to an organic approach.

I would take this a step further. A mechanistic organization would probably be better suited to a strategic planning model that provides the kind of detail and structure inherent in both the military model and the *hoshin* planning model. An organic organization would have a need for a strategic planning model that is less complex, less detailed, and perhaps more flexible.

The problem, however, is that it's often difficult to characterize companies as either mechanistic or organic. These terms might be better treated as opposite ends of a continuum, the extremes of which could be total anarchy and total regimentation. Most companies will lie at some intermediate point on that continuum, exhibiting characteristics of each to some degree.

HOSHIN KANRI AND THE SCHOOLS OF STRATEGIC THOUGHT

Where would *hoshin kanri* fit into the 10 strategic schools of thought (chapter 1)? Clearly, the detail of its pedagogy would suggest the *formal* planning school. To a lesser extent, characteristics of other schools might also apply. The whole Japanese approach to management from which *hoshin* springs has elements of the *cultural* and *environmental* schools embedded in it.

CONCLUSION

The *hoshin kanri* model was originally intended to be a process improvement tool and policy deployment model, not a strategic planning model. But as I mentioned in chapter 1, it's possible to synthesize elements of different systems to form a new creation. The strategic planning model introduced in chapter 4 is such a synthesis. It includes overtones of *hoshin kanri,* but it's also intended to resolve the apparent dilemma of "too much detail versus too little." It will provide a basic framework, like a Christmas tree, upon which individual companies can hang their chosen decorations. Those companies that prefer the heavily decorated tree can hang as much of *hoshin* planning's detail on it as they like. Those companies that prefer an understated tree, where the beauty of individual ornaments isn't visually overwhelmed by volume, can limit their effort to just what is offered in this book.

> *Act after having made assessments. The one who first knows measures of far and near wins—this is the rule of armed struggle.*
>
> —Master Sun
> *Sun Tzu and the Art of War*

ENDNOTES

1. M. Cowley and E. Domb, *Beyond Strategic Vision: Effective Corporate Action with Hoshin Planning* (Boston: Butterworth-Heineman, 1997): 16.
2. Ibid, 2–3.
3. W. E. Deming, *Out of the Crisis* (1986): 88.
4. Cowley and Domb, *Beyond Strategic Vision.*
5. H. Mintzberg, *The Rise and Fall of Strategic Planning* (New York: The Free Press, 1994): 82–90.
6. Ibid, 60.
7. T. Burns and G. M. Stalker, *The Management of Innovation* (London: Tavistock Publications, 1961).
8. H. Weihrich and H. Koontz, *Management: A Global Persective*, 10th ed. (New York: McGraw-Hill, 1993).

3

The Military Strategic Planning Model

Plans get you into things, but you got to work your own way out.

—Will Rogers

Creating and executing a business strategy is not unlike planning and prosecuting a military campaign. Many of the same attributes that make for good military plans are equally applicable—and translatable—to civilian uses, in both commercial business and government agencies. In this chapter we'll examine the military approach to strategy development and execution and see the strengths and weaknesses of the military planning process. In chapter 4, we'll see how the strengths of the military approach can be adapted for general use.

If there's any activity that demands planning, it's military operations. Battles are lost when the wrong tactics are used. Wars are lost when strategies fail. Sometimes such failures can result as much from poor execution as from poor planning. But for now, let's assume that our military forces are capable of executing strategy and tactics.

The challenges of planning a large, complicated military operation are significant, and the risk is high. I'm not referring to something small, such as the 1983 rescue operation in Grenada, or the overthrow and capture of General Noriega in Panama in 1989. I'm talking about something on the order of Operation Desert Storm, the largest deployment and application of military force in the history of the world—even bigger than the "D-Day" invasion of Europe in 1944.

WHY THE MILITARY DOES PLANNING

The U.S. military has a well-deserved reputation for meticulous planning, but it wasn't always that way. For 170 years of America's existence, from the Revolutionary War through World War II, the military wasn't what we would call "proactive"—it was decidedly reactive. In each case, a peacetime military waited for its nation's call, then decided what to do *after* it was engaged in hostilities.

You might think that the executive branch and Congress would have learned a lesson about this after World War I, but you'd be wrong. After the armistice was concluded in 1918, America demobilized its military and retreated back into isolationism, secure behind its ocean barriers. Consequently, it was only marginally more ready to engage the Axis powers in 1941 than it was the Kaiser in 1917.

But after World War II, cooler heads prevailed. The President and Congress recognized that isolationism was no longer a realistic option. The development of nuclear weapons, the evolution of the means to deliver them over intercontinental distances, and the polarization of East and West with an "iron curtain" between them made that impossible. The demobilization following World War II was not as drastic as the one that happened after World War I. America recognized its security responsibilities around the world and refrained from retreating into an isolationist cocoon.

Shortly thereafter, the rapid precipitation of the Korean War made it clear that military operations would have to be anticipated—not just a reaction—in potential strategic trouble spots around the world.

HOW THE MILITARY DOES PLANNING

U.S. military planning is a well-defined hierarchical process. It begins at the highest levels with the formation of national strategy. (See Figure 3.1.) The President and the National Security Council (NSC) consider America's principles, domestic and foreign commitments, policies, and politico-economic-military capabilities in determining national interests and objectives. These interests and objectives, in turn, provide the basis for the President and NSC to determine U.S. military policy—the national security objectives and worldwide defense commitments required to realize them. This policy becomes the planning guidance to the Department of Defense.

THE JOINT STRATEGIC PLANNING SYSTEM

Armed with the national military objectives and commitments, the office of the Joint Chiefs of Staff begins a five-phase process called the joint strategic planning system (JSPS). (See Figure 3.2.) These fives phases are:

• *Strategic assessment.* This first phase combines several inputs to determine what the national military strategy should be. One of these inputs is the U.S. military policy provided by the President and the National Security Council. Another is a long-range evaluation—a 20-year projection—of what the international economic, political, and security situations will be. A third is a capability forecast: what kinds of military technologies lie on the horizon in the foreseeable future? Each of these factors is compared with the existing military strategy, and a new or modified strategy is created.

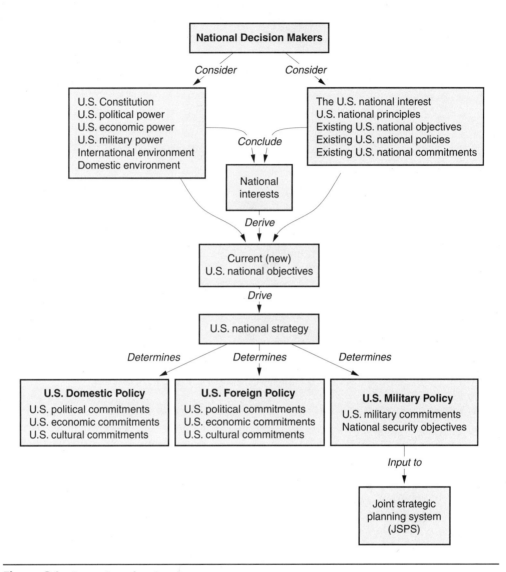

Figure 3.1 Formation of national strategy.
Adapted from the *Joint Officer's Staff Guide* (1984), Armed Forces Staff College.

• *Strategic direction.* The second phase of the JSPS is intended to produce a definitive statement of military missions—objectives and tasks—for the U.S. military to achieve throughout the world. This phase also allocates the required forces—equipment, supplies, and personnel—to geographic regional commanders, so that they can successfully complete their missions. The inputs for this direction are the same long-range security projections and the national military strategy from the strategic assessment phase.

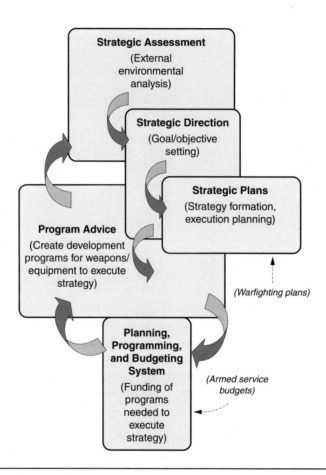

Figure 3.2   The joint strategic planning concept.

• *Strategic plans.* With the specific military tasks and allocated forces as a starting point, the regional commanders use a process called the Joint Operation Planning and Execution System (JOPES) to create the actual combat plans for their operating theaters. These are the so-called "war plans" that will guide the prosecution of combat in a geographic area.

• *Program advice.* Besides guiding war planning, the same output from the strategic direction phase—regional military missions and required force structures—provide the input to guide the creation of military hardware acquisition programs, force capabilities, and personnel/training to enable the armed services to fulfill their regional missions successfully in the future.

• *Planning, programming, and budgeting system (PPBS).* Hardware and force development programs are inevitably multi-year efforts. They are also the responsibility of the individual services (Army, Air Force, and Navy). The Department of Defense uses the PPBS to craft annual armed service budgets out of multi-year programs. A five-year defense plan (FYDP) is created to guide long-term budgeting. The FYDP includes the current (budget) year, and rough projections for the next four years into the future. Each year, the most recent year's budget drops out of the picture, the next year's projection becomes the new budget year, and a new out-year is added to the "front end."

This five-phase strategic planning model is designed to start with very broad guidance on the role the military is expected to play in supporting national strategy. Then, through a progressive analytical process, it creates successively more specific levels of programs, war plans, and tactics until national strategy is connected completely through a vertical hierarchy to individual combat units.

How effective is this planning hierarchy? Consider Operation Desert Storm. The U.S. deployed a military force to the Persian Gulf, with no advance notice, to throw the Iraqi forces out of Kuwait. In four months, a logistical task equivalent to moving the entire city of Des Moines, Iowa, halfway around the world was completed successfully. In another six weeks a 500,000-man army, along with its equipment, was largely destroyed, and the mission was accomplished.

But what is not obvious is the strategy and planning behind the victory. The U.S. Central Command had built a theater strategic war plan over the preceding 10 years, and the JSPS made possible the capabilities to execute it. Though Central Command's strategic plan was conceived with a different adversary and objective in mind, the essential foundation was there from which to improvise. The JSPS and the JOPES provided that capability.

STRENGTHS OF THE MILITARY PLANNING SYSTEM

As a strategic planning model, the military approach has several definite advantages:

1. *Goal/objective oriented.* The overall goal is well-defined. At each level, critical success factors—necessary conditions that *must* be satisfied—are clearly established, as well as the intermediate objectives needed to fulfill them.

2. *A vertically integrated, traceable hierarchy.* The national military strategy is traceable through successively lower levels all the way to the tasks of individually deployed units. Those operating "where the rubber meets the road" have excellent visibility on how their contributions support higher-level strategic objectives.

3. *A "family of plans."* (See Figure 3.3.) The national strategy begets a series of parallel regional operation plans. Each regional operation plan is supported by the component plans of its army, navy, and air forces. Tactical plans of army corps, naval fleets, and air force units, in turn, support their service component plans.

4. *Lateral, as well as vertical, coordination.* The component plans in each operating theater are, by nature, integrated. Everything the Air Force and Navy do is designed to support, or to take pressure off of, the Army and Marine ground forces. Likewise, the Army depends on naval and air forces completing their assigned tasks in

order to complete its own mission quickly and effectively. Coordination and communication among components is not just expected—it's "engineered" into the war plan.

5. *Delegation.* For the U.S. military, the essence of executing military operations is delegation. The "family of plans" is designed for a situation in which authority is delegated and commanders are encouraged to exercise initiative at each successive level of the hierarchy. Micromanagement almost never happens, either in the plan or the execution, for two reasons. First, the plan is relatively static—a "snapshot in time" based on assumptions made in peacetime that may not be valid anymore by the time war occurs. Subordinate commanders are expected to modify the plan as required to suit the actual situation, yet still achieve the higher-level objectives. Second, things never unfold on the battlefield exactly as expected, even if the plan seems to mirror reality to begin with. What Clausewitz called the "fog and friction" of war take over.[1]

U.S. military planners *expect* this to happen, and they deliberately design plans to allow—even encourage—innovation and creativity, both of which can happen only if the plan is based on a policy of delegation.

6. *A repetitive process.* As just noted, plans are based on best-estimate static assumptions, and because uncertainty prevails, adjustments will inevitably be necessary during both planning and execution. The military planning system prescribes cyclic reviews and revisions of strategic and operation plans, generally on an annual or biennial schedule. As soon as it becomes clear that a particular plan is likely to be executed, planners immediately evaluate the planning assumptions in light of the actual situation and determine how execution should differ from the plan. Execution orders then reflect these differences.

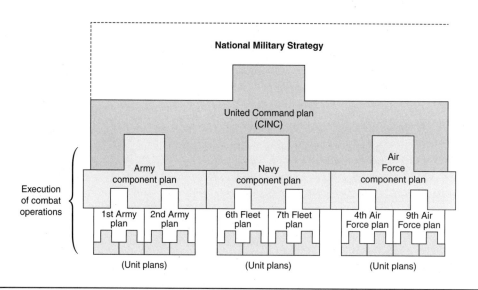

Figure 3.3 Family (hierarchy) of plans.

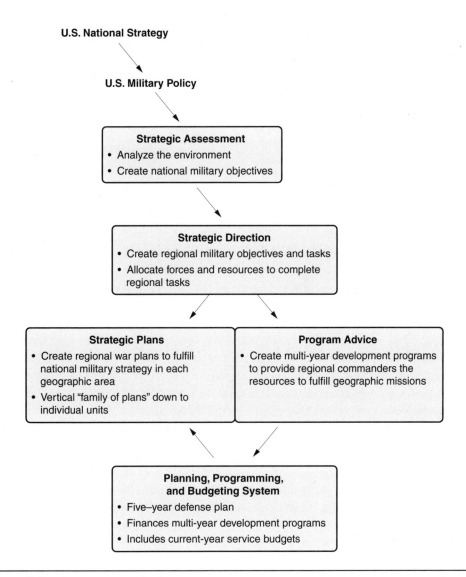

Figure 3.4 The JSPS summarized.

WEAKNESSES OF THE MILITARY PLANNING SYSTEM

What we've just seen is a very elaborate, complex construction (summarized in Figure 3.4). Where the national defense is concerned, it functions reasonably well. There are, of course, disconnects and breakdowns, particularly in the Department of Defense's planning, programming, and budgeting system, which is the mechanism designed to translate military missions into the resources—hardware and people—needed to accomplish them.* Instead, let's focus on the characteristics of the whole military model that make it impossible to overlay it, intact, onto a nonmilitary domain.

• *Specification of detail.* The JSPS, JOPES, and PPBS are all highly pedagogical. They are filled with specific, detailed information and instructions, in typical "bureaucratese," that describe how the system operates, who's responsible for what, and how to dot every "i" and cross every "t."

• *Complexity.* The processes themselves are very complicated, with scores of internal iterations and exchanges of requests, reviews, and approvals. The PPBS alone, for example, sends working documents back and forth between the Joint Chiefs of Staff, the Secretary of Defense, the White House, the services, and the unified commands many times before even one cycle of the PPBS is complete. If you don't have a process map, a clock, and a calendar, you can find yourself playing Abbott and Costello's game, "Who's on first?"

• *Time-intensive.* It takes time to go through each of the steps of these three planning processes (JSPS, JOPES, and PPBS). Some of the JSPS documents are on annual cycles, while others are multi-year. PPBS is an annual exercise, but it takes 18 months to complete one cycle, so there are usually two cycles in process at any given time. Operation plans are reviewed and updated on a two-year cycle. About the time an approved operation plan is ready from the preceding cycle, it's time to start a new cycle all over again. This, of course makes JOPES a "planner's heaven" and a "planner's hell" at the same time: on the one hand, there's job security in knowing that the process never ends, but on the other hand there's frustration in knowing that about the time you finish, it's time to start all over again.

• *Inflexible and unresponsive.* The military model leaves something to be desired in these areas. A heavily prescribed and regulated process doesn't lend itself to changing direction when changing or volatile international situations do.** As we saw earlier, the joint operation planning and execution system accommodates this shortcoming by allowing enough ambiguity in the plans themselves to provide battlefield commanders the flexibility to run the war as changing situations dictate, within broadly defined limits. JOPES even anticipates the "brushfires" that the deliberate planning process is totally unequipped to deal with by providing *crisis action planning*—an orderly procedure for planning and fighting small engagements "on the fly, by the seat of the pants."

---

* We won't get into the sins and failings of the PPBS here, but it's somewhat of a disaster. It has worked, often in spite of itself, but it's inefficient, often wasteful, and sometimes ineffective. Its failures are well documented. For an excellent critique of the PPBS, see *The Rise and Fall of Strategic Planning* (Mintzberg: 1994), pp. 121–22. Mintzberg concludes: "The simple fact is that they never did put P [planning] and PB [programming, budgeting] together into a S [system] that worked."

** The U.S. military response in Afghanistan in October 2001 can be considered more of a crisis action response than execution of a deliberate plan. Can you imagine how long it would have taken for the DoD to go through the whole JSPS/JOPES and budget process (2+ years) to develop an orderly, deliberate response to the terrorist attacks in New York and Washington? Only the crisis action planning part of the military model can be considered truly responsive in the short term.

BOYD'S THEORY OF MANEUVER WARFARE

From a practical perspective, it's not possible—nor desirable—to separate the creation of the strategy from its execution. Moreover, because the operating environment is both highly uncertain and variable, often in ways that can't be completely foreseen, it's not possible to operate for long with a static strategy. In much the same way that the presence of even a passive observer influences the observed environment (a major element of the Heisenberg uncertainty principle), any action to execute a strategy, however minimal, changes the strategic environment. And in a changed environment, the originally conceived strategy may no longer be optimum, which generates a need to adjust the original strategy and re-execute.

This kind of design–execute–adjust–execute cycle is well known—now—to the business world in a more microcosmic form: the Shewhart cycle, used to guide continuous quality improvement (plan–do–check–act). But such a feedback loop, though often applied to make tactical adjustments in both military and civilian worlds, has never been formally applied at the strategic level. John Boyd changed all that in 1976. The engine for cycling through successive refinements of strategy and execution is Boyd's "OODA loop." (See sidebar, page 28.)

Upon his retirement from the U.S. Air Force, Boyd set about a comprehensive effort to study the evolution of strategy from the time of Sun Tzu to the present. But he did so from a much broader perspective than just military history alone. Boyd's reading list in his multi-year research effort includes 318 references that run the gamut from military and political history to philosophy, science fiction, physics, creativity and innovation, psychology, economics, culture, high technology, political science, management, intelligence and espionage, and mathematics. In other words, he employed perhaps the broadest-based systems approach ever to synthesize his strategic philosophy into an intensive two-day military briefing he called "Patterns of Conflict." This briefing was subsequently captured in a document called *A Discourse on Winning and Losing.**

The centerpiece of Boyd's strategic philosophy, which applies equally effectively to competitive business as well as warfare, is the so-called "OODA loop." (See Figure 3.5) OODA is, of course, an acronym. It stands for "observe–orient–decide–act." Of these steps, "orient" is the most challenging and the most important. It sounds deceptively simple, but there is much more to it than a procedural cookbook.** The OODA loop is a meta-level template for creating and deploying overall strategy, but at a micro level it can do the same for tactics. At the same time, it's also a closed-loop feedback mechanism for the refinement or complete reinvention of both strategy and tactics. At one end of the combat spectrum, it can help define winning strategy at the level of Operation Desert Storm. At the other end of the spectrum, it can help turn your average fighter

---

 * More popularly known in defense circles as "The Green Book," because of its distinctive cover, *A Discourse on Winning and Losing* was informally printed and bound (not formally published) in limited quantity by the Marine Print Plant at Quantico, Virginia, around 1981.

** So much so, in fact, that Boyd expected that his close friends would absorb his 318-reference reading list before he would discuss his *A Discourse on Winning and Losing* with them.

"40-Second Boyd"

Colonel John R. Boyd, USAF (retired), was the greatest military theoretician since Sun Tzu. Academicians, and most generals and admirals, would undoubtedly contest that assertion, but the record is persuasive. "Who the hell is John Boyd?" you're undoubtedly wondering.

Boyd was the greatest pilot ever to strap on a fighter and go head-to-head with another in aerial combat. That he never shot down a single opponent in combat is merely an accident of fate. In more than ten years of daily air-to-air engagements against "the best of the best" at the USAF Fighter Weapons School, Boyd was *never* defeated—and a lot of very good fighter pilots tried. He beat every opponent every time in less than a minute (usually less than 20 seconds), which led to one of his many nicknames: "40-Second Boyd." Other—later—nicknames included the "Mad Major," the "Ghetto Colonel," and "Genghis John." (Are you beginning to see a pattern here?)

Boyd's remarkable success in aerial combat prompted him to wonder what he was intuitively doing differently from others, many of whom had as much or more air-to-air engagement experience than he did. Boyd's pursuit of the answer to this question produced his "energy-maneuverability theory," which, in turn, provided the foundation for the complete (and revolutionary) restructuring of modern aerial combat tactics. It also formed the basis of his subsequent arguments for fighter aircraft design. Boyd's bulldog insistence that his energy-maneuverability principles guide fighter design resulted in the F-15 and F-16 programs.

The F-16, in particular, is the most successful weapon system development program in history, for two noteworthy reasons that no other program has been able to match—or perhaps ever will. First, the F-16's air combat performance has been unequalled anywhere in the world for the past 30 years, and that performance dominance is not likely to change anytime soon. Second, it's the only weapon system in history ever to cost *less* (significantly so) than the generation that preceded it.

However, it wasn't until after John Boyd retired from military service that he produced his most profound contribution—a complete paradigm shift in the conduct of warfare. Boyd's synthesis of strategic and tactical military theory from Sun Tzu through Belisarius, Musashi, Clausewitz, Liddell Hart, and Patton, integrated with his own conclusions about energy and maneuverability, led him to create the "OODA loop." (See chapter 4 for a more detailed discussion of the OODA loop.)

Despite the fact that Boyd's strategic theories have been repeatedly borne out in combat engagements—land as well as air—since the 1980s, the mainstream military establishment has only grudgingly accepted them, and in some quarters, they are still ignored or resisted today. Though he never set foot in the Middle East combat theater, Boyd was unquestionably the architect of the strategy that produced the stunning victory with minimal casualties against Iraq in Operation Desert Storm.

The face of warfare is changing in the 21st century, as terrorism challenges the set-piece thinking of mass military engagements. Yet just as Boyd's OODA loop is applicable to individual air-to-air fighter and traditional military unit engagements, it's eminently transferable to the kind of unconventional "fourth generation warfare"* posed by terrorism.

---

*For a sobering, prescient discussion of the war on terrorism, read Lind, Nightingale, et. al., "The Changing Face of War: Into the Fourth Generation," in the *Marine Corps Gazette,* October 1989, p. 22–26, accessible on the Internet at http://www.d-n-i.net/fcs/4th_gen_war_gazette.htm. This article was written 12 years before the World Trade Center/Pentagon terrorist attacks.

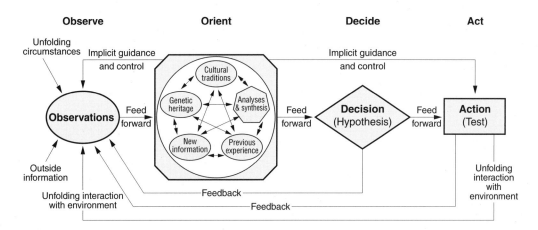

Note how *orientation* shapes *observation,* shapes *decision,* shapes *action,* and in turn is shaped by the feedback and other phenomena coming into our sensing or observing window.

Also note how the entire "loop" (not just *orientation*) is an ongoing many-sided implicit cross-referencing process of projection, empathy, correlation, and rejection.

John R. Boyd, 1992

Figure 3.5   Boyd's OODA "loop."

pilot into a "40-Second Boyd" in tactical engagements with individual opponents. This applicability up and down the spectrum of warfare and across the range of different kinds of competitive environments (that is, warfare, business, athletics, and so on) makes the OODA loop a truly fundamental advancement in competitive thinking.

Boyd's OODA loop not only implicitly accepts the uncertain, continually changing nature of the external environment, *it's designed to thrive on it.* Rather than striving for stability and predictability, it suggests that instability and unpredictability should be promoted (to the detriment of an opponent), because the OODA loop enables its users to be comfortable with the ambiguities inherent in such situations, and to control the competitive environment.

Boyd discovered that the key to winning was twofold: an effective pass through the O–O–D–A steps initially, followed by fast successive adjustments to the changed environment through repetitive OODA cycles. To the extent that a combatant (military or business) can navigate through the observe–orient–decide–act cycle faster than the opponent, control of the initiative accrues to the OODA user, while confusion, disorientation, and ambiguity accrue to the opponent. (See Figure 3.6.) In its ideal state, Boyd suggested, "it's like commanding both sides in a conflict." Notice in Figure 3.6 that the OODA loop is depicted more like a spiral. The reason for this will become apparent in chapter 4.

Traditional military strategists placed a high premium on reducing "friction" and "the fog of war,"* and bringing an adversary to a big, decisive battle. Fog is generally

---

* Clausewitz is generally credited with coining these terms in the 19th century.

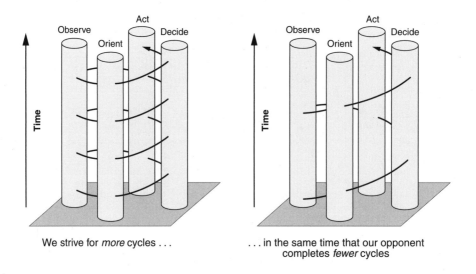

We strive for *more* cycles . . .   . . . in the same time that our opponent
                                           completes *fewer* cycles

Figure 3.6   Operating inside the opponent's decision cycle.

interpreted to mean incomplete, unclear, erroneous, or no information concerning adversaries' strength and intentions. Sometimes fog is the result of chaos in the battlefield. Friction is a physical obstacle to action. It can be a communication breakdown, confusion, or a loss of coordination resulting in collisions or contradictory actions or efforts. Friction can result from fog. Obviously, a military commander wants to cut through the fog and reduce or eliminate friction on his own side, and much attention is devoted to doing so.

Boyd, on the other hand, reveled in the idea of also maximizing the enemy's friction, sowing confusion, and causing the enemy to "unravel before the fight."[2] What allowed Boyd to do this was the ability to cycle through the O–O–D–A steps faster than his adversary—whether that adversary was a fighter pilot being "hosed" by 40-Second Boyd, or the Republican Guard being hosed by the coalition forces in Desert Storm. Boyd called this "getting inside the mind and decision cycle of the adversary."[3]*

Speed alone is not the most important aspect of executing the OODA loop. At its highest form, the loop must be so completely understood that its execution becomes implicit, not explicit. In other words, if you have to think about the step you're on and incremental transition to the next step, you're not cycling through implicitly. This is difficult to do with the most critical step in the process, orientation.

---

* I haven't even come close to doing justice to the Boyd philosophy and the OODA loop, for which I sincerely apologize to those who were close to Boyd and his work. Readers who are inclined to learn more about the OODA loop—and certainly any who entertain ideas of applying it—are well advised to educate themselves first. While the 318-reference reading list prescribed by Boyd himself might be a little intimidating, I can suggest two starting points. In order, they are *Boyd: Fighter Pilot Who Changed the Art of War,* by Robert Coram, and *The Mind War: John Boyd and American Security,* by Grant T. Hammond. (All terrorists, and terrorist "wannabes," please ignore all of the preceding advice, as well as everything in this book on Boyd and the OODA loop.)

CONCLUSION

So, where does the military model fit in relation to the schools of strategic thought (chapter 1)? It's definitely in the category of traditional, deliberate approaches—*design, formal, and positioning*. It's very much about control and positioning. Given the nature of military missions, objectives, and operations, it's very much appropriate that it be so. But as the discussion of maneuver warfare demonstrates, there must clearly be enough flexibility to respond to uncertainty in the strategic, operational, and tactical environments. To that extent, there are strong overtones of the *learning, power,* and *environmental* schools as well. And because the military is a ponderous, stable kind of organization, it tends to resist change. In that respect, there are certainly elements of the *cultural* and *configuration* schools—especially the *configuration* school—at work.

In chapter 4, we'll see how the military model can be translated and synthesized for nonmilitary uses, so that you can realize the benefits of applying the time-tested principles of war without toting the "anchor" that typically goes along with them. Chapter 9 will introduce the key characteristics and elements of successful military operations planning and relate them to a nonmilitary environment.

> *Therefore, I have heard of military operations that were clumsy but swift, but I have never seen one that was skillful and lasted a long time. It is never beneficial to a nation to have a military operation continue for a long time.*
>
> —Master Sun
> *Sun Tzu and the Art of War*

ENDNOTES

1. G. T. Hammond, *The Mind of War: John Boyd and American Security* (Washington, D.C.: Smithsonian Institution Press, 2001): 163–65.
2. R. Coram, *Boyd: The Fighter Pilot Who Changed the Art of War* (New York: Little, Brown and Co., 2002): 332.
3. Coram, *Boyd*, 335.

4

The Constraint Management Model

*Systems almost always have the peculiarity that the characteristic of
the whole cannot be understood from even the most complete understanding of the individual components.*

—Ernst Mayr (biologist)

PROBLEMS WITH TRADITIONAL AND CONTEMPORARY METHODS

As we saw in chapter 1, there's no shortage of evidence that traditional schools of
thought on strategic planning (*design, formal,* and *positioning*) leave a lot to be desired.
And while the contemporary schools address many of the deficiencies of the traditional
schools, they have shortcomings of their own.

Discontent with traditional approaches seems to center on four characteristics:

1. Disregard for dependencies

2. Inflexibility

3. Greater emphasis on "the plan" than on "the strategy"

4. Difficulty in implementation

Disregard for dependencies. Perhaps the most serious failing of traditional strategic
planning methods is the way they compartmentalize the functions of an organization. In
effect, it treats each of the various major organizational functions—marketing/sales, operations, and finance—as largely independent of one another. Certainly, lip service is paid
to the interdependency among them, but planning rarely considers this interdependency.

Inflexibility. The process of planning itself breeds a basic inflexibility in organizations, which includes a resistance to significant change. Mintzberg contends that planning is fundamentally a conservative process, serving the basic (established) orientation of the organization. Any changes it promotes tend to lie within the context of the organization's established orientation. Planning seems to work best when the broad outlines of a strategy are already in place, *not* when strategic change is required from the process itself. So, rather than creating new strategies, planning generally can't proceed without their prior existence.[1]

"The plan" versus "the strategy." What Mintzberg implies is that strategy "form" seems to follow existing organizational "function." Companies develop their plans in terms of the subunits they already have—be they functions, divisions, or departments.[2] This might be acceptable to many companies in a relatively stable environment, where the underlying assumptions and paradigm don't change very much, or evolve slowly over long periods. Agriculture and automobile manufacture spring to mind as examples. Changes in such cases are, at best, changes in strategic position, rather than in the strategies themselves.

However, for organizations operating in dynamic, rapidly evolving environments, the rules of the game are more Darwinian by an order of magnitude. "Adapt or die" is a daily operating philosophy. Inflexibility is the kiss of death, and the formal strategic planning processes of companies such as General Electric or General Motors are casually dismissed as irrelevant by companies in information technology, computer hardware or software, or the Internet.

Keep in mind, however, that the strategic environment is probably more like a continuum than a structure of absolutes, with stability at one end of the continuum and chaos at the other. Toward the unstable end there are probably varying degrees of "ordered chaos," with evolutionary cycle times ranging from the very short to the medium term. Toward the stable end are also varying degrees of stability, from almost glacial paces of change to more orderly evolution in the medium term. So while companies at the stable end can tolerate a strategic planning process that embraces incremental change based on predetermined strategy, companies at the unstable end need a process that can emphasize the "strategy" part, while holding the "plan" part to an absolute minimum.

Moreover, Minztberg also emphasizes that, contrary to conventional wisdom, successful strategies tend to *emerge* from environmental situations or from within the recesses of the organization as often as they're *deliberately planned* from the top down. Witness, for example, the unanticipated, unsought success of Post-It notes for the 3M Company—clearly an emergent strategy for a company previously known mostly for tape and other industrial adhesives.

Difficulty in implementation. Assuming strategy can be effectively developed and expressed in some kind of plan, implementing the strategy is often a challenge. In a survey in the 1980s, 87 percent of respondents expressed disappointment and frustration with their planning systems. Almost two-thirds attributed this "discontent mainly to difficulties encountered in the implementation of plans, not the plans themselves or the process of planning."[3]

Criticisms of the contemporary schools (*entrepreneurial, cognitive, learning, power, environmental, cultural,* and *configuration*) seem to be centered on three characteristics:

1. Limited control by those charged with leadership of the organization

2. Overemphasis on relatively narrow factors

3. A predilection for the status quo (that is, not changing)

Limited control. CEOs, administrators, executive directors, and military commanders are expected to lead, not allow the organization to wander in the direction of whatever current "opportunity" presents itself. Most of the contemporary schools encourage a reactive, rather than a proactive, attitude. Senior leaders are usually uncomfortable with that. They'd rather be the "captain of their own ship, master of their own fate." Following the *environmental* school seems to leave one exclusively at the mercy of external events. Even the *learning* school, as popular as it has proven to be (thanks to Peter Senge), risks fiddling while Rome burns to some extent.

Overemphasis on narrow factors. For some, the *power* school puts too much emphasis on politics and relationships, both internal and external. The *cultural* school seems too preoccupied with the socialization relationships for others. And the *cognitive* school risks spending too much time thinking at the expense of acting.

A predilection for the status quo. The *cultural* and the *configuration* schools, in particular, put an organization at risk of valuing stability too highly, at the expense of creative growth and change.

PROBLEMS WITH THE *HOSHIN* APPROACH

The *hoshin* planning approach is a considerable improvement over the traditional strategic planning model. It's substantially better focused on the ends–means relationship. It is, however, pedagogically intensive, emphasizing measurement and documentation at every turn,* and stressing almost obsessive reviews. It's considerably more process-oriented than system-oriented. There are also tools for every possible taste, preference, and need.** In the right situations, these tools and techniques are all useful, and the bigger the toolbox, the more choices people have.

But the big toolbox is a heavy toolbox, too. And sometimes it's difficult to find the small screwdriver at the bottom. The examples cited for *hoshin* planning (and the tools

---

* For example, there are review tables, process overview maps, flowcharts, correlation tables, annual business plan matrices, annual plan tables, performance measurements tables, Gantt-type charts, manpower loading charts, fact sheets, and abnormality reports.

** For example, there are the original *seven quality control tools* (flowcharts, checksheets, Pareto charts, run charts, control charts, histograms, and scatter plots), the so-called *seven new tools* (matrix diagrams, affinity diagram, radar charts, relations diagrams, tree diagrams, process decision program charts, and activity network diagrams), fishbone charts, and the PDCA cycle. There are also techniques, such as brainstorming, team work, consensus-building, conflict management, benchmarking, process management, and the "house of quality" (voice of the customer).

and techniques) are largely focused on process improvement, confirming Mintzberg's contention that strategy formation has already preceded *hoshin* planning. Such strategies as *hoshin* planning *does* address are closer to being changes to strategic position in a predetermined organizational orientation.

Also, for many people, especially those at the organizational levels in which strategy is determined, *hoshin* planning is a little too intensive. To develop effective strategy and turn it into action, often "less is more." *Elegance in simplicity.* That's the ultimate objective of the best strategic planning models. (Or, if it isn't, it should be!) To paraphrase the New Testament, "Sufficient unto the day is the detail thereof."* Which is another way of saying, "Keep it simple, stupid!"

PROBLEMS WITH THE MILITARY APPROACH

As indicated in chapter 3, the military model of strategic planning has some decidedly desirable characteristics. Chief among these is a clear and unequivocal traceability between the overall national security strategy and the operational theater war plans. The strategic construct that results from the joint strategic planning system (JSPS) is also very well aligned with the world geopolitical environment. And there is a coherent (if ponderous) funding process—the planning, programming, and budgeting system—to provide the capabilities and resources needed to support the strategy.

But using the military strategic planning process is a lot like driving an eighteen-wheel tractor-trailer on a Formula One racetrack. As long as the truck is driving the straightaways, things are fine. The irregular curves and banks, however, demand high-speed, maneuverable race cars rather than trucks. Likewise, when the geopolitical environment presents the military establishment a tight curve, it's a challenge to clear the turn and still stay on the course.

For example, the U.S. military has long had a force structure designed for the massed armor, infantry formations, and frontal engagements prevalent in World War II and Korea. The unconventional (guerrilla) warfare of Vietnam and the geopolitical-military situation related to terrorism in the 1990s presented problems for such a force structure, with predictable results: ultimate defeat in Vietnam, and an uncertain future in the war against global terrorism.

The American military establishment does reasonably well changing strategic positions within its basic orientation, as characterized by Mintzberg. Witness the fact that it adapted admirably from the idea of fighting the Warsaw Pact in the central European plains to a *blitzkrieg* against the Iraqis in the Middle East desert. But this adaptation was actually one of position, rather than orientation. Even today, some 10 years after the Persian Gulf War, the Department of Defense is still grappling with the reorientation of its forces from the massed formations and pitched frontal battles of World War II to fast

---

* *The Christian Bible,* New Testament, Gospel of St. Matthew, 9:34.

deployments and lighter but highly violent units capable of near-instantaneous response to regional brushfire engagements.

Fortunately for the military, its competitive environment is closer to the stable end of the continuum than to the chaotic. But it still demands constant vigilance and a willingness to change strategy, even if that happens over longer time horizons. And the JSPS is well suited for such an environment.

The military's emphasis, however, is still more on "the plan" (and the planning) than on "the strategy." And implementation is a lot like the mating of elephants: it requires high-level contact, it's accompanied by a lot of screaming and shouting, and it takes years to show results.

STRATEGIC NAVIGATION

In light of what Mintzberg and others have said concerning the disconnect between "strategy" and "planning," I almost hesitate to use the two words together. Instead, a better concept might be *strategic navigation.*

Let's picture ourselves as captain of a ship. Let's assume that we're hired by the owners, though we could also be an owner-captain. Either way, the owner decides the destination of the ship before it embarks. The captain is responsible for determining the best route to the destination—the one that avoids foreseeable obstacles, adverse weather, maybe even enemy submarines. If we're talking about an around-the-world race, there are also competing ships (owners and captains) to consider.

Once the owner has established the destination, the captain plots the course on a chart. We estimate the time it will take to reach that port, and we hire the crew and provision the ship for the journey. This is often an expensive undertaking, which the owner is expected to support.* With a sailing plan in hand, the cargo secure below, all hands aboard, and the ship fully provisioned, we then order the deck crew to "cast off."

Let's assume this particular ship is leaving Virginia, on the east coast of the United States, and is heading for the Strait of Gibraltar, which separates Europe from Africa on the eastern side of the Atlantic Ocean. (See Figure 4.1.) For the sake of simplicity, we've determined that the shortest distance between two points (our port of embarkation and Gibraltar) is a straight line. We've established preplanned "milestones" on the navigation chart, so everybody knows where the ship *should be* each day: on the course line, at successive predetermined distances from Gibraltar.

Each day, the navigator fixes the position of the ship, either by celestial means or (these days) by global positioning satellite. We do two things with this updated position. First, by measuring the distance traveled and dividing that by the time elapsed, we come up with an average speed since the last known position. By measuring the distance between our most current position and our destination, an estimated time of arrival at

---

* It's been said that a boat is "a hole in the water into which you pour money."

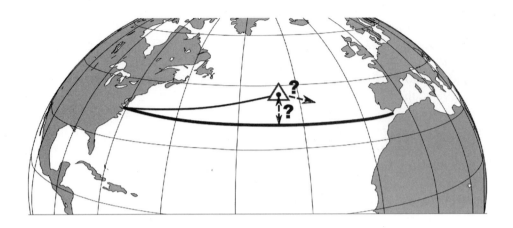

Figure 4.1   "Strategic navigation" (example).

Gibraltar can be predicted. In other words, we can tell the owner with assurance when we're going to be there.

The second thing a captain does with the updated fix position is to determine how far off course the ship might be. Triangulation between the fix position, the planned course line, and the destination will tell us how far left or right to turn the ship so that it reaches Gibraltar, rather than the English Channel. It's much easier on everybody if the captain makes small adjustments to heading and speed early, rather than waiting until Europe comes over the horizon and making a 90-degree turn at full steam to reach Gibraltar on time.

Strategic planning is really only part of the strategic navigation of business—whether that business is commercial competition, effective government, or military engagement. The owners of the business (or system) decide what the destination will be. It's the job of senior management to decide on the best course to get there and what will be needed to do the job.

Sometimes, however, the owner decides to change the destination of the ship, often without any prior warning. In our nautical example, let's say the owner has come to the bridge from her cabin and said to us, "I don't really want to go to Greece. Let's go to Singapore instead!" We're now two-thirds of the way across the Atlantic, on a heading of zero-nine-zero, making 25 knots. We have to replan the entire trip while underway, including new, unanticipated stops for fuel and provisions (and maybe mosquito repellant). Depending on the time of year and the weather in the South Atlantic and Indian Oceans, the entire strategy for reaching the new destination might have to change.

Does this happen in business? Of course it does! And sometimes it isn't the owner who decides to change destinations. Often it's circumstances beyond the control of either the owner or the captain. Maybe a market for a certain kind of product collapses. Maybe new technology renders our existing products, services, or processes obsolete almost overnight. Or perhaps we're visionary enough to see such a paradigm shift coming and make a smaller heading change earlier. Any of these circumstances can completely invalidate a strategic plan, perhaps even an entire organizational orientation.

Consider, for example, the Mothers' March of Dimes. In the 1940s, this organization was formed to wage war on polio, a cruel crippler of children and young adults. By the early 1960s, the Salk and Sabin vaccines had solved the polio problem, and today it's virtually nonexistent on the face of the earth. The original business of the Mothers' March of Dimes evaporated in a very short time. But the March of Dimes is still with us, because the organization reinvented itself, rebuilding its strategy to focus on the elimination of birth defects and infant mortality—a mission sure to require a very long time to accomplish. This change was an exercise in strategic navigation.

DEFINING STRATEGY

We've seen in chapters 1 through 3 that different groups have a different concept of what strategy and strategic planning are. Before we can effectively assess the value of different strategy development methods, we need a common definition of what "strategy" is. This book, and the constraint management model introduced here, is based on the following definition of strategy:

> Strategy is the means and methods required to satisfy the conditions necessary to achieving a system's ultimate goal.

Good strategy satisfies the necessary conditions quickly, effectively, and efficiently. Bad or faulty strategy fails in one or more of these characteristics (see sidebar on page 40). Creating and executing a good strategy requires:

- A clear and unequivocal understanding of the system's overall goal.

- A complete, accurate determination of the discrete conditions—the critical success factors—required to achieve the system's goal. Satisfying these requirements alone may not be sufficient to realize the goal, but failure to satisfy even one will prevent goal attainment. In other words, necessary conditions are "showstoppers."

- Selecting a methodology and determining the means (resources) to realize the conditions/success factors necessary to achieve the system's goal.

- Effective leadership and everlasting focus ("eye on the ball"), self-discipline, and accountability at all levels of the system's organization.

CHARACTERISTICS OF A ROBUST METHODOLOGY

If you accept the idea that moving into the future is an exercise in strategic navigation, the next question is: "By what means shall we navigate?" We've seen that the traditional, military, and *hoshin* approaches to strategic planning all leave something to be

---

"Critical Success Factors" or "Necessary Conditions?"

The constraint management model for strategy development and execution assumes that for any goal to be achieved, a discrete set of necessary conditions (NC) must be satisfied. "Necessary conditions" is a term used by E. M. Goldratt in his work on the *theory of constraints.* The term refers to a very few high-level requirements—usually no more than 3–5—that must be met, or the system's goal will not be achieved. Goldratt cited three necessary conditions common to all business organizations: satisfied customers; secure, satisfied employees; and making money—all of these now as well as in the future. (Goldratt Satellite Program (#8), 2000.) There may be others pertinent to specific circumstances, industries, or environments.

In business circles, necessary conditions are often referred to as *critical success factors* (CSF), meaning, in effect, "show-stoppers": those requirements that will doom the organization to failure if not effectively satisfied.

For the purposes of this book, the two are synonymous and interchangeable. You'll see both used. Keep in mind that they mean the same thing.

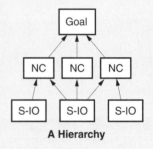

A Hierarchy

Another term you'll see in this book is strategic intermediate objective (S-IO). This is a somewhat lower-level milestone or outcome that may be required to satisfy a necessary condition. Chapter 5 will differentiate the system goal, necessary conditions (or critical success factors), and strategic intermediate objectives more completely. For now, it's sufficient to say that these constitute a kind of hierarchy.

---

desired. So, what's the alternative? Whatever the answer might be for your organization, it ought to satisfy four criteria:

1. *Systems approach.* Organizations live or die as complete systems, not as a collection of independent parts. A strategic planning approach that fails to recognize this characteristic of organizations runs a high risk of *suboptimizing:* improving a part of the system at the expense of the whole.

To make sure we're all singing from the same sheet of music, let's establish a definition of a system. Figure 4.2 shows four different definitions related to systems. For the purposes of what follows in this book, we'll use this synthesized definition of a system:

> A set of interrelated things encompassed by some arbitrary boundary, interacting with one another and an external environment, forming a complex but unitary whole and working toward a common overall objective.

Notice the key words in this definition: "interrelated," "interacting," "unitary whole," and "common overall objective." The first two words imply *dependencies,* both internal and external. The idea of a unitary whole implies *coordination.* And common overall objective implies an overarching *goal* of some kind.

2. *Flexible.* A robust methodology for developing and deploying strategy should be simple and flexible enough to permit frequent, rapid adjustment when the environment changes. Ideally, it should enable decision makers to anticipate changes in the

---

a. *System.* An assemblage or combination of things or parts forming a complex or unitary whole. (*Webster's New Universal Unabridged Dictionary,* 1989.)

b. *Systems approach.* Analyses of the interrelatedness of systems and subsystems as well as the interaction of organizations with their external environment. (Weihrich and Koontz, *Management: A Global Perspective,* 1993, p. 47.)

c. *System.* Any set of components that *could* be seen as working together for the overall objective of the whole. (Athey, *Systematic Systems Approach,* 1982, p. 12.)

d. *Organizational system.* A collection of physical resources, financial resources, people, and a clearly specified set of relationships between them, such that together the financial resources, physical resources, and people optimize a common objective function.

Figure 4.2 System-related definitions.

environment, or actions by competitors, and act *before* the need becomes pressing—it should facilitate a faster decision cycle. In other words, steering the organization should be more like driving a jet ski than the Exxon *Valdez.*

3. *Visible.* Executives should have instantaneous visibility, from top to bottom, on programs, individual projects, and capital budgeting. For example, an executive hearing a capital budgeting proposal should be able to see instantaneously its relevance to the ultimate goal of the company. This is an area where the capital budgeting process is notoriously ineffective.[4,5]

4. *Verifiable.* Within the limitations imposed by uncertainty, the executive should also be able to trace an unbroken logical connection between a proposal and attainment of the company's goal. A strategy development and deployment methodology should include a dependable set of rules to help decision makers evaluate and verify the validity of arguments for a particular course of action. A CEO should be able to demand—and receive—a step-by-step guided tour from the approval of *any* initiative or change to its ultimate contribution to goal attainment. There should never be any steps equivalent to ". . . and then, a miracle occurs!"

DELIBERATE, EMERGENT, OR A COMBINATION?

Some writers have advocated that the strategy process must be as "deliberate as possible."[6] In other words, a "controlled, conscious process of thought."[7] This approach naturally seems to ignore the idea that strategy can emerge from situations—such as 3M Corporation's Post-It notes—or be intuitively developed. Mintzberg stressed the idea that strategy formation was different from strategic planning. He suggested that strategy spontaneously emerges at least as often as it's deliberately planned, and, in fact, strategies are almost always partially emergent, even when a formal formulation process is used.[8]

Without discounting Christensen et al., I would suggest that Mintzberg is right. Moreover, a prudent approach would be a combination of the two positions. Since intuition and emergence probably can't be forced on a predetermined schedule, it would be smart to follow the military's lead: *In the absence of any intuition or emergence, follow a deliberate strategy formation process, but remain flexible enough to change course if intuition or emergence occur.*

The strategy development model that follows, then, is intended to be a little of both. It's deliberate, in that it offers leaders a degree of control, a loosely structured process, and robust tools with which to build strategy. But it's also flexible and agile enough to accommodate learning and emerging strategy that results from unexpected results and changes in the operating environment.

It's as simple and flexible a deliberate process as I can conceive of. The basic concept—what to change, what to change to, and how to cause the change—and the tools to effect it were originally conceived by E. M. Goldratt.[9] I've merely applied them here to the challenge of robust strategy formulation. This process (which I refer to as the *constraint management model*) begins with a framework similar to the military model, in that it's composed of a vertical hierarchy: a goal, objectives (the satisfaction of necessary conditions), and the discrete tactical actions needed to fulfill them. At the same time, however, it encourages an outward-looking effort to stimulate creative, intuitive thinking and consider external changes in the environment that might provide emergent strategies as well. If such opportunities present themselves, the constraint management model is "lean" enough to accommodate almost immediate changes in direction.*

Here's another way of looking at it. Absent other, more attractive alternative opportunities that might subsequently come up, we'll start with a deliberate approach. We'll use whatever intelligence resources we can muster to assess what the external environment will be like, from the present out to our planning horizon. We'll make some basic assumptions about how our competition will play out during that time, and we'll lay out a strategy that will: (a) help us reach our goal under our assumed scenario, and (b) provide a flexible position from which to change to a better alternative strategy, should one emerge from the environment or spring intuitively from within. Then we'll be ready to adjust our strategy in real time as the environment diverges from the circumstances we've prepared for.

ANALYSIS AND SYNTHESIS

At its core, strategic navigation is essentially an exercise in analysis and synthesis. *Analysis* is a process of breaking down complex situations into their component parts to learn as much as possible about how they work and fit together. *Synthesis,* on the other hand, is a process of combining often disparate parts into a new type of whole. One might say that analysis is a process of "destruction," and synthesis is a process of "creation."[10] Here's an example of a combination of the two processes.

---

* I use the word "lean" only with great trepidation. No allusion or similarity to *lean manufacturing* is intended.

Let's consider a small *gedunken* (thinking) experiment. We'll start with four different kinds of locomotion, or transportation: snow skis; a boat with an outboard motor; a bicycle; and an earthmover with tracks/treads, rather than wheels. These are four radically different modes of transporting people or things. By way of *analysis,* let's mentally disassemble these four things into their components. Now we have four distinct piles of parts. How can we *synthesize* at least one piece from each pile into a completely new concept?

First, let's take the ski "boards." We'll discard the boot bindings and shorten the skis by about 50 percent. Then let's take the outboard motor from the boat—just the engine and transmission, not the propeller or the casing. Next we'll steal the *idea* of the tracks/treads from the earthmover. The tracks themselves would be too big and heavy. We'll reduce the size of the tracks/treads substantially, to a scale approximating the skis and outboard motor. And we'll use only one of the tracks. Last, we'll take the handlebars and the saddle from the bicycle. Then we'll combine (synthesize) these components in a new way:

Skis + engine/transmission + track/tread + saddle and handlebars
= *snowmobile!**

John Boyd characterized the whole analysis–synthesis process as "inventing snowmobiles."

Now let's transfer this same analysis–synthesis process to the strategy arena. In this case, we'll synthesize elements of three prescriptive theories: the Department of Defense's approach to strategic planning, Boyd's theory of maneuver warfare, and Goldratt's theory of constraints. The result will be. . .

. . .the *constraint management model for strategy development and execution.*

A SYNTHESIS OF THEORIES

If the CM model is a synthesis of selected components—a "snowmobile," as it were—of other theories, just what are these components?

From the military strategic planning system, we'll adopt its hierarchical character, which vertically integrates the highest goal and objectives of the whole organization with the tactics of the lowest-level units—in other words, the concept of a "family of plans" described in chapter 3. Each set of day-to-day tactics will be designed to support a higher-level strategy for attaining major necessary conditions/critical success factors and, ultimately, the system's overall goal. The Joint Strategic Planning Systems and the Joint Operation Planning and Execution System contribute this hierarchical concept.

From Boyd's theory of maneuver warfare, we'll adopt the concepts of shaping the strategic environment, adapting to the fluidity of modern competition, coping with

---

* Colonel John Boyd used this example to demonstrate how his OODA loop was a synthesis of Gödel's proof, Heisenberg's uncertainty principle, and the second law of thermodynamics.

uncertainty, using time as an ally, and degrading a competitor's ability to cope.[11] The instrument for doing these things is the OODA loop (observe–orient–decide–act), which is really more of a spiral than a closed loop. Even though the four steps are repeated ad infinitum, they happen from a different set of environmental circumstances. In the words of Heraclitus, "It is impossible to cross the same river twice," because neither the person crossing nor the river are quite the same the second time. Our objective will be to operate inside the decision cycle of others—to strive for more cycles of the OODA loop in the same time that our competitors, or the environment itself, complete fewer, as we saw in Figure 3.6.

Those of you familiar with *hoshin kanri* will recognize the similarity of the OODA loop to Shewhart's plan–do–check–act (PDCA) cycle for process management. The OODA loop is aimed at a much higher system level and it prescribes more discrete functions (observe, orient, and decide), where the PDCA cycle says only "plan."

Goldratt's theory of constraints encompasses a comprehensive picture of systems, including assumptions about how they function and behave, their internal and external dependencies, prescriptions on how to manage them effectively, and various tools to do so.* The constraint management model borrows more heavily from the theory of constraints than from the other models—thus, the origin of the name.

From Goldratt's theory, we'll adopt his concept of a system constraint limiting what an organization can accomplish, and his logical *thinking process.* The thinking process is designed to answer three basic system management questions: *What* to change, what to change *to,* and *how* to cause the change? The thinking process will be the constraint management model's preferred tool for integrating the selected aspects of the military planning process and Boyd's theory on maneuver warfare. Figure 4.3 shows the relationship among the theories. We'll see how the constraint management model and its tools, which we'll examine in detail shortly, constitutes a synthesis of these theories.

The net effect of this synthesis of theories should be the creation of an organization that is adaptive and capable of rapidity, variety, harmony, and initiative.

THE CONSTRAINT MANAGEMENT MODEL

The constraint management (CM) model relies heavily on understanding cause and effect in organizational systems, a key foundation of the theory of constraints. None of the other strategic planning models place the importance on understanding cause-and-effect that the CM model does. If there is one overriding advantage to the CM model, it's this foundation in cause and effect.

---

* We won't delve into constraint theory here, except those aspects that are relevant to strategy development. For a more comprehensive discussion of the theory of constraints, its applications and tools, refer to the bibliography, specifically Caspari, Corbett, Dettmer, Goldratt, Leach, Newbold, Noreen et al., Scheinkopf, Schragenheim, and Smith.

Shewhart (Hoshin)	Military Planning	Boyd	Goldratt
Plan	Strategic assessment (1)	Observe (1) Orient (1)	(*Why* change?) *Not originally part of the theory* *What* to change?
	Strategic direction; program advice	Decide	What to change *to*?
Do	Strategic plans	Act	How to cause the change?
Check; Act	Strategic assessment (2)	Observe (2) Orient (2)	

Figure 4.3 A synthesis of theories.

The result of the CM model is a framework that is:

- *Optimal.* It permits users to "strap on" as much or as little detail as they choose. It's intended to be "lean and mean," but it can be as comprehensive as necessary.

- *Fast.* Strategy can be constructed in a matter of days, versus weeks or months with the other models.

- *Flexible.* It lends itself to relatively easy, rapid change as strategic or tactical situations dictate.

- *Integrated.* It articulates all the dependencies within the system, both vertical and horizontal, so that it's clear to everyone which actions or elements are within a group's span of control and which require support from others.

- *Deployable.* Because actions required at the operating level to support the strategy are vertically "nested" and clearly displayed along with the overall strategy, deployment is relatively straightforward.

- *Visible.* Specific groups within the organization can see the overall strategy and parts pertinent to themselves at all times—especially the system objective and their contributions to it. Nobody can "hide."

- *Accountable.* It's easy to assign and monitor accountability for the actions required to fulfill the strategy.

It's important to realize at the outset that this model does *not* include every tool, technique, aid, or procedure your organization might need to fulfill its chosen strategy.

There are other perfectly suitable methods that can provide such details. What this model *will* do is to tell you when such supplementary methods are needed. It's then incumbent upon management to select the right tool for the job.

SEVEN STEPS OF THE CONSTRAINT MANAGEMENT MODEL

The constraint management model (Figure 4.4) has seven basic process steps. The first six develop and deploy the strategy. The seventh is an evaluate-and-adjust step.

1. *Define the paradigm.* The constraint management model begins with a determination of the system's boundaries and its goal. It then identifies the necessary conditions—critical success factors—without which the goal cannot be achieved. These constitute the expectations of the system's owners as far into the future as the organization decides its planning horizon will be. That might be two years or 20. Once the goal and critical success factors are identified, they represent the standard against which all subsequent plans, actions, and performance are measured.

2. *Analyze the mismatches.* The second step in the model is to determine the nature and scope of the deviation, or "gap," between the system's current condition and performance, and that which will be required to achieve the goal and critical success factors by the expiration of the time horizon. The characteristics of this gap might be considered

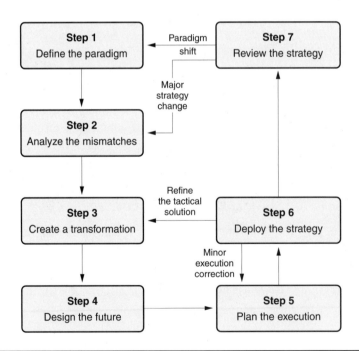

Figure 4.4 The constraint management model.

undesirable effects. They're undesirable because their very presence indicates a mismatch between what *is* and what *should be.* The critical mismatches represent the constraints to global system success. They're considered *effects,* because the theory of constraints contends that measurable, tangible deviations are the ultimate result of a chain of interrelated cause and effect that begins with an elemental cause. This step of the constraint management model is designed to reveal the underlying causes of the "gap" between where the system *is now* and where it *wants to be* in the future. In other words, *what to change.*

3. *Create a transformation.* The third step is the most fun—it's the part of the process where you get to design the future! Once you've determined the nature and scope of the gap between your current situation and your desired future, you get to create strategies to close that gap. The objective here is to minimize your own mismatch between reality and expectations while increasing that of your competitors.

The emphasis in transformation is on the word *create.* The ease or difficulty in doing this is directly proportional to your willingness to challenge your cherished assumptions about why things have to be the way the are now, and to "think outside the box"—in other words, unconventionally.

Invariably, you'll run into conflicts in considering the new strategies you'll need to follow in order to make your newly-designed future unfold. You'll probably even find yourself in conflict with the other participants in the strategy design process, especially when considering possible courses of action. Part of the third step involves resolving those conflicts in a way that everybody can live with, if not eagerly endorse. The third step of the constraint management model tells the organization *what to change to.*

4. *Design the future.* The fourth step verifies that the proposed new strategies will really deliver the desired results—that the system will actually satisfy the conditions necessary for the future to unfold the way the organization wants it to, and achieve the system's goal. It's also a "mine detection" step, raising warning flags when any of the proposed strategies can be anticipated to produce devastating problems that don't exist now.

5. *Plan the execution.* The fifth step is the formulation of the technical activities needed to deploy the new strategies. Sequence and dependency of discrete actions are determined, along with accountability assignment and projected completion dates. This is very much a "how to" step, with the details left to those assigned to complete the tasks. Leaders and subordinates are jointly responsible for creating ways to assess progress and success. Corrections to execution are applied as deployment proceeds.

When this part of the model is completed, the "navigation plan" for reaching the system's goal is both complete and visible to all.[*] The fifth step of the constraint management model tells the organization *how to make the change happen.*

---

[*] A poem dating back to the days of the American Revolution characterizes this model: "For want of a nail, the shoe was lost. For want of a shoe, the horse was lost. For want of a horse, the rider was lost. For want of a rider, the message was lost. For want of a message, the battle was lost. For want of a victory, the war was lost—all for want of a horseshoe nail." The CM model identifies and verifies the dependencies between horseshoe nails and successful wars, and it does so in the simplest way possible.

6. *Deploy the strategy.* With the execution plan completed (by those responsible for its execution), the next step is to "just do it."* Effective strategy deployment is a product of leadership, delegation, accountability, initiative, and trust. During deployment, management must watch that deployment and correct or adjust it as necessary to ensure success and preclude delay.

7. *Review the strategy.* The final step has two evaluation and correction actions associated with it. First, assuming that deployment was successful, the performance of the entire system, and all the new strategy elements, must be measured and evaluated. If the organization isn't progressing satisfactorily toward its goal, the strategy should be evaluated and adjusted as needed to improve progress.

Second, even if progress is satisfactory, at a somewhat longer interval the basis of the strategy itself—the system boundary, goal, and critical success factors—should be reviewed. External environments *always* evolve. It's just a matter of time. As this happens, the organization itself may expand or contract. The competitive environment may change, either because new competitors have entered the arena or because new technologies are beginning to change the state of the art. As an analogy, steps 1 through 6 represent a system view "from ground level." Correcting deviations in the deployment might be considered a "10,000-foot view." Step 7 would be a "40,000-foot view." And the long-term strategy review is more like the view from "low earth orbit."

Now that the constraint management model is defined, how do we convert it into an actual strategy? The logical *thinking process* created by Goldratt provides the tools to do that.**

A LOGICAL STRATEGY DEVELOPMENT PROCESS

The theory of constraints provides a graphical tool set—the *thinking process*—to support the first five steps in the constraint management model. Those first five steps represent a cycle of analysis–synthesis on the organization and its operating environment. The outcome of applying these logical tools is a flexible strategy, concisely represented in a single graphic picture that enables everyone to see his or her part in the organizational process and how it relates to others.

This graphical strategy permits senior executives to see and understand the causal dependencies between the ultimate company objectives and the day-to-day activities that must succeed in order to achieve them. The logic trees of the constraint management model allow the CEO, at any time, to "drill down" to the working level and determine the status of progress in executing the strategy. Noise is separated from signal, so that management can focus on the issue—the system constraint—that limits the organization's

---

* *Just Do It* is a registered trademark of the Nike Corporation.

** Goldratt created the logical *thinking process* (Dettmer, 1997, 1998; Scheinkopf, 1999) to facilitate the analysis of complex systems for the purpose of identifying constraints to improved performance. That same logical analysis rigor can be translated to the development of strategy, too.

performance at the moment. Instead of having to watch a wide range of company indicators, the senior executive knows exactly what needs attention and when that attention should shift to something else.

THE LOGICAL TOOLS OF THE CONSTRAINT MANAGEMENT MODEL

Figure 4.5 shows the relationship of the thinking process tools to the steps of the constraint management model. An overview of the logic trees follows. Chapters 5, 7, 8, 10, and 11 explain how to use each of them in detail.

Strategic Intermediate Objectives Map. The first step in the logical process—the one that satisfies the need to establish the system boundary, its goal, and critical success factors—is the Strategic Intermediate Objectives (S-IO) Map. It's the starting point for determining where the organization is going and what major milestones must be reached on the journey. Once the S-IO Map is completed, Step 1 of the constraint management model is done. Chapter 5 describes the Strategic Intermediate Objectives Map in more detail.

Strategic Current Reality Tree. While the Strategic IO Map represents the organization's desired destination, before the organization can determine the direction that

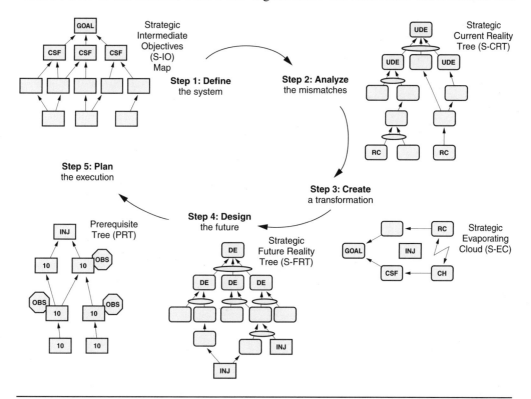

Figure 4.5 The constraint management methodology.

will take it there, it must first figure out where it is. This is basically a gap, or vector analysis. The Strategic Current Reality Tree (S-CRT) identifies the root causes behind the mismatch between where the organization is now and where it wants to be at the end of the planning horizon. The *undesirable effects*—statements of variance between current and desired performance—are only visible indications of much deeper, underlying root causes. These are usually very few in number, and most often existing or accepted policies governing how the organization runs. The S-CRT ferrets out those policies or practices that prevent the organization from eliminating the undesirable effects—which, in turn, means achieving the goal. It does so by revealing the interlocking structure of cause and effect (a domino chain, if you will), connecting the few root causes with the many undesirable effects. One of these root causes is the system's ultimate constraint. Once the S-CRT is done, Step 2 of the constraint management model is complete. Chapter 7 explains the Strategic Current Reality Tree.

Strategic "Evaporating Clouds." Identifying the underlying root causes of the gap between "present position" and destination isn't enough. Changing the root causes of that gap is often a real challenge because resistance, either internal or external, can stagnate the change effort. Step 3 of the constraint management model calls for rooting out and resolving the conflicts behind such resistance, which in many cases is not obvious. Yet these underlying conflicts can forestall progress toward a new future. The Strategic Evaporating Cloud (S-EC) is most effective at doing this. Chapter 8 discusses the S-EC in more detail.

Strategic Future Reality Tree. Step 4 in the constraint management model calls for constructing the strategy, verifying its effectiveness, and "clearing the future path of mines." The tool for this is the Strategic Future Reality Tree (S-FRT), a comprehensive cause-and-effect diagram that represents the entire strategy in a single graphical map. In doing so, it provides unprecedented visibility for everyone on where the organization is going and what their individual roles are in the journey.

There are two key elements in an S-FRT: *injections* and *desired effects.* Injections are the new initiatives and breakthrough ideas created to deliver the desired effects—satisfied critical success factors (necessary conditions) identified in the Strategic Intermediate Objectives Map. The S-FRT shows the unbroken chain of causality between the two.

But the S-FRT does more than just provide assurance that changes will achieve the strategic goal. It also affords the organization the opportunity to anticipate where new initiatives may create more (or worse) problems than they solve, and head those problems off.

Prerequisite Trees and Critical Chain Project Plan. Step 5 in the constraint management model is planning the execution. There are two tools available to support execution. The first is the Prerequisite Tree (PRT). This tool is designed to identify the significant tasks and milestones—called *intermediate objectives*—that must be accomplished in order to say, unequivocally, that an S-FRT injection has been completed. Some of these component tasks have significant obstacles associated with them that must be overcome. Others don't. All of them are necessary for the completion of an injection, and there is invariably a specified sequence in which they must be done.

Each of the intermediate objectives can be treated as a discrete task in a project, the deliverable of which is a completed injection. To ensure that the Prerequisite Tree is completed on time, and in the shortest possible time, the second tool used in strategy deployment is *critical chain project management.*[12–14] *Critical chain,* the first truly innovative advance in project planning and management since PERT/CPM, provides a means of ensuring the shortest possible promised completion dates for the execution of the strategy depicted in the S-FRT.

MANEUVER WARFARE, THE OODA LOOP, AND THE CONSTRAINT MANAGEMENT MODEL

There is an important relationship between the OODA loop and the constraint management model. You could consider it a "bridge" between strategy development/revision and tactical deployment.

The CM model is a prescription for creating strategy in the first place and updating it as the need occurs. But it doesn't really address the self-discipline required—and the reasons self-discipline is needed—to go through the feedback part of the process once the original strategy is deployed. In fact, more often than not, in the execution of cyclic prescriptive loops complacency sets in, sometimes before the first cycle is even completed.* Boyd's OODA loop provides the concrete theoretical basis for motivating people and organizations to continually evaluate results and adjust inputs quickly.

The CM model describes a kind of OODA loop, though it's not as elegantly simple as Boyd's four-part creation. Refer to Figure 4.6. The first two steps of the CM model, *define the paradigm* and *analyze the mismatches,* are essentially a combination of Boyd's *observe* and *orient* steps. A mismatch analysis starts with the gathering of intelligence, data, information, knowledge, and experience about the organization and its competitive environment—in other words, amassing *observations.* The creation of a Strategic Current Reality Tree is a way of *orienting* ourselves in relation to all these observations—in other words, defining the causal relationship and interdependencies among ourselves, our objectives, and the realities of our environment.

The third and fourth steps of the CM model, *create the transformation* and *design the future,* correspond to Boyd's *decide* step. These are the places in the process where we resolve the conflicts inherent in changing the status quo, bench-test our strategies (which are the product of creative effort), then "bulletproof" them before we implement. Strategic Evaporating Clouds, the Strategic Future Reality Tree, and trimmed *negative branches* provide the input for the next step.

The fifth and sixth steps of the CM model, *plan the execution* and *deploy the strategy,* are equivalent to Boyd's *act* step. Prerequisite Trees and critical chain project plans contribute to complete, efficient, effective execution of the strategy.

---

* Consider the Shewhart cycle. Most practitioners go through the plan–do–check–act process at least once, but how many actually make it a continuous, repetitive practice?

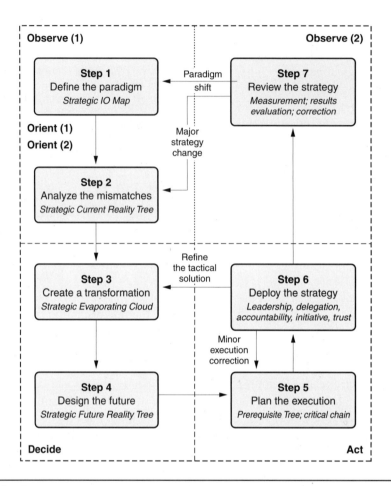

Figure 4.6 The constraint management model, tools, and the OODA loop.

Step 7 of the CM model, *review the strategy,* is comparable to Boyd's feedback loops, in which the effects of our actions on the environment are observed and a new orientation (a second-generation Strategic CRT) is articulated.

CYCLE TIME

Naturally, the cycle time for this process at the organizational strategy level is nowhere near as rapid as it is for a fighter pilot in aerial combat. It's hard to envision anyone in a tactical combat situation thinking, "We'd better develop a Strategic CRT on this ambush!" As observed earlier, the OODA cycle has to be implicit and almost instantaneous at this level.

But the organizational strategy level is a horse of another color. As we've seen, strategic plans can take a long time to develop—months, perhaps as much as a year—

using traditional models. The U.S. Department of Defense's operation plans take even longer. Yet the constraint management model, executed with the urgency of the OODA loop, can compress that time substantially, creating a winning strategy ready for execution in a matter of weeks.

COMPETITIVE AND NONCOMPETITIVE ENVIRONMENTS

At this point some of you may be thinking, "The constraint management model sounds as if it applies to a competitive environment alone. But I operate in a noncompetitive environment. Does this mean the CM model is irrelevant to me?" Rest assured, the CM model for developing and executing strategy applies to all types of organizations—commercial for-profit, not-for-profit, and government agencies.

Since the CM model draws so heavily on concepts from the military model—the military planning systems and maneuver warfare—it might be tempting to assume that it applies only to competitive situations, which are most often commercial. Certainly, maneuver warfare and Boyd's OODA loop concept originated in battlefields, which represent the ultimate in competition. But most people have heard the saying, "Adapt or die." This statement implies a completely different kind of competition: a struggle with the environment in which one exists. (Refer to the sidebar, "Reaction versus Initiative: The U.S. Postal Service.")

Even organizations without direct competitors operate in constantly evolving environments that demand regular change to avoid stagnation (and possible irrelevance). So

---

Reaction versus Initiative: The U.S. Postal Service

In August 2000 the U.S. Postal Service indicated that it was considering adding e-mail service to counteract a major penetration of its $35 billion-per-year first-class mail business by e-mail communication and online billing services. (*USA Today,* August 8, 2000.) Eight months later the Post Office indicated that it was considering terminating Saturday deliveries because "As people begin to communicate with each other by means of the Internet . . . we're seeing declines in volumes of first-class mail." (*Seattle Times,* April 3, 2001.) Clearly, these moves—one strategic, one tactical—are the Post Office's attempts to respond to a changing strategic environment.

But are these moves the result of a conscious effort to adjust a strategy deployment (Step 6), or to refine a previously developed strategy (Step 7)? The chances are these changes are merely reactions to a changing environment, not initiated to reduce mismatches with a baseline strategy.

Had the Postal Service used the constraint management model to create a high-level, long-term strategy in the first place, it would have been easy to observe changes in the external environment and recognize the impact of these changes on their strategy more quickly. They could have acted "ahead of the decision cycle" of the (new) potential competitors: Internet service providers.

even if your organization has no head-to-head competitors—government agencies and not-for-profit groups, for example—you're still competing with an ever-changing, often insensate environment for continued survival. In such situations, the constraint management model is still eminently useful.

SUMMARY

Where does the constraint management model fit in the scheme of the schools of strategic thought (chapter 1)? It embodies characteristics of almost all the schools, but it probably favors one from the traditional category (the *design* school) and one from the contemporary category (the *learning* school). The military model contributes the structure preferred by *design* school fans, and Boyd's OODA loop contributes the flexibility to accommodate external chaos (*environmental* school), the historical social experience of the *cultural* school, and the continual refinement of the *learning* school.

In summary, the constraint management model is a synthesis of several other theories and processes, which are equivalent to a foundation upon which a house is built. (See Figure 4.7.) It may not be the optimum balance of all the strategic schools of thought, but it's flexible enough to be used both for long-range strategy development and deployment and for short-term crisis management. And the process is virtually

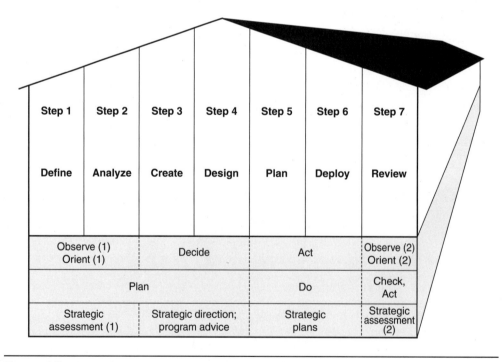

Figure 4.7   Constraint management model structural foundation.

Shewhart (Hoshin)	Military Planning	Boyd	Goldratt	CM Model	CM Tools
Plan	Strategic assessment (1)	Observe (1) Orient (1)	(*Why* change?) *Not originally part of the theory*	**Step 1: Define the paradigm** (Where do we *want* to be?)	Strategic Intermediate Objectives (S-IO) Map
			What to change?	**Step 2: Analyze the mismatches** (where *are* we?)	Strategic Current Reality Tree (S-CRT)
	Strategic direction; program advice	Decide	What to change *to*?	**Step 3: Create the transformation** (What direction should we take?	Strategic Evaporating Cloud (S-EC)
				Step 4: Design the future (What does the solution look like?)	Strategic Future Reality Tree (S-FRT)
			How to cause the change?	**Step 5: Plan the execution** (How to change course?)	Prerequisite Tree (PRT); critical chain project management (CCPM)
Do	Strategic plans	Act		**Step 6: Deploy the strategy** (Start on the journey)	Leadership, delegation, accountability, initiative, trust
Check; Act	Strategic assessment (2)	Observe (2) Orient (2)		**Step 7: Review the strategy** (Are we getting closer to where we want to be?)	Measurement; results evaluation; correction

Figure 4.8 Relationship of the synthesized theories.

the same, which is comforting to planners. Only the focus (strategic versus operational) is different.

The CM model draws its strength from valid theory (theory of constraints and Boyd's OODA loop) and proven practices (*hoshin kanri* and military strategic planning). It provides flexible tools that can instill a "big picture" vision for everyone within the organization. Yet these tools are easily mastered and they support the rapid observe–orient–decide–act cycle times required to "get inside the adversary's decision cycle."

Figure 4.8 shows in more detail the relationship of the constraint management model with each of the theories and processes from which it is synthesized.

Over the next several chapters, we'll see how each of the first five steps unfolds, whether the challenge is long-term strategy development or crisis action planning.

> *The individualist without strategy who takes opponents lightly will inevitably become the captive of others.*
>
> —Master Sun
> *Sun Tzu and the Art of War*

ENDNOTES

1. H. Mintzberg, *The Rise and Fall of Strategic Planning* (New York: The Free Press, 1994): 175–76.
2. Ibid.
3. D. H. Gray, "Uses and Misuses of Strategic Planning," *Harvard Business Review* (January–February 1986).
4. Mintzberg, *Rise and Fall*, 128–58.
5. T. Pyzdek, *The Handbook for Quality Management* (Tucson, AZ: Quality Publishing LLC, 2000): 240.
6. K. R. Andrews, *The Concept of Corporate Strategy* (Homewood, IL: Richard D. Irwin, 1971): 24
7. C. R. Christensen et al., *Business Policy: Text and Cases*, 5th ed. (Homewood, IL: Richard D. Irwin, 1982).
8. Mintzberg, *Rise and Fall*, 26.
9. H. W. Dettmer, *Breaking the Constraints to World-Class Performance* (Milwaukee: ASQ Quality Press, 1998).
10. G. T. Hammond, *The Mind of War: John Boyd and American Security* (Washington, D.C.: Smithsonian Institution Press, 2001): 155–56.
11. Hammond, *Mind of War*, 194.
12. E. M. Goldratt, *Critical Chain* (Great Barrington, MA: The North River Press, 0997).
13. R. C. Newbold, *Project Management in the Fast Lane: Applying the Theory of Constraints* (Boca Raton, FL: CRC/St. Lucie Press, 1998).
14. L. P. Leach, *Critical Chain Project Management* (Boston: Artech House, 2000).

5

Defining the Paradigm

*System Boundary, Goal, Critical Success Factors,
and Measures of Progress*

By losing your goal, you have lost your way.

—Friedrich Nietzsche

*Obstacles are those frightful things you see when you take your eye
off the goal.*

—Hannah More

DETERMINING THE SYSTEM BOUNDARY

The first step in establishing a strategic direction is to decide *who the strategy is for.* In other words, who's included and who isn't. For many organizations, this isn't too difficult to do, because the "inclusion–exclusion" boundary is relatively obvious: it's the physical boundary of the organization. This might be a plant or office location. More than one physical location might be included within such a boundary—a warehouse located separately from a manufacturing facility, for example.

For some organizations, however, the determination of a system boundary isn't so easy. If there are several divisions within the company—these are often called *strategic business units*—the system boundary may include them all. But by definition, strategic business units are semi-autonomous, perhaps even pretty well self-contained. They might well be considered systems on their own.

A good "rule of thumb" could be to determine the *degree of decision autonomy.* No system is completely independent of the environment in which it operates, but different systems have varying levels of autonomy in decision making. A division of a company that can't make major operational decisions without approval from another group (probably corporate headquarters) should probably include that group in its system definition. A different division, with more latitude to decide its operational future, might be considered a system on its own, even if it exists within a larger system.

For example, since its inception, the Saturn Division of General Motors has been treated somewhat differently by the corporate headquarters. Although major strategic decisions, such as capital expansion, undoubtedly require corporate approval, the creation and execution of Saturn's strategy is left largely to its own executives. To the extent that other General Motors divisions enjoy a comparable level of autonomy, they might also be considered discrete systems. Suppliers and customers are substantially external to these systems, though they may be closely coordinated.

On the other hand, Ford Motors used to operate its own electronics division (since spun off into an independent company called Visteon). The Ford Electronics Division was an internal supplier to Ford, providing almost all radios, sensors, and other types of electronics to the automobile manufacturing plants. Nearly all of its output went to support these manufacturing plants. The electronics division's annual business objectives were undoubtedly driven by their requirement to support the auto plants, so considering their system boundary as stopping at their own organizational border would probably not have been very useful.

Once a system has been defined by establishing some natural or arbitrary boundary, the goal of that system should be determined. In our strategic navigation analogy, this would be akin to deciding the ship's ultimate destination. If you don't know (or care) where you're going, then any path will do.

GOAL, OBJECTIVE, OR MISSION?

It's easy to get bogged down in semantics. Is a goal the same as an objective? Or a mission? Some people use "goal" and "objective" interchangeably. In some interpretations, a goal connotes a higher purpose, while objectives represent milestones en route to the goal. We won't split hairs here.

But for the purposes of this book, we *will* distinguish between a *goal* and a *mission*. A mission is the basic function of an enterprise or agency, or any department of it. Another way of describing a mission is "the business we're in." This is different from a goal, which is the end toward which activity is aimed—the end point of planning.[1] The *goal* is some result, preferably measurable, that we're trying to achieve. The *mission* is the kind of activity we engage in to achieve that goal.

Why is the distinction between *mission* and *goal* important? *Because missions can change, but goals might not.* Also, goals might change, but missions might not. Remember the Mothers' March of Dimes? Its mission changed, but its goal was clearly something else—some higher good. Were this not the case, the organization would have disbanded once the goal had been achieved. But for them, eradication of polio was a mission, not a goal.

Since this book contends that the military strategy model is transferable to nonmilitary contexts, let's consider a military example. The mission of the U.S. Air Force is:

To defend the United States through control and exploitation of air and space.[2]

Clearly this is a statement of the business the Air Force is in—national defense through air and space operations. It's *activity* oriented. But the goal is not specifically articulated in this statement, though it is implied. That goal would undoubtedly involve some definable state of security for the United States. One might conceive of an Air Force at some time in the future in which control and exploitation of air and space is not the mission, but the goal of effective national security would probably still remain.*

In the commercial sector, consider Toyota, well known to the world as a manufacturer of automobiles. Yet in Toyota's long-range view, the company would diversify into other areas, emphasizing low-cost prefabricated housing and telecommunications technology. Hiroshi Okuda, Toyota's president, observed that a single business line rarely prospers for more than 60 years. Undoubtedly, Toyota will focus on automobiles for the foreseeable future. It won't likely see a significant shift in its core business, possibly for decades. But a shift in a company's core business—its *mission*—isn't unprecedented. Toyota was originally founded more than 60 years ago as a textile company and only later moved into automobiles.[3] However, in spite of this shift in missions, both past and potentially in the future, I submit that Toyota's goal hasn't changed.

Clearly, Toyota's goal is something other than "making the best automobiles in the world." At best, considering their long-term perspective, this would be the mission of the moment. But it's not likely to be their goal—not if they expect automobile market expansion to level off. Outwardly, it would appear that their overall goal is long-term financial success, and their mission—the horse they choose to ride to that goal—is automobiles for now. But stand by for a change of mounts!

Does this mean that goals *never* change? Certainly not. For example, not-for-profit corporations sometimes become for-profit, and vice versa. The goal of such organizations would likely change under these circumstances. And when goal changes occur, the mission may well change, too, though perhaps not always. I suggest that as environmental circumstances evolve, missions change more frequently than goals.

So, strategically, what systems should be focusing on over the long term is a *goal,* not necessarily a mission, which might be subject to change. But as we'll see shortly, a mission statement can be a useful tool in zeroing in on a goal and the requirements needed to achieve it.

THE GOAL

What, then, is your system's goal? What *should* it be? Obviously, it's related in some way to the mission—the kind of activity the system engages in. But what *is* it?

---

* The U.S. Air Force's mission statement has changed over the years. But its goal—national security—hasn't.

The simple answer is that the goal is whatever the system's owners say it is. So we need to ask: Who *owns* the system? Ownership is usually determined by some kind of equity investment. A commercial, for-profit company is either privately held or publicly traded. In either case, the owners are the stockholders, whether that's one person, a family, a couple of partners, or everyone who holds as little as one share of the company.

In the case of not-for-profit organizations—for example, the Sierra Club, the United Way, the Ford Foundation, or any formally established church—the "owners" aren't stockholders in the traditional sense of the word. But to the extent that money must be provided to operate such organizations, those who provide the money certainly have some influence in determining the goal, if only in that they can cause the collapse of the organization by withholding it.

Government agencies are another type of organizational system. The owners in this case are those who provide the money to operate them: the taxpayers.* So, to determine the goal, we should probably start with the question: What do the system's owners think it is?

The answer to this question will vary. If the owners' goal is not to make money, it can certainly be something else, but generating financial support, either through profits, donations, or appropriations, will certainly occupy a position of importance—what we'll call a *necessary condition.*

CRITICAL SUCCESS FACTORS (NECESSARY CONDITIONS)

Having a goal alone—and knowing what it is—is generally not enough. One of the characteristics of complex systems is that their goals inevitably have several preconditions that must be satisfied if the goal is to be achieved. These might be considered *critical success factors* (CSF). They're discrete elements whose presence is required for success. Having them alone is *not* a guarantee of success, but *not* having them is a guarantee of failure. Consequently, these critical success factors might also be considered *necessary conditions.* In this book, I'll refer to necessary conditions and critical success factors interchangeably.

Let's consider a sports example to demonstrate the difference between a goal and a necessary condition. In a football game, the goal is to win—which is usually defined as amassing at least one more point than your opponent by the time the game clock expires. A typical football team has players, coaches, equipment, uniforms, and a field to play on. It also has competitors (the opposing team). But to win the game, there are some necessary conditions that must be satisfied. In some cases, that satisfaction is relative (that is, execute plays better than the other team). In other cases, it's absolute (for example, field the required number of players, no more and no less).

---

* It's exceedingly tempting to get into the issue of political interference, influence-buying, and other ways that the business of government agencies is corrupted, but I'll resist that temptation here. For our purposes, we'll assume that the taxpayers determine the goals of government agencies, through their elected representatives and executives.

There are other necessary conditions as well. Some of these might include:

- Talented players

- Coordination and teamwork

- An effective game plan

- Discipline (minimal penalties, player ejections)

- Individual conditioning

- Good coaching

Even having all of these necessary conditions doesn't guarantee victory. Luck certainly plays a part, often in the avoidance of injuries to key players. The weather can also influence outcomes. In other words, the combination of causative factors *sufficient* to ensure victory may be more inclusive than the necessary conditions alone. But the necessary conditions are the limited number of factors that are individually and collectively critical to success.

TWO TYPES OF NECESSARY CONDITIONS

Necessary conditions can originate from different sources. Generally, these sources can be classified as *external* or *internal* with respect to the boundary of the system in question.

External. External necessary conditions are imposed from outside an organization. They might be considered part of the environment. Natural laws, laws of science or mathematics, legislative laws, "common sense"—even the personal fiat of someone with the power to shut down the system—can all be sources of necessary conditions. So can the competitive environment, the nature of a product, or the paradigm of an industry.

For example, there's an inherent logical cause-and-effect connection between the need to produce a particular product and the profit that a company realizes from doing so. So, assuming that a commercial company's goal is profitability, effective production (timely, with high quality) would be a necessary condition for the company's success. Compliance with environmental protection laws has no inherent logical cause-and-effect connection with the production of that product, but failure to comply can lead to the government shutting down the company. In that respect, environmental responsibility is no less a necessary condition—a critical success factor—than effective production, even though it's administratively imposed, rather than by natural law.

Paradigm shifts can render some necessary conditions moot, while introducing new ones. To the extent that a company's management can engage in "breakthrough thinking"—creating new ways of dealing with the external or internal environment—it's possible to exercise willful control over necessary conditions, and perhaps eliminate

"To provide our customers with the world's best and most innovative communications systems, products, technology, and customer support.

"Powered by excellent people and technology, we will be a customer-driven, high performance company that delivers superior, sustained shareholder value."

Figure 5.1   Mission statement for Lucent Technologies.

them entirely. An organization with fewer, or different, necessary conditions to satisfy can find itself with a significant advantage over its competitors.

Internal. Internal necessary conditions are those an organization imposes upon itself. In the early 1990s, many organizations involved with total quality management went through an exercise of creating mission, vision, and values statements to help them crystallize the direction they wanted to take. In many cases, the content of these statements—especially the values statements—expressed or implied self-imposed necessary conditions.

Take, for example, the mission statement of Lucent Technologies, shown in Figure 5.1. By citing communications, Lucent establishes a necessary condition of working in products and technology pertinent to that area alone. In turn, this imposes external necessary conditions—critical success factors—that apply to this industry and not to, say, the agricultural industry. By citing "excellent people and technology" and committing itself to be "customer driven," Lucent imposes other necessary conditions on itself.

Bear in mind that internal necessary conditions are *choices,* which makes them *policies.* And policies can represent system constraints. The most devastating constraints on the success of any system are often the policies it imposes upon itself. Perhaps the most insidious of policy constraints is the often heard statement, "That's *not* the way we do things around here." Or, conversely, "*That's* the way we do business around here."*

The central lesson from this discussion is that whether internal or external, necessary conditions are potentially both requirements that must be satisfied and constraints that may limit what an organization can do. To the extent that organizations are willing to challenge the assumptions that underlie these necessary conditions—either paradigms or self-imposed policies—great breakthroughs in system performance are possible.

FEW BUT CRITICAL

In most organizations, the number of truly necessary conditions (or critical success factors) is relatively few—certainly more than one, but maybe no more than three to five.

---

* I remember asking one client why they didn't diversify their product line from purely metal-stamping to include precision laser-cutting and machining. The general manager replied, "We're a metal-stamping business. We've always been a metal-stamping business. We stick with what we do well." This could constitute an informal but potentially devastating policy constraint.

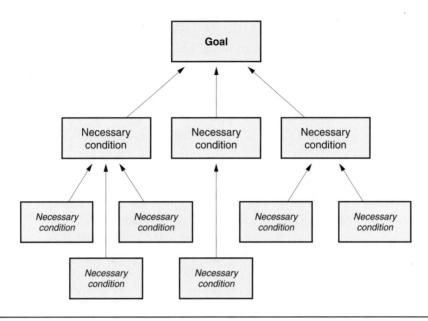

Figure 5.2 The Strategic Intermediate Objectives Map—a hierarchy of conditions necessary to achieve the goal.

Each of these may be composed of lower-level, subordinate CSF, but, again, probably no more than a very few. The conditions necessary to achieve the system's goal may be arranged in a hierarchy, which I'll call a Strategic Intermediate Objectives Map. (See Figure 5.2.) More about that in later in this chapter.

GOAL OR NECESSARY CONDITION? MAKING THE RIGHT SELECTION

There has been some discussion among students and practitioners of constraint management about whether making money can actually be a legitimate goal for an organization. Some have said that it can't or shouldn't be, citing various experts and scholars in management as sources. They contend that the goal is, or should be, some "higher" purpose,[*] and that making money is no more than a necessary condition in achieving that ultimate goal. Others have defended making money as a legitimate goal.

This issue is closely related to the difference between a mission and a goal. If the goal is really some higher purpose than the crass generation of money, there's some risk that the goal may obsolesce itself into irrelevance (much as the original Mothers' March

---

[*] The whole concept of a "higher purpose" seems to imply some kind of judgment about political correctness in selecting goals. Personally, I detest the whole concept of political correctness, because it tends to distort facts and impose the standards (read: "opinions") of someone else. Readers should keep in mind that opinions are like . . . well, noses: everybody has one, and they often smell!

of Dimes goal did), maybe even without the system's stewards ever noticing! Some people have advocated selecting a goal that might be considered a "race without a finish line"—a journey along a continuum, rather than a finite destination. Doing so allows for mission changes along the way, as previously discussed, and in fact very likely improves the probability that an obsolescent mission will be detected in the natural course of evaluating progress toward the goal.

Moreover, selecting a goal that doesn't lend itself to easy quantification of progress increases the risk that the system might stray off course without noticing. The ultimate result of that could be the "Nero effect"—spending too much time fiddling while Rome burns.[4*]

This is a particular risk faced by not-for-profit organizations, charitable or civic groups, and government agencies, because their goals really can't be easily and directly quantified. Leaders of these groups—whose goal is generally *not* making money—should exercise special care in choosing what the goal should be. With that in mind, here are some thoughts on identifying necessary conditions and choosing goals.

A group of factors. Necessary conditions might be considered a collection of conditions (some interdependent but others not) that must be met in order to achieve success in any given situation. In my flying days, especially when the airplane gave us problems, we'd occasionally refer to the aircraft as a collection of parts flying in loose formation in the same direction at the same time. This is a useful metaphor in considering necessary conditions: a collection of factors "flying in loose formation" along the path to success. The formation isn't complete without all the factors, so it's crucial that leaders identify *all* of the critical ones and make sure they're accounted for.

The goal. However, among all of these myriad factors is one that probably stands out as the most widely applicable, reliable standard of system success. All the factors are necessary—otherwise, they wouldn't be necessary conditions. Their attainment enables system success. But the one most significant factor among them, worthy of being singled out for special attention, represents the goal of the system. It's the one factor for which we can confidently say, "If we've done (or achieved) *this,* we've succeeded." Figure 5.3 illustrates the idea of selecting a goal from among the complete group of truly necessary conditions.

Multiple goals. Can there be more than one goal? Certainly. The owners of a system can have as many goals as they like. However, having more than one goal is an invitation to conflict. Most people have probably encountered conflicting goals in organizations at one time or another. As a matter of convenience, it would be easier if there were only one goal and all other requirements for success were treated as necessary conditions.

With these ideas in mind, I suggest the following approach to determining the system goal and the necessary conditions required to achieve it:

1. *Identify all the critical success factors pertaining to the system.* This is an exercise in idea generation. It should probably not be confined to the "leadership brain trust" alone. Other people occupying key positions in the organization—people with visibility

---

* See the section entitled Measuring Progress toward the Goal, in this chapter, for a more detailed examination of this challenge.

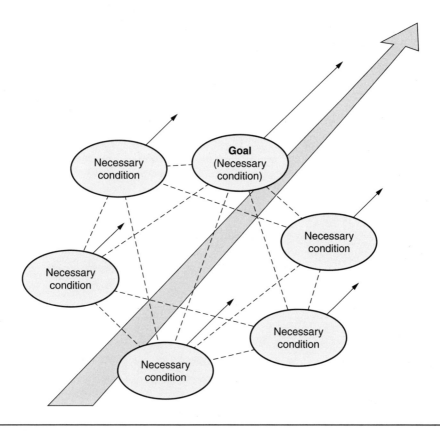

Figure 5.3   The relationship between necessary conditions and the goal.

on more than just one isolated part of the system—should also be surveyed. The *Crawford slip method,* discussed in chapter 6 and described in more detail in appendix A, is a good way to do this quickly and effectively. Figure 5.4 provides some useful things to consider in determining these factors.

Consolidate critical success factors into "wraparound" statements that encompass similar or equivalent ideas. Even a consolidated list might be somewhat lengthy, having 10 or more CSF statements. Try to separate out the ones that seem to be broader system-level statements from those that might represent supporting components of them. Even a long list should "shake out" to no more than about three to five factors really crucial to success.

Remember that CSF are necessary conditions. They have the characteristics described in Figure 5.5. They can be absolute or magnitudinal. An absolute necessary condition might be characterized as a "zero-or-one" condition. In other words, it's either present or it's not. And it *must* be present for the goal to be achieved. Compliance with the law would be an example of an absolute necessary condition.*

---

* I know, I know . . . laws are anything but absolute—that's why we have lawyers. But once the interpretation of the law is decided upon by the courts, compliance with it becomes more or less an absolute requirement.

Potential Sources of CSF

- Mission statements
- Vision statements
- Values statement
- Laws, government regulations
- Board of directors mandate

Potential CSF

For-Profit	Not-for-Profit
• Make money, now and in the future • Establish a competitive advantage • Establish effective "intelligence" on the market and competitors • Maintain robust marketing and sales functions • Satisfy customers • Provide a safe, satisfying, secure work environment for employees • Maintain "cutting edge" technology	• Revenue exceeds expense (long term) • Preserve assets (long term) • Preserve reputation/good name • Develop and nurture revenue base • Sustain integrity/legality • Satisy beneficiaries/beneficial effect • Assure satisfactory employee/ volunteer work environment

Figure 5.4   Determining critical success factors (CSF).

Necessary Conditions

Absolute	Magnitudinal	
"Zero-or-One"	"Satisficed"	"Continuously Improvable"
A "yes-or-no" condition. Only two states: either it's present or it's absent. Presence is required for the system to benefit.	A modified "yes-or-no" condition. Some minimum threshold level required. May be increased (or decreased) with benefit to the system until some threshold is reached. After that, increasing or decreasing results is of no further benefit to the system.	No theoretical limit (though probably a practical one). Can be continuously increased (or decreased) and produce incremental improvements in system benefits.

Figure 5.5   Characteristics of necessary conditions.

If it's not absolute, the CSF might be magnitudinal. In other words, it can be present or absent to varying degrees. Within the magnitudinal category, CSF might be "satisficed"* or continuously improvable. Employee satisfaction would be an example of a satisficed necessary condition. No employee can expect infinite satisfaction, nor is any company likely to try to provide it. But there is some threshold below which there's a need to improve, and above which further improvement doesn't make much—if any—difference.

A continuously improvable CSF is one that doesn't have a threshold; in other words, satisfying the condition to a greater degree will lead to greater system success. Profitability would be a good example of a continuously improvable CSF.

2. *Select one critical success factor to be the goal.* The system's leaders (owners or their designated executives) choose one factor from among the consolidated list to be the ultimate determinant of success or failure—the goal. The rest of the critical success factors will be necessary conditions for achieving that goal.

3. *Select a minimum number of supporting measurements.* Once the goal and necessary conditions are determined, some measurements will have to be chosen to help assess success in attaining the goal and satisfying the necessary conditions. Absolute necessary conditions generally don't need measurements. Their satisfaction is usually verifiable "by inspection," since they constitute a "yes or no" condition. But magnitudinal necessary conditions and the goal usually need some kind of "how are we doing?" check, which generates the need for standards and measures.

MEASURING PROGRESS TOWARD THE GOAL

Whatever the owners say the goal is, there must be some way of measuring progress toward reaching it. In the strategic navigation example, the goal is a geographic location. Attaining that goal means arriving there (presuming, of course, that we started from somewhere else). But how can we know whether we're making progress toward our destination? In the navigation problem, we use a rectangular coordinate system called latitude and longitude to determine both where the destination (goal) lies, and where *we* are. The difference between the two is expressed as a compass bearing and distance. As we apply engine power and steer a heading equivalent to that bearing, we move closer to the goal. Over time, we can check both our rate of progress (speed) and the accuracy of our aim by fixing our position. We then measure a new bearing and distance between our current position and the destination, and we correct our heading as necessary to eliminate any deviation from our course line. If time of arrival is critical, we might also adjust our speed as well.

Steering an organization is similar. But instead of a geographic measuring system, an organization needs other measures of progress toward the goal. Ideally, measurements

---

* *Satisficed* is a hybrid of "satisfy" and "suffice" introduced in the organizational behavior literature in the 1970s. It's intended to convey the idea that a certain level of satisfaction will be "enough."

will tell us how far we've come, how far we have yet to go, and suggest when changes to our direction might be needed. So, clearly, the determination of a system goal is crucial to success. If people within the system don't agree on what the goal is, there's a high probability that they'll be using different measurement systems to determine progress. And different measurement systems can send conflicting signals about which way to turn or what decision to make at a particular time.

CONSTRAINT MANAGEMENT MEASURES

The constraint management approach to strategic navigation makes use of three system-level measures in determining progress: *throughput, inventory* (or *investment*), and *operating expense.* Throughput is a direct measure of progress toward the goal. Inventory, or investment, is a measure of the capital needed to establish the operation for its mission. And operating expense is the recurring cost to turn on the lights and open the doors for business. In the nautical navigation analogy, throughput would be the distance covered in some period of time—let's say in a day. Investment would be the cost of acquiring, fueling, and provisioning the ship, and operating expense would be the cost of operating it after it's acquired. If all we did is rent or hire the ship, there isn't any investment, only operating expense.

In a business, inventory/investment and operating expense are invariably expressed in financial terms. Throughput may or may not be, depending on the goal that the owners decide upon. If the system is to be self-sustaining—that is, the source of money needed to acquire inventory and pay operating expenses comes from the generation of throughput, then throughput will also have to be expressed in monetary terms. Profit-making organizations (and some not-for-profit organizations) fall into this category.*

In government agencies and civic or charitable organizations, money is not generated by the activity of the business. The source of funds needed to defray inventory/investment and operating expenses usually comes from a budget. This budget, in turn, is funded each year from outside the organization, but without any direct connection to the throughput the agency generates.

For example, the Defense Department's budget comes from taxes collected from every citizen and company in the country (and some lucky people get to pay more than once!). Progress toward its goal—throughput—is clearly not measurable in terms of cash. You never hear any military commander say, "Well, we generated $3 million worth of national defense today!" Rather, throughput in a case like national defense is probably better measured in terms of the *undesirable effects that were avoided.*

Let's say that the nuclear forces of the United States cost an average of $100 billion a year over the last 50 years. That's a total of $5 trillion. And what did we get for that

---

* Whether a company is considered "for-profit" or "not-for-profit" is exclusively a function of how the income is intended to be distributed. This intention is codified in the legal documents that charter incorporation. It should be noted that there are not-for-profit companies that make a lot of money, and there are for-profit companies that don't (though it wasn't intended that way!).

expenditure (both investment and operating expense)? We got no nuclear detonations in anger during that time. Or another way of looking at it: the combined military investment and operating expense of both the United States and the Soviet Union over that time bought an uneasy peace—survival. To the extent that we avoided undesirable effects—total destruction of our respective economies, death of untold millions worldwide, and cities that are not puddles of coagulated steel and fused glass—we can say that the goal of those expenditures on both sides was achieved: we didn't experience global annihilation.

In a charitable organization, such as Doctors Without Borders, funding is supplied from external sources, too. Usually these are large corporate contributions, charitable foundation grants, or other types of donations, rather than tax dollars. The goal of Doctors Without Borders isn't financial, either. Consequently, neither can its measure of throughput be. In this case, however, throughput might be expressed as undesirable effects avoided, but it might also include some positive nonmonetary benefits—*desirable effects*—as well. For example, one measure of throughput might be a reduction in the incidence of communicable disease in a developing country. Another might be an increase in overall life expectancy.

THE USE OF SURROGATES

One characteristic is common to both for-profit and not-for-profit companies, government agencies, and charitable or civic organizations. They all use some kind of *surrogate* to measure their success in progressing toward their goal. By definition, a surrogate is a substitute. It's not a direct measure of progress, it's an indicator tied to that progress by an *assumption*. That assumption is that there is either a *direct* or an *inverse* correlation between the change in the indicator (surrogate) and progress toward the goal.

Here's an example of the classic surrogate used by most commercial for-profit businesses: *direct and indirect costs.* These are easily quantifiable. The assumption (often unspoken) is: *If we reduce costs (a progress measure), we become more profitable (move closer to our goal).*

Even such surrogates themselves have components. At an operational level, we see all kinds of quotas and aggregate figures: units sold, sales closure rates, process efficiency, defect rates, and a whole slew of customer satisfaction dimensions (complaints, repeat sales, and so on). Underlying each of these measures is the assumption that if we do well in these surrogate measures, we can assume that we're making progress toward our goal!

This is not necessarily the case. A few years ago, the Rohr Corporation's Riverside, California, plant reported impressive financial results: a 55 percent improvement in profit over the same quarter in the preceding year.[5] The plant's managers superiors patted them on the back for the great job they'd done. All the measures of cost and efficiency were sterling. Conveniently downplayed, however, was the fact that this impressive profit improvement came while the plant experienced a three percent reduction in sales in the same period. The Rohr treasurer observed that costs had dropped faster than sales revenue had decreased—and that this was cause for celebration! When questioned further, he admitted that layoffs had a lot to do with the "improved" efficiency—but that the layoffs were a thing of the past.* Rohr's workforce over the preceding five years had shrunk from 4,000 to only 550.

The overall lesson here is very important: *The system optimum is* not *the sum of the local optima.*[6] Local optima are typically determined by measuring local efficiencies. Managers who use local efficiencies as surrogate measures for the satisfaction of system-critical success factors often delude themselves into thinking they're making the right "course correction" decisions, when, in fact, they might be making the worst possible decisions for the successful "strategic navigation of the ship." So, it's critical to be sure that the *right* surrogate measures are chosen—ones that truly reflect the satisfaction of the system-level necessary conditions. And it's just about as important for management to limit these measures to the absolute minimum number necessary to get the job of satisfying necessary conditions done. Otherwise, there's a risk of "losing signal in the noise."

THE STRATEGIC INTERMEDIATE OBJECTIVES (IO) MAP

Now that we have a good definition of the system, a well-defined goal, and a complete set of valid necessary conditions, *what do we* do *with them?* The answer is that these become the core of our strategy. Obviously, the goal is the ultimate focus of our efforts, and satisfying the necessary conditions enables progress toward the goal. But there's likely to be a hierarchy among the necessary conditions. Some of them are probably going to be more general, meta-level factors, while others will probably be more discrete.

Let's take, for example, one of the critical success factors mentioned in Figure 5.1 (The Lucent mission statement): *satisfied customers.* There are undoubtedly several fairly specific subordinate conditions that must be fulfilled if we're to say we have satisfied customers. One might be a high-quality product. Another might be fast delivery or installation. A third might be high-quality follow-up service. And some of these subordinate necessary conditions might also be required to support other critical success factors, too. Obviously, this implies an interactive hierarchy of some kind. So it makes sense to depict the goal and necessary conditions that way—a kind of Strategic Intermediate Objectives (IO) Map, similar to the one depicted in Figure 5.2.

AN EXAMPLE: LUCENT TECHNOLOGIES

Let's consider a practical example. Some years ago, Lucent Technologies (formerly Bell Laboratories) developed mission and values statements, probably as part of a total quality

---

* "Trust me. . . *really!*"

management effort. Assuming that this wasn't just a "feel good" exercise—that the company *really* embraces this mission and these values—let's see how they might be rendered into a Strategic IO Map.

Lucent's mission and values statements read[*]:

Mission: To provide our customers with the world's best and most innovative communications systems, products, technology and customer support. Powered by excellent people and technology, we will be a customer-driven, high performance company that delivers superior, sustained shareholder value.

Values:

1. An obsession with serving our customers

2. A commitment to business excellence

   - Speed

   - Innovation

   - Quality

3. A deep respect for the contributions of each person to the success of the team

   - Mutual respect and teamwork

   - Personal accountability

   - Integrity and candor

4. A strong sense of social responsibility

If we deconstruct these two statements into key component phrases and words, a nice list of necessary conditions results:

- World-class communication systems and products

- Innovation

- World-class customer support

- "Leading edge" technology

- Customer satisfaction

- Maximum profitability, now and in the future

- Speed of development, response

- Innovation

---

[*] The author found these statements under glass in a frame on the wall of a public reception area in a Lucent facility.

- High-quality products (both software and hardware)

- High-quality, secure, satisfied workforce

It's a good possibility that you won't be able to extract all the critical success factors from mission, vision, or values statements like these. You'll have to assess what you *can* get from such statements and "interpolate or extrapolate" any important missing elements. For example, for a company the size of Lucent, dominant market share is important. And an effective research and development program is essential to successful innovation.

So are highly competent associates. It should be obvious that the high-quality products and services don't come from incompetent employees. Lucent's stock in trade, in particular, demands highly intelligent, energetic, "self-starting" people.* And if you're lucky enough to find and hire highly competent people, you don't keep them very long if you don't fulfill their individual needs. And highly competent people in high-technology fields have important needs to consider, other than just financial compensation alone.

Taken together, these critical success factors can be structured into a hierarchy we call an Intermediate Objectives (IO) Map. The goal resides at the top of the hierarchy, and the critical success factors are arranged by layers of successive dependency. (See Figure 5.6.) The arrows in this map indicate a general direction of flow. Outcomes lie at the head of each arrow, lower-level requirements at the tail.

The Strategic IO Map is a derivative of a tool developed by Goldratt called a Prerequisite Tree. There are specific procedures for constructing Prerequisite Trees, but they aren't included here. Readers unfamiliar with Goldratt's logical thinking process should consult one of the other published books on the thinking process.[7]

LUCENT'S GOAL AND CRITICAL SUCCESS FACTORS: A POST-MORTEM

How valid is a Strategic IO Map such as this likely to be? While the Lucent mission and value statements may not have been so succinctly articulated until after the company was spun off from AT&T, the company had adhered to those same values and mission for the preceding 115 years, since the invention of the telephone. Those objectives helped make AT&T the "800-pound gorilla" in communications for over a century, even after the U.S. Department of Justice won its antitrust case against the company in 1984. In fact, when Lucent entered the competitive arena as an independent company, it did so with the predominant market share in the industry. And for the first two years, things just got better for Lucent.

---

* The very antithesis, one might say, of Dilbert's company, as portrayed in the popular comic strip of the same name by Scott Adams (coincidentally, a former Pacific Bell employee!).

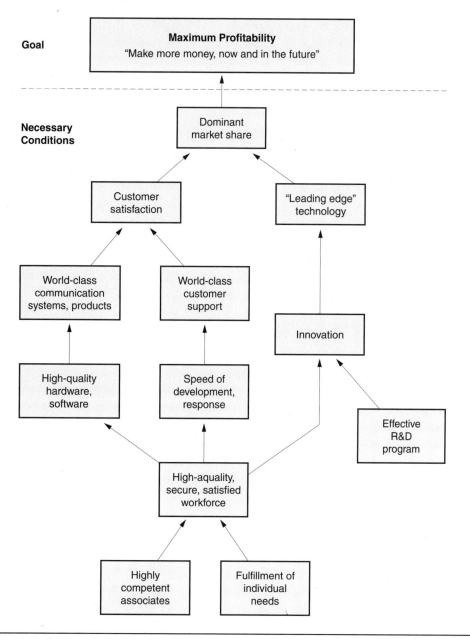

Figure 5.6 Strategic IO Map example for Lucent Technologies.

Then the roof fell in. Between April 2000 and May 2001, the company lost huge amounts of money, suffered an 82 percent drop in its stock price,* and eliminated 10,000 jobs.[8] In the spring of 2001, there were even rumors that the company was on the verge of bankruptcy.

Various Wall Street analysts offer much the same reasons for Lucent's "crash," most of which boil down to the company's failure early on to recognize the importance of the need to develop an optical network capability, and their subsequent loss of early market share to Cisco Systems and Nortel Networks. Lucent tried to make up for this strategic oversight by scrambling to acquire companies with such capability, saddling itself with substantial long-term debt just as the demand for optical network systems began to slack off.

But I submit that somewhere along the line, Lucent lost sight of its necessary conditions. In fact, whether they ever recognized a connection between those necessary conditions (critical success factors) and their ultimate goal is questionable. Refer to Figure 5.6. Notice that one of the necessary conditions for dominant market share is "leading edge" technology, which in turn results from innovation. Innovation comes from an effective research and development (R&D) program. Though Figure 5.6 doesn't show it, another level of necessary condition might have been included: an effective R&D program depends at least in part on an active effort to discern the future direction of technology evolution. The military establishment would call this a "long-range intelligence assessment."** If Lucent actually did this, then their executives didn't pay attention to it when it came time to make program decisions. Given that Cisco and Nortel both recognized the value of pursuing optical networks early on, any argument that this technological direction couldn't have been anticipated is suspect.

TEMPLATES

By now, many of you have the picture clearly in your minds. The framework of a strategy for your system resides in a hierarchy of critical success factors pertaining to the nature of the business you're in, your own capabilities, and the environment in which you compete. One of these factors is assigned special significance as the overriding goal of your system. The rest of the critical success factors form a dependent hierarchy beneath (and leading to) that goal.

Many of you may find it easy to convert your organization's mission, vision, and values statements into such a goal–necessary condition hierarchy. Others may not

---

* Some credit rating agencies considered degrading Lucent's debt rating to "junk bond" status.

** Recall our discussions of the Joint Strategic Planning System in chapter 3. Three blocks near the top of Figure 3.3 indicate a joint strategy review, a joint vision, and the National Military Strategy. These steps in the JSPS process constitute a deliberate attempt to look into the future and determine what the nature of the competitive environment will be. For big, bureaucratic organizations not nimble enough to change direction quickly (such as the defense establishment—and Lucent!), this kind of effort at the strategic level is crucial. And Lucent clearly dropped the ball.

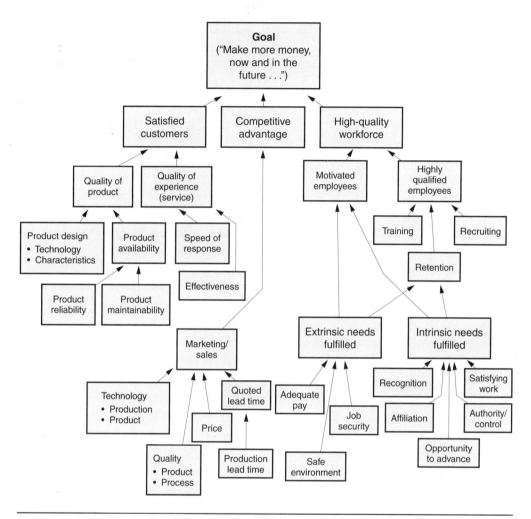

Figure 5.7   Template #1: goal and necessary conditions ("critical success factors").

enjoy the advantage of having mission, vision, or values statements to start with. Still others may have difficulty visualizing the goal–necessary condition hierarchy that pertains to their particular situation. For those of you who might benefit from some kind of defined starting point, two templates you might consider using are shown in Figures 5.7 and 5.8.

Obviously, these templates are generic, so parts of them might not apply to your circumstances. A government agency, for example, would normally not have a need for the "competitive advantage" branch* in Figure 5.7. The financial aspects of Figure 5.8 might not apply to a not-for-profit system, either. So feel free to cut and paste pieces, or

---

* An exception might be a self-sustaining government organization, such as the U.S. Postal Service, which competes in some areas with commercial couriers (e.g., FedEx, UPS, DHL, etc.).

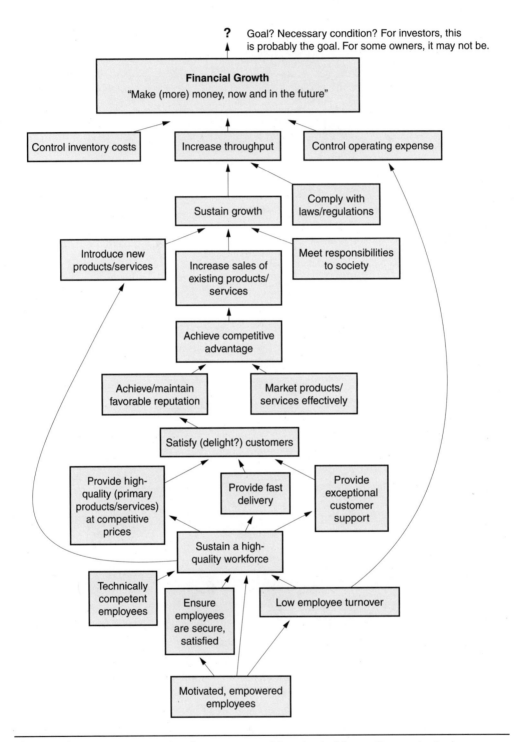

Figure 5.8   Template #2: goal and necessary conditions (typical for-profit organization).

customize the templates to your own environment. If your effort works, others in your organization will affirm it. If not, they'll certainly be glad to tell you where you went wrong and how to correct it.*

Whether or not you use this template, you *need* a concise, accurate representation of your goal–necessary condition hierarchy to safeguard the rest of your strategy (which we'll develop in later chapters) from the pitfalls of suboptimization—winning the battle, but losing the war!

CONCLUSION

This has been a lengthy, somewhat intensive chapter. But it's probably the most important one in the book, because it lays the foundation for everything that follows. One might make the argument that tools other than the ones suggested in subsequent chapters of this book could achieve the same results (though maybe not as quickly or painlessly), and that would probably be true. But *no* strategic methodology can succeed if the goal and critical success factors (necessary conditions) aren't clearly established in the first place. Having good tactical and operational plans and the skill to execute them can keep the company on the centerline of the highway and out of the ditch. But if you haven't clearly identified the goal and necessary conditions, it's highly probable that you could find yourself on the centerline of the wrong highway. The time and energy devoted in accurately articulating the goal and necessary conditions will save you much heartburn later.

Once you're reasonably confident that you have a good fix on the goal and necessary conditions for success, you're ready to begin figuring out how big the divergence is between the path that you're actually on and the one that you *should be* on. One word of caution, however: perfection is rarely achieved the first time around, especially in qualitative, intuitive activities such as strategy development. To avoid "paralysis by analysis," at some point we have to say, "This is close enough for us to go on to the next step." But in doing so, recognize that sometimes the true nature of the forest doesn't become visible until after you pass some of the trees. Strategy development and deployment is an iterative process, even while it's going on. So don't treat the Strategic IO Map, or any other logical tool in this entire process, as set in stone when you decide to move on to the next step. Be prepared to go back and adjust preceding logic trees as better information becomes available later in the process.

And above all, when the strategy is ready for execution, recognize that the assumptions it's based on can be invalidated overnight. As an object lesson, one only need consider the hundreds of assumptions made in all aspects of society that were invalidated by the terrorist attack on the World Trade Center and the Pentagon on September 11, 2001. Whole paradigms must be rethought as a result of those dastardly deeds. This is

---

* "Those who cannot do, criticize!"

a catastrophic example that affects the whole world, but the continual evaluation and reassessment of the strategic environment is no less important in more modest systems and circumstances of business as well.

If you don't know what the destination is, then any path will do.

—Unknown

ENDNOTES

1. H. Weihrich and H. Koontz, *Management: A Global Persective*, 10th ed. (New York: McGraw-Hill, 1993): 716.
2. *U.S. Air Force Handbook*, 1999.
3. D. Holley, "Toyota Heads Down a New Road," *Los Angeles Times* (16 March 1997).
4. E. Schragenheim and H. W. Dettmer, *Manufacturing at Warp Speed: Optimizing Supply Chain Financial Performance* (Boca Raton, FL: St. Lucie Press, 2000): 28.
5. O. R. Soto, "Rohr Reports Big Increases in Earnings; Riverside Plant Said Safe from Being Closed Down," *The Press-Enterprise* (Riverside, CA) (22 May 1996).
6. Schragenheim and Dettmer, *Manufacturing at Warp Speed*, 16.
7. Dettmer, H. W., *Breaking the Constraints to World-Class Performance* (Milwaukee: ASQ Quality Press, 1998); Dettmer, H. W., *Goldratt's Theory of Constraints* (Milwaukee: ASQ Quality Press, 1996); Scheinkopf, L., *Thinking for a Change* (Boca Raton, FL: St. Lucie Press, 1999).
8. Reuters News Service (CNN Financial Network), "Lucent Ousts Hopkins As CFO," (6 May 2001).

6

Knowledge, Creativity and Idea Generation

So it is said that if you know others and know yourself, you will not be imperiled in a hundred battles; if you do not know others but know yourself, you win one and lose one; if you do not know others and do not know yourself, you will be imperiled in every single battle.

—Master Sun
Sun Tzu and the Art of War

Strategy in war is intended to achieve victory. Superior commanders use several resources to construct a winning strategy. First and foremost is a thorough knowledge of the capabilities of both the enemy and their own forces. Another very important asset is knowledge of the battlefield environment: Will forces engage on flat terrain, in the mountains, or near the sea? Will they have to traverse swamps, forests, or deserts? Knowledge of the adversary and the battlefield environment usually comes from intelligence-gathering activities. Knowledge of one's own force capabilities is a function of how close the commander is to his units' day-to-day activities, and how much information about these activities the commander demands. Good commanders combine this knowledge with a thorough understanding of operational art: the principles of war and combat engagement. Inevitably, the convergence of knowledge about the environment, the enemy, one's own forces, and operational art suggests some possible strategies and discourages others.

Clearly, success in battle depends on knowledge. But knowledge alone isn't enough. We must assume that our adversary has knowledge of the same factors, knowledge that is at least equivalent to our own. Consequently, to achieve a decisive advantage, we must be prepared to do new and unexpected things with both our knowledge and our capabilities. The "unexpected" *is* unexpected precisely because it represents a creative synthesis of things that are known or have been done before with things that have not been done before. So success depends on creativity to some extent, too. The element of surprise, a key ingredient in any victory, depends very heavily on creativity.

Creativity is an elusive talent. Not everybody is equally creative. It's an inherent characteristic in some people, but largely absent in others. Yet it's essential to success. So, how do we obtain the creativity we need to build a winning strategy? There is often "security in numbers." An effective commander recognizes that he or she personally may not have the degree of creativity that the mission demands, but there's a good chance that this creativity is resident within one or more people within the organization. Success may depend on eliciting that creativity from whoever might have it. The best military commanders don't try to develop the strategy all by themselves. They solicit the inputs of their subordinates and staff. In many cases, a method of generating ideas is required. Sometimes that method must come from outside the organization.

Let's summarize. To develop a winning strategy, we need knowledge of the enemy and our engagement environment—what's known in the military world as *intelligence.* We also need a thorough knowledge of ourselves and our own capabilities. We must also be creative, and to achieve creativity we need a way to elicit the best ideas quickly from a number of people. Then we need to synthesize our knowledge and creativity into a winning strategy.

The situation is no different in a competitive business environment. To be effective, a chief executive officer (commander) needs a winning strategy. That strategy is a synthesis of the sum of the company's knowledge and creativity. A company requires knowledge about itself (its own forces), its competitors (the enemy), the market environment (the battlefield terrain) and effective business methodologies (operational art). Creativity comes from harnessing the ideas of its employees. It's risky to assume that creativity will just naturally appear when needed, so some reasonably structured method of idea generation is advisable to ensure that management maintains some degree of influence or control over the process. The relationship of these factors is reflected in Figure 6.1.

KNOWLEDGE

On a recent trip to Korea, I was assisting colleagues in Seoul in analyzing the problems affecting a chain of discount retail stores. My colleagues had set up the six-day session and asked me to facilitate a complete strategic analysis: what their current capabilities were and where they needed to focus their energies for the next several years. At the conclusion of the visit, the client was somewhere between satisfied and disappointed. They were satisfied, because they had a much more complete understanding of the breadth and depth of their problems, as well as the challenges posed by the solutions required to resolve them. But they were disappointed, too, because they expected a complete, detailed "road map" to follow at the end of the six days. They didn't get that.

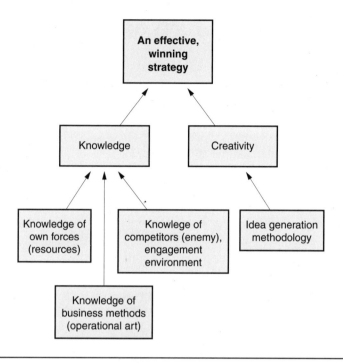

Figure 6.1   Elements of a winning strategy.

There wasn't enough time to thoroughly penetrate what they found they didn't know enough about.

A large part of the client's dissatisfaction resulted from one critical factor: *the precision of the solution and the length of time it takes to develop it are directly related to the quality of the knowledge of competitors, environment, and self that goes into the analysis.* This sounds obvious, but it's not.

If people are ever going to experience disappointment with the results of a strategic analysis, even the kind proposed in this book, it's most likely to happen on their first exposure to it. There's a good reason to avoid such disappointment: the potential beneficiaries may give up on the method without ever trying it a second time. But you can avoid this reaction ahead of time if you: (a) understand what the strategy development process is designed to do, and (b) if you set realistic expectations for the outcome.

When my daughter was much younger, she thought all you had to do to get money was put a plastic card into the machine at the bank. Just as her incomplete understanding of automatic teller machines led her to unrealistic expectations, some people can have unrealistic expectations about strategy development. They expect it to produce neat, clean, completely packaged solutions quickly. In many cases, this *is* possible. But if this *does* happen, it's the result of a major contributing cause other than the strategy development methodology itself: *knowledge.*

COMPLEXITY

Another factor bearing on the quality of our knowledge or understanding of our systems is complexity. Goldratt has likened complexity in organizations to the physicist's concept of it.[1]

Consider the systems shown in Figure 6.2. Which would you consider to be the more complex of the two systems, A or B? Most people would choose B, owing to the greater number of elements and the complex appearance of their interactions. But for a physicist, the number of elements is less important than the *ability to control* the system. Control depends on the number of degrees of freedom inherent in the system.

Based on the depiction in Figure 6.2, System A, without any apparent interaction between its four elements, would be more complex, because it has four degrees of freedom—four elements capable of variation independent of one another. System B, on the other hand, is less complex because of the interactions of its elements, as indicated by the arrows and dependency ellipses. It has only one degree of freedom.

Consider System A to be the circus lion tamer, locked in a cage with four fractious big cats. Consider System B to be the driver of the Budweiser beer wagon, with eight huge Clydesdale horses hitched to the wagon (and a Dalmatian to tell the driver where to go!). Which of the two do you think faces the more complex job, the lion tamer or the wagon driver?

The fewer the number of variables in a system, the fewer the degrees of freedom it has, and the easier it should be to manage. But how many degrees of freedom does your system have? In other words, how complex is it? If you don't have a full appreciation for the dependencies—the cause-and-effect relationships—operating within your system, your system may be as difficult for you to manage as System A, even if it actually has fewer degrees of freedom, like System B.

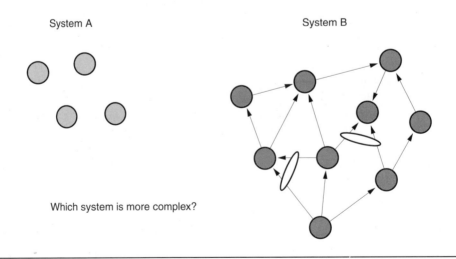

Figure 6.2   Complexity.
Source: Necessary and Sufficient, a lecture prepared by E. M. Goldratt. Used with permission.

THE ROLE OF KNOWLEDGE IN STRATEGY AND EXECUTION

In chapter 4, we saw that the foundation of the constraint management model for strategy development and execution is Boyd's OODA loop (observe–orient–decide–act). It's in the *observe* and *orient* stages—especially in the *orient* part—that knowledge comes into play.

Take a look at Figure 6.3. It highlights the *orient* part of the OODA loop. The arrows in the orient block reflect the interactions among cultural traditions, genetic heritage, new information, and previous experience. These factors are analyzed, then synthesized—an inherently creative activity—to feed the next stage of the OODA loop: *decide*.

The constraint management model provides the tools to complete this analysis-synthesis in the logic trees of the *thinking process*. But the thinking process depends on having something—knowledge—to analyze first.

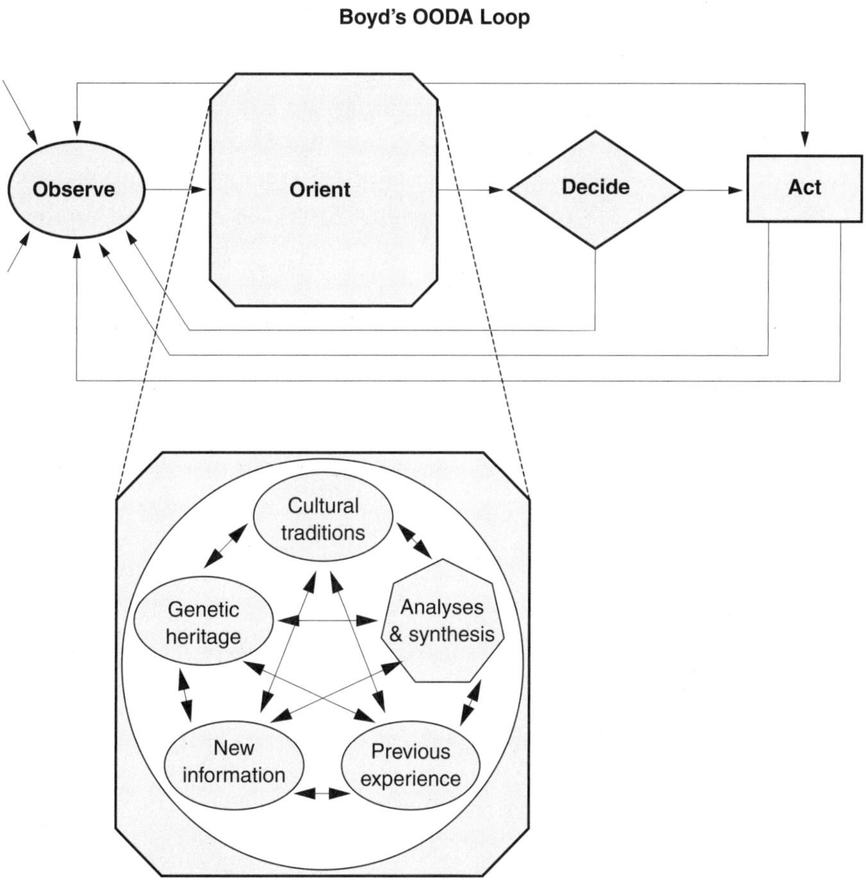

Boyd's OODA Loop

Figure 6.3 The *orient* step.

Adapted from *A Discourse on Winning and Losing,* by John R. Boyd (1987).

The thinking process can be equated to a computer. Computers can do wonderful things, but they require accurate data to be inserted into them. What kind of data does the thinking process need? It needs *facts* (verifiable through measurement or naturalistic observation) pertaining to the situation being analyzed. These facts may be either quantitative or qualitative.*

However, never lose sight of one key detail: *the thinking process itself does not create knowledge.* It merely arranges and configures what we already know into a logically sufficient structure of dependencies. And it does so in a graphical way that allows us to see easily the impact of changes in key variables.

But if you don't *know* anything about the situation, you have nothing of value to put into the logic trees, and, of course, you'll get nothing of value out of them. Some people overcome this lack of verifiable knowledge by speculating—"I think . . ." or "It seems to me . . ." They may even speculate without realizing it.** The most important standard you can apply in using any strategy development tool, the thinking process included, is *verifying the factuality of the knowledge that goes into it.* You can overcome cause-and-effect weaknesses through logical methods, but these methods won't save you from a fallacy in factual validity. Like a computer, it's a "garbage in, garbage out" effect.

This book describes how a logical thinking process[2‡] can be used to develop and operationalize strategy. It does this by structuring the collective knowledge of many people into a rigorous chain of cause and effect. In other words, it *makes* System A more like System B (Figure 6.2). In doing so, it can help create a strategy that provides a greater margin of control. The next several chapters describe how to apply this thinking process to strategy development.

THE JOHARI WINDOW

There's a way of looking at knowledge called the *Johari window.*[3‡‡] The original model characterizes human behavior in groups. But with a little adaptation, it lends itself very effectively to our *knowledge* of things and our *awareness* of that knowledge. Figure 6.4 illustrates the Johari window concept, as applied to epistemology (the philosophy behind the origin, nature, and limits of human knowledge). "Knowledge," as we refer to it here in this book, is the synthesis of information based on verifiable data, or highly reliable intuition—*not* speculation. "Awareness," as referred to below, is our conscious recognition that we possess certain knowledge, and we understand its relevance.[†]

---

  * That's one of the great things about the *thinking process:* it's probably the best tool in the world for dealing with qualitative inputs.

 ** If the knowledge you put into the trees is "half vast," the resulting trees will be "half vast," too.

 ‡ This thinking process was conceived by Eliyahu M. Goldratt in the early 1990s.

‡‡ The name sounds a little "eastern-mystical." It's actually a contraction of its creators' names—Joe Luft and Harry Ingham. It was first applied to group development at the Western Training Laboratory in 1955.

 † The author is indebted to Mr. Tim Sellan for his clear and concise explanation of the Johari window and its significance.

Awareness

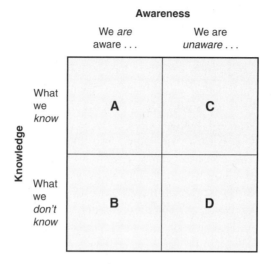

Figure 6.4   The Johari window (adapted for epistemology).

In our modified Johari window concept, the four cells in Figure 6.4 represent different states of knowledge, at two levels: the conscious and the unconscious.

• *Cell D: We are not aware of what we don't know. ("I didn't know that")* This is knowledge that exists "out there" but we haven't yet discovered it. Once we gain such knowledge, it no longer resides in Cell D. Instead, it has migrated to either Cell C or Cell A.

• *Cell B: We are aware of what we don't know. (Ignorance-aware)* The one great truth about science is that when you answer one question, it brings up a dozen more. Being *aware* of what we *don't know* is the basis of scientific curiosity.

• *Cell C: We are not aware of what we know. (Archived knowledge)* Einstein once said, "The secret to being a genius is knowing what to forget." Most information we come across that has any potential value to us is archived in the back of our minds. It only comes to the fore when it becomes relevant for some reason. Most scientific advancement comes from taking seemingly unrelated pieces of archived knowledge and discovering new relationships between them.

• *Cell A: We are aware of what we know. (Conscious knowledge)* At some point, we learn enough about something, and we're sufficiently aware of its potential relevance that it stays in the forefront of our minds. We continue to work with it and explore potentially complementary knowledge to see how far such knowledge can take us. Only when we have knowledge, and are aware of its potential significance, can we apply it in a practical manner to achieve our goals. Applied research uses this type of knowledge. Eventually enough knowledge from different sources comes together to make something practical and useful. For example, someone combined knowledge of how microwaves work (makes things hot) with other types of knowledge (mechanical engineering and merchandise marketing) to create . . . wait—here it comes! . . . the *microwave oven!*

RELEVANCE OF AN ANALYSIS PROCESS TO THE FOUR STATES OF KNOWLEDGE

Knowledge is like water. It flows and pools into one of the four states (cells) at any given time. No analysis process creates original knowledge. Rather, it's a critical thinking tool that allows you to "channel" the flow of knowledge from a less useful form (Cells B, C, and D) to the preferred state of conscious knowledge (Cell A). Decisions made from conscious knowledge that are based on solid verifiable data, not speculation, are the foundation of smart strategic thinking and problem solving. The quality of what comes out of any analysis process is only as good as the quality of the knowledge that goes into it. If people understand this before beginning an analysis, their expectations will be more reasonable, and their chance of success will be greatly improved.

How does all of this relate to developing a business strategy, and how does the "knowledge" version of the Johari window relate to the thinking process, or any other analysis methodology? When we decide to begin such an effort, we have a substantial amount of knowledge about ourselves, our competitors, and the field of competition. In the military analogy we saw earlier, these would be our forces, our enemy, and the terrain.

The thinking process can give us a clear sense of *how little* we know about ourselves, our competitors, or our competitive environment, and *what* we need to find out. The Johari window can help us appreciate *where* the knowledge we still need to obtain might lie. Together, these tools can help us set realistic expectations about what we can achieve, how much effort will be required (and what kind), and maybe how long it will take. The value of the thinking process in particular is that it can help *move* information from one cell to another. Refer to Figure 6.5.

We'd like for everything to be in Cell A—what we know, and know that we know. When this happens, any problem-solving or strategic analysis comes together 'slicker than water through a goose.' But it's not easy to achieve this kind of "profound knowledge."[4] Going into a situation, we don't usually have it. Yet for us to achieve the kind of results embodied in a complete, detailed strategic analysis, we need to put as much relevant information as we can about our system, our competitors, and the environment into Cell A.

By configuring bits of information about our systems in a logical structure of cause and effect, two things happen. First, we begin to realize things about our system that we were only marginally aware of before, if at all. That represents a transfer of knowledge from Cell C to Cell A. Second, the enlightenment produced by a problem or strategic analysis makes us aware of specific limits to our knowledge. That's a transfer from Cell C to Cell B, and this is important knowledge, because it can point us toward things we need to educate ourselves about.

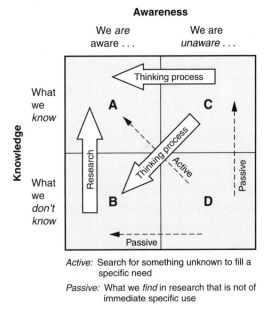

Figure 6.5   The Johari window—knowledge "migration."

A logical analysis shows us new relationships between things that we weren't aware of (transfer from Cell C to Cell A), but it also prompts us to go outside our own knowledge boundaries (that is, "We now realize that *this* is important, and we don't really know enough about it"). To the extent that it forces us to look outside our systems, it facilitates the movement of knowledge first from Cell C to Cell B, then from Cell B to Cell A. (But this last transfer doesn't result from the analysis tools themselves—it comes from other research.)

That leaves us with Cell D. There are only two ways that knowledge moves out of this cell and into our conscious domain (either Cells A or B). One is by the "Eureka!" effect. In other words, we stumble over it and recognize its significance.* If we don't recognize its significance, it goes into Cell C. The other way knowledge comes out of Cell D is by a conscious effort to actively search for it, without really knowing what we're looking for. In academic and government circles, this is known as basic, or "blue sky" research. Some of what we find this way is complete knowledge. In other words, it goes straight to Cell A. The rest goes to Cell B (the things we need to become smarter about) or Cell C—temporarily "useless" data.

So to summarize, the *thinking process* helps us structure information that we already know into easily identifiable dependent relationships. It also prompts us to search out information we know we need, but don't already have, to complete the cause-effect

---

* On the other hand, as Winston Churchill once observed, "Man will occasionally stumble over the truth, but usually he just picks himself up and continues on."

picture. And it helps us fit nuggets of information we already had, but didn't see the significance of, into our cause-and-effect picture to make it more complete.

The more verifiable knowledge (Cell A) you can gather in one place, the more likely you are to come up with the neatly wrapped package solution quickly. The more your foray goes into unexplored territory (Cell B), the less complete your first pass through the analysis will be, and the longer it may take to reach a fully executable solution. If you're totally clueless (Cell D), you're dead before you start.*

Sometimes you *think* you know everything you need to know to analyze and solve your problem, and you don't discover the limits to that knowledge until you're well into the analysis. In a situation like this, it's the analysis process itself that shows you the limits of your knowledge. It's almost impossible to predict that something like this will happen in advance. The best thing to do is to look at any analysis—whether for problem solving or for strategy development—as a kind of treasure hunt. When you start, you're not quite sure where you'll end up, or how long it might take you to get there.

SOURCES OF KNOWLEDGE FOR A STRATEGIC ANALYSIS

One of the best sources of knowledge about one's own system is the people closest to the work or problem. But even they might not know everything they need to know about the situation. Outside experts on the subject matter of specific problem areas might be needed. Either way, you need people who *know,* otherwise you'll just be shooting in the dark with speculation. This is particularly true of tools or methodologies— what the military strategists refer to as "operational art." If you don't understand them well, you may need outside help.

CREATIVITY

Creativity is perhaps one of the most elusive traits on the planet. Everybody has it to some degree. Very few have it to an exceptional degree. There's an ironic relationship between creativity and organization: *extremely creative people very often aren't well organized.* If they're good at generating new ideas, especially artistic ones, they're often not very good at structured organizational skills. To substantiate this hypothesis, consider the truly creative people who work in arts such as sculpture, painting, or other artistic media—they usually have the most messy, disorganized studios, and often they don't have what many would consider an organized way of coming up with their creations and executing them.

A similar phenomenon applies in organizations. The "idea" people are usually good conceptually, but not as often good at organizing and executing what they come up with.

---

* An old saying goes, "Winners *make* things happen. Losers *let* things happen. Idiots *watch* things happen and wonder *what* happened."

Neither are they often able to articulate a structured approach to doing what they do so well: generate good ideas. Unfortunately, too, there are usually significantly fewer "idea" people than organizers.

In combat, creativity is essential to victory, especially when forces are evenly matched, or when one's own side is outgunned by the other. Even more important, the chaos of the battlefield and its ever-changing environment make it important that the combat commander who wants to be successful produce this creativity *on demand* and *quickly*. Creativity, flexibility, and the ability to maneuver are often as important as superior firepower, sometimes more so. If you can combine creativity and flexibility *with* superior firepower, you're virtually unbeatable.

SIZE VERSUS MANEUVERABILITY

In business, as in combat, there is usually an inverse relationship between flexibility or maneuverability and superior mass of forces or firepower. The bigger a company is, the more bureaucratic it's likely to be. This, in turn, tends to constrain responsiveness, flexibility, and creativity to levels only slightly above the personal. Over the years, however, the military has learned an important lesson that most businesses haven't: how to shorten response time to unexpected developments and build flexibility into the system. They do this by avoiding detailed policy and guidance from the highest levels— micromanagement—concentrating instead on establishing the overall objectives and rules of engagement alone.

For example, supreme headquarters might say, "Our objective is to win the war in minimum time by controlling the battlefield [a defined geographic area] and the airspace above it, neutralizing enemy forces, and minimizing friendly casualties and collateral damage." The component commanders (army, navy, marine, and air force) would then each develop their own plans to fulfill this charter from supreme headquarters, using the forces they have available to them. But they, in turn, would do no more than specify overall objectives of the land, sea, and air battle, leaving the decisions on tactical operations to the various large unit commanders.*

These commanders, in turn, would develop their own operation plans, providing tactical objectives and general rules of engagement to their component small-unit commanders. Then, when forces are actually engaged, small unit commanders have the widest possible latitude in decision making. Since they have also been trained and authorized to make important force employment decisions on their own, they are easily able to respond quickly to rapid, drastic changes in the battlefield environment without having to call higher headquarters for guidance or approval.

They can do this in wartime, because throughout their peacetime training these small-unit commanders are mercilessly hammered by their trainers for being slow to

---

* Actually, they would do a little more than that. Chapter 10 discusses in some detail the concept of the commander's intent and a tool called "METT-TC" to translate the higher-level objectives into guidance for unit commanders that is sufficient without being overly restrictive.

assess their tactical situations and create new ways to react to changes on the battlefield. Large-unit commanders are like master chess players, supervising a dozen of their protégés, each of whom is playing a high-speed chess game with an individual opponent. The quality of the chess master's training of the protégés, both in the content of operational art and in independent, creative decision making, enables the small unit commander to achieve exactly the results the large unit commander would want them to when time is of the essence. And they can do this without calling the boss and saying, "I've run into a problem—what do you want me to do now?"

This was the crucial difference between the NATO and the Warsaw Pact forces during the cold war. And it was a difference that would have been decisive for NATO forces, in spite of their numerical inferiority, had a war with the Warsaw Pact ever broken out in central Europe.[5]*

In business, a similar effect can be observed. Large companies, because of their ponderous size and many layers of management, don't respond quickly to the need for change, even when that need is recognized. And when they do begin to respond, both their creativity and their actions are often constrained by the organization structure and its operating policies. These factors serve to impart all the maneuverability of a supertanker, while smaller, more agile competitors change direction with the responsiveness of a speedboat—and often without the big organization's restrictions on their creativity.

HOW TO BREAK THE CHAINS CONSTRAINING CREATIVITY

Making large, bureaucratic organizations agile and responsive isn't easy. But the example of the U.S. military demonstrates that it *can* be done. Consider how quickly the Department of Defense shifted from plans and tactics designed for major force movements in focused geographic battlefields to the kind of unconventional warfare required to root out terrorists in Afghanistan and other places. This kind of flexibility and creativity requires, first, a will to *be* flexible and creative. Second, it requires the right tools and practice in their use.

There are many group creativity tools available. Brainstorming,[6] the nominal group technique,[7] and the Crawford slip method[8] are examples of three. There are certainly others.** These tools are intended to elicit creative ideas from groups of people. I've

---

* This situation is described in detail by General Fred Franks, USA (Ret), in his autobiographical account of his experiences leading the VII Corps, both in Europe and in Iraq. Warsaw Pact doctrine gave almost no authority to field commanders to deviate from carefully constructed plans when the chaos of the battlefield changed the tactical situation, and the assumptions on which the plan was based became invalidated. In all cases they had to get instructions on what to do from higher headquarters. This left them extremely vulnerable to "decapitation" through interdiction of communications, a reality that actually beset Iraqi forces (who followed Soviet doctrine) during Operation Desert Storm.

** The Delphi method and TRIZ come to mind. But Delphi is not a group tool, and TRIZ was designed primarily to solve engineering problems.

tried all three of these. My personal preference is for the Crawford slip method, which is described in some detail in Appendix A.

THE CRAWFORD SLIP METHOD

As creativity tools go, the Crawford slip method (CSM) is perhaps more sophisticated than brainstorming, but less technically structured than TRIZ.[9]* The CSM's primary features are the ability to survey large numbers of people quickly and simultaneously, the ability to target either specific or general topics, and anonymity.

The CSM is usually applied in a workshop-type setting. Several people are gathered in a room where a facilitator leads the workshop. This number can be as few as two or three, or as many as you can fit into the room comfortably.

Selection of the people who participate is critical. Participants should include those who *know* something about the topic and who are likely to be able to offer creative ideas about it.**

A short stack of paper slips cut from standard bond paper is distributed to each participant. The facilitator then reads a short statement explaining the objective of the workshop—in other words, "Why are we here?" Immediately thereafter, the facilitator introduces the target question (refer to Appendix A for an example), and the participants are given 10 minutes to write as many ideas in response to the question as they can, one idea per slip. (See Figure 6.6 for an example of Crawford slips.)

The facilitator collects the slips after the 10-minute writing period is finished. If there are additional target questions (the facilitator might introduce three or four in the same session), the group moves on to writing about the subsequent targets, in turn. After the writing about the last target is concluded, the facilitator divides the participants into groups of three, segregates them in different parts of the room, and allows them another 10 minutes (maximum) of open discussion concerning the targets they've just written ideas about. Then the facilitator convenes everyone into a single group again and introduces a kind of "summary" target that asks the participants to suggest any final ideas that may have grown out of the 10-minute discussion period. These slips are collected, and the participants are dismissed, the workshop having required no less than about 30 minutes and probably no more than about an hour.

After the workshop session, the facilitator reads all the written slips, which contain the ideas of the participants, and sorts them by topical category. Duplicates are consolidated into unified statements, and the ideas, by category title, are typed into a single paper document or computer file for review by problem solvers or decision makers.

---

* TRIZ is a Russian acronym standing for "theory of inventive problem-solving."

** This is not a time to be "politically correct" or worry about individuals' feelings. The facilitator should include those with something worthwhile to contribute (signal) and exclude "straphangers" who might only be able to offer speculation or empty opinions (noise).

Target B: Achieving our goal—What critical success factors (necessary conditions) are absolutely essential?

We need thorough, current knowledge of the market

We must be fast to market with new products

Our product quality levels must be high

Our order-to-delivery lead times must be shorter than our competitors'.

Our customer service must be the best in our industry

Figure 6.6 Crawford slips (example).

It's not unusual to realize 10 ideas per person on every target question. If 10 people participate, and there are four target questions, that could be as many as 400 ideas collected in less than an hour. Obviously, the value of different ideas will vary. Some will be nearly useless. Others will be moderately useful. A few, properly verified and included in a broader strategy, may turn out to be "million-dollar" ideas. Even in the least productive cases, the outcome is almost always worth the investment of an hour of people's time.

Anyone interested in trying the Crawford slip method to support strategy development should refer to Appendix A.

CRAWFORD SLIP WORKSHOP: AN EXAMPLE

Here's an example of how the Crawford slip method might be used in strategy development. Let's assume that you've been asked to assist with the development of a business strategy for a mid-sized company. Because you realize that it's important to have all of senior management "on the same page," you've decided to determine the organization's goal and critical success factors (refer to chapter 5). You choose 3-inch by 5-inch Post-It notes for your medium and obtain a sufficient number of pads so that each executive participating has one. You convene the group around a conference table, distribute the pads and a bold felt-tip permanent marking pen to each participant.

Using either an overhead slide projector or a digital data projector, you show your first two slides. One is a summary of the points you'll use to motivate the "idea generators." The second slide gives them the directions they should follow in writing their slips. When they're ready to write, you show the third slide, containing your first target question, which asks them to state the organization's goal as they perceive it. They write for five minutes (most will finish sooner). You collect all the Post-It notes, paste them on a blank wall or whiteboard, and overlap them like shingles, so that each one can be easily seen from the conference table. Separate out duplicates, so that only one copy of each version of the goal statement remains in the column of overlapped slips. Look for similarly worded slips, propose consolidated wording, and replace all those related slips with a new slip (which you write) that concisely states the same idea. Dispose of the original slips.

If there are distinctly different statements remaining about the goal—for example, one suggests that the goal of the organization is "to make money," while another suggests it's "to satisfy customers"—call for a consensus on one or the other, and save the ones not chosen for inclusion as a critical success factor.

Then show the next slide to introduce the second target, which calls for the executives to contribute ideas on what critical success factors are absolutely indispensable in achieving the goal statement just developed. Give them 10 minutes to write on this particular target. Then collect the slips, and repeat the same process to consolidate duplications and similar wordings, until you obtain a well-defined list of different critical success factors.

Appendix A illustrates some typical examples of a motivational orientation, directions for writing Crawford slips, and generic targets for the first part of a strategic analysis. A detailed "how to" for the Crawford slip method is beyond the scope of this book; however, anyone interested in learning more about it may contact the author directly.

CONCLUSION

Okay, where do we go from here? So far in this book, we've seen the deficiencies in traditional strategic planning, and we've briefly discussed alternatives, including the military model and *hoshin* planning. Chapter 4 introduced the constraint management model for strategy development, and chapter 5 explained the importance of knowing what an organization's goal and critical success factors (necessary conditions) are. In chapter 6, we've discussed how crucial it is to have concrete knowledge of one's own organization, the competition, and the market. And we explored ways of eliciting creativity in developing strategy. Now we're ready to apply the foundation inherent in chapters 5 and 6 to begin our strategic analysis-synthesis.

In chapter 7, we'll see how to create a visual representation of our mismatches with respect to our stated goal and necessary conditions. We'll determine the size and scope of the gap between where we are now and where we expect to be when our goal and necessary conditions are satisfied. And we'll see how this visual picture zeroes in on the few root causes of these deficiencies—our system constraints.

In later chapters, we'll see how to "fix" these root causes, test our strategy, and plan its deployment.

> *Foreknowledge cannot be gotten from ghosts and spirits, cannot be*
> *had by analogy, cannot be found out by calculation. It must be*
> *obtained from people, people who know the conditions of the enemy.*
>
> —Master Sun
> *Sun Tzu and the Art of War*

ENDNOTES

1. Source: *Necessary AND Sufficient,* a lecture prepared by Eliyahu M. Goldratt, 2001.
2. H. W. Dettmer, *Breaking the Constraints to World-Class Performance* (Milwaukee: ASQ Quality Press, 1998).
3. J. Luft, *Group Processes: An Introduction to Group Dynamics*, 2nd ed. (Palo Alto, CA: National Press Books, 1970).
4. W. E. Deming, *Out of the Crisis*, 1993.
5. T. Clancy and F. Franks, Jr., *Into the Storm: A Study in Command* (New York: G. P. Putnam's Sons, 1997): 113–14.
6. C. Clark, *Brainstorming: How to Create Successful Ideas* (CA: Melvin Powers Wilshire Book Company, 1958).
7. A. Delbecq, A. Van de Ven, and D. Gustafson, *Group Techniques for Program Planning: A Guide to Nominal Group and Delphi Processes* (Middleton, WI: Green Briar Press, 1986).
8. G. B. Siegel and R. Clayton, *Mass Interviewing and Marshalling of Ideas to Improve Performance* (Lanham, MD: University Press of America, Rowan and Littlefield Publishing, 2001).
9. J. Terninko, A. Zusman, and B. Zlotin, *Systematic Innovation: An Introduction to TRIZ* (Boca Raton, FL: St. Lucie Press, 1997).

7

Analyzing the Mismatches

Therefore use these assessments for comparison, to find out what the conditions are. That is to say, which political leadership has the Way? Which general has the ability? Which has the better climate and terrain? Whose discipline is effective? Whose troops are the stronger? Whose officers and soldiers are the better trained? Whose system of rewards and punishments is clearer? This is how you can know who will win.

—Master Sun
Sun Tzu and the Art of War

Developing an effective strategy for the future starts, of course, with a decision about what that future should look like. We ought to have the destination firmly in mind before we begin the journey. Since that destination is, in most cases, beyond our "visible horizon," it makes sense to have a compass bearing to follow. However, as in our strategic navigation example (chapter 4), charting a precise course to a known destination requires concrete knowledge of *both* our goal and our present position. Knowing that we're aiming for the Strait of Gibraltar is only part of the equation. When we choose our initial heading, we also must know where we're starting from. It makes a huge difference knowing we're embarking from Virginia, rather than South Africa—otherwise, we might end up in Buenos Aires.*

If we're to have confidence in the strategic direction we choose, we must know, with as much certainty as possible, exactly where we're starting from and exactly what

---

* In an old comedy routine, Bob Newhart, posing as a submarine commander about to surface at the end of a two-month submerged voyage, tells his crew, "Men, in a moment you'll be gazing at the familiar skyline of . . . either New York or Buenos Aires!"

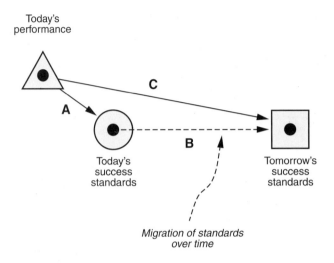

Today's
performance

C

A

Today's
success
standards

B

Tomorrow's
success
standards

*Migration of standards
over time*

Figure 7.1 The nature of the "gap."

our destination is. In chapter 5, we clearly defined our desired destination in a statement of our goal and the necessary conditions (critical success factors) for achieving it. Now it's time to fix our present position. The difference between the two is a well-defined gap, or mismatch, between reality and expectations, which might be represented as a vector—a magnitude of distance and a direction.

Notice that, unlike day-to-day problem solving, this mismatch is not a comparison between today's standards and today's performance. It's really a comparison between today's performance and *tomorrow's* standards. Comparing today's performance against today's standards, the gap may not look very significant. But in comparison with the requirements for success in the future, it might be considerably larger. Figure 7.1 illustrates this point.

Most management activity is normally focused on reducing the deviation between current performance and existing standards, or "benchmark" metrics. In Figure 7.1 this is represented by vector A. But we all know that time doesn't stand still, nor do standards of performance. The technology of 2002 is capable of much higher performance than that of even 1990, and the standards of 2002 reflect commensurate selectivity.[*] The magnitude and direction of the evolution of standards is represented in Figure 7.1 by vector B. This means that if we're to plan today for success in the future, we should be considering the gap represented by vector C, not A. A duck hunter might call this "leading the target."

---

[*] I remember in 1990 thinking that my 386 computer, with its 33 MHz processor and 1,024 kilobytes of random access memory (RAM) was pretty fast. Today, writing this with my 1.3 GHz processor and 750 megabytes of RAM, I almost want to laugh at what I considered acceptable state of the art. For a larger perspective, consider the IBM System/360 Model 70 computer of 1964, IBM's top-of-the-line model: 1,064 kilobytes of memory and a 7.5 megabyte hard disk, costing more than a million dollars and filling a whole room! (Lilly, pp. 28-29.)

So, with the goal and necessary conditions (chapter 5) representing the new standards of future success (our destination), we're now ready to determine the size and scope of the gap between that future outcome and our present position. We'll do this by means of a Strategic Current Reality Tree (S-CRT).

Figure 7.2 illustrates the concept of a Strategic Current Reality Tree. It represents the mismatches between present performance and the future goal/necessary conditions as statements of *undesirable effect*. The S-CRT then reveals all the layers of direct and unavoidable causality between those effects and the deepest factors producing them that

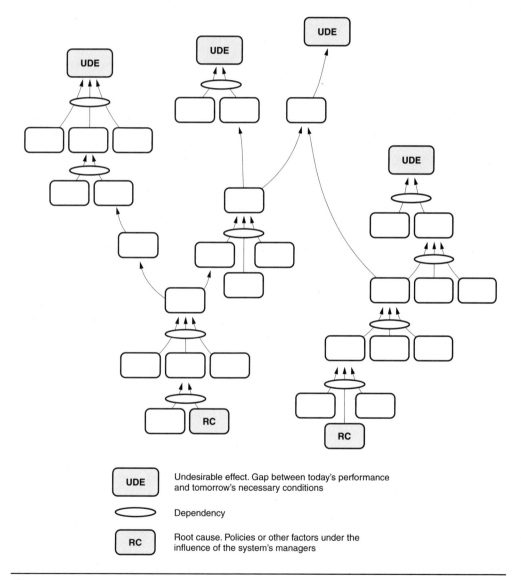

Figure 7.2 Current Reality Tree (conceptual).

it is possible (or practical) to change. It also indicates the lateral dependencies between one chain of cause and effect and another.

The revelation of the critical root causes is the intended product of an S-CRT. These are policies or other factors under the influence of system managers that combine to produce the performance of today that compares unfavorably with the future standard. In other words, these are the factors that *must* change if the gap between current performance and future expectations is to be eliminated. Let's consider an example that almost everyone is familiar with by now: the airline industry.

TERROR ATTACKS AND AMERICA'S AIRLINES

Even before the terrorist attacks, the major commercial airlines were in troubling financial straits. Through September 30, United Airlines had lost $1.8 billion in 2001. American Airlines wasn't much better, with a loss of nearly a billion. Much of that red ink was already on the books before 9/11.[1] The terrorist attacks only drove the profit curves downward more steeply.

The air traffic control system, especially access in and out of major airports, had been saturated for a long time, meaning that any schedule disruptions resulting from weather or mechanical failures caused chain reaction flight delays and cancellations throughout the country.[2] The summer of 2000 had been particularly bad because of acrimonious labor disputes between United's management and its pilots and mechanics. Delays and cancellations reached an all-time high for nearly all airlines, and "air rage" incidents among passengers upset with customer service skyrocketed.[3]

Passengers of commercial airlines have long been dissatisfied with airline service anyway, from the deterioration of in-flight meals to the shortage of overhead storage space and cramped seating.[*] Following the "law of unintended consequences," the terrorist attacks had a subtle additional effect. Besides questioning whether it was really safe to fly, prospective passengers began to question whether it was really worth the hassle.[4] The inconveniences of increased airport security included much earlier arrival at airports, long check-in lines, long (and frequent) security screening queues, and, after the "exploding shoe" incident, removal and x-ray of people's shoes. Reduced flight schedules decreased opportunities to connect, making for long layovers at major hubs. Inevitably, people began to look for less stressful, more comfortable ways to travel when they *had* to travel, and alternatives to traveling at all when they could avoid it. Telephone conferencing and videoconferencing increased among business travelers.[5] Leisure travelers found things to do closer to home, or traveled by car or train. Demand for airline seats dropped precipitously immediately following the terror attacks, and airlines eliminated 20 to 30 percent of their scheduled flights to compensate for the lower loads.

---

[*] In *Hannibal,* author Thomas Harris's sequel to his best-selling novel *Silence of the Lambs,* Hannibal Lecter, flying in a Boeing 747 middle coach seat, observes that "Shoulder room is 20 inches. Hip room between armrests is 20 inches. This is two inches more space than a slave had on the Middle Passage." And some flights seem about as long!

As new security measures began to restore some of the public's confidence in the safety of air travel, the airlines became eager to win back passengers who had curtailed flying. They lifted normal restrictions and offered a variety of enticements to lure customers back. Competing for a perceived limited market, they even began "raiding" each other's customer bases. Alaska Airlines openly tried to take away United's frequent fliers by offering instant "elite" status to any who would change allegiance.[6] For their part, airline customers began to be more discerning and less tolerant of the airlines' past cavalier behavior toward them.

COMPARING TODAY'S PERFORMANCE AGAINST FUTURE REQUIREMENTS

Overshadowing the problems commercial airlines were experiencing prior to September 11, 2001 (equivalent to vector A in Figure 7.1), the terrorist attacks on that day changed the whole paradigm of air travel forever. While the airlines' goals have undoubtedly remained the same, the necessary conditions—critical success factors required to achieve them—have changed dramatically. This change in the environmental requirements for success is equivalent to vector B in Figure 7.1. That leaves the airlines—the smart ones, anyway—staring directly at vector C: the difference between where they stood financially, operationally, and security-wise on September 10, and where they needed to put themselves in 2002, if they were to survive.* Essentially, this means that the airlines must analyze the new paradigm and reevaluate their strategies in light of this new reality. It remains to be seen whether they will actually do that, or just revert to business as usual while the economy and air travel demand begin limping back to normalcy.

STRATEGIC CURRENT REALITY TREE: AN EXAMPLE

The final outcome and "shakeout" of the paradigm shift the airlines have undergone is yet to play out as of this writing, though some of them are apparently starting to wake up. (See the accompanying sidebar, page 105.) So, how has the "current reality" of airlines changed since September 11, 2001? Figure 7.3 shows a generic example of a Strategic Current Reality Tree on the airlines' situation. It simplifies, somewhat, the situation as we know it today. But it shows how this situation would be structured to display logical cause and effect. It isn't intended to characterize one particular airline, even though some of the entities seem to be worded that way. However, in many respects, it characterizes *all* airlines at the moment. Your organization's Strategic Current Reality Tree might be considerably more complicated than this one. I offer this example only to give you a sense of what's possible.

---

* And some of them won't. Sabena and Swissair already haven't. Both declared bankruptcy in the aftermath of the terrorist attacks. Since then, even major U.S. air carriers such as US Air and United have also sought refuge in bankruptcy.

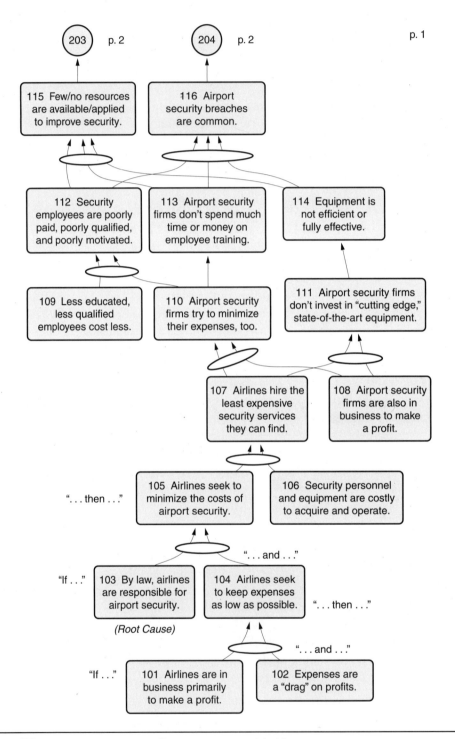

Figure 7.3a Strategic Current Reality Tree—commercial airlines.

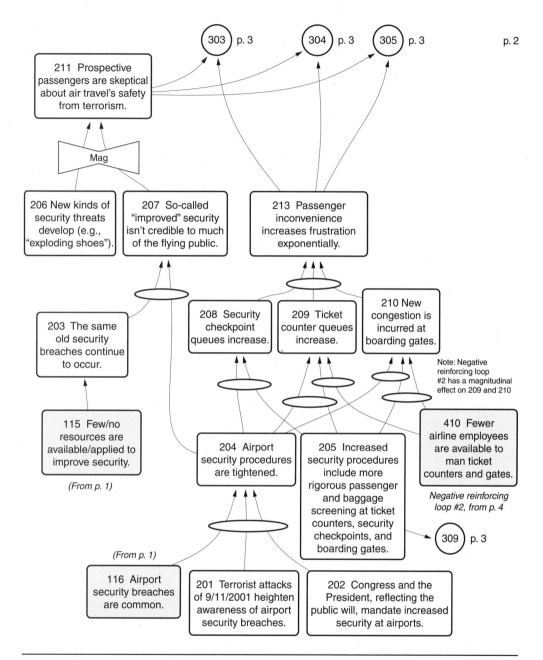

Figure 7.3b Strategic Current Reality Tree—commercial airlines.

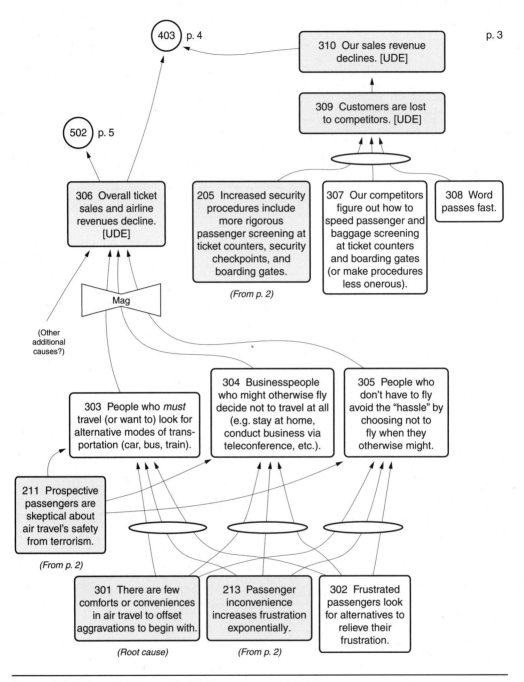

Figure 7.3c Strategic Current Reality Tree—commercial airlines.

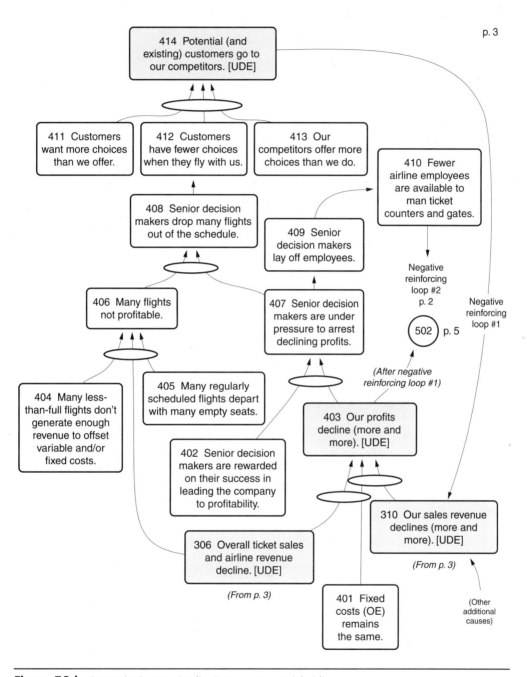

p. 3

414 Potential (and existing) customers go to our competitors. [UDE]

411 Customers want more choices than we offer.

412 Customers have fewer choices when they fly with us.

413 Our competitors offer more choices than we do.

410 Fewer airline employees are available to man ticket counters and gates.

408 Senior decision makers drop many flights out of the schedule.

409 Senior decision makers lay off employees.

Negative reinforcing loop #2 p. 2

Negative reinforcing loop #1

406 Many flights not profitable.

407 Senior decision makers are under pressure to arrest declining profits.

502   p. 5

(After negative reinforcing loop #1)

404 Many less-than-full flights don't generate enough revenue to offset variable and/or fixed costs.

405 Many regularly scheduled flights depart with many empty seats.

403 Our profits decline (more and more). [UDE]

402 Senior decision makers are rewarded on their success in leading the company to profitability.

310 Our sales revenue declines (more and more). [UDE]

(From p. 3)

306 Overall ticket sales and airline revenue decline. [UDE]

(From p. 3)

401 Fixed costs (OE) remains the same.

(Other additional causes)

Figure 7.3d   Strategic Current Reality Tree—commercial airlines.

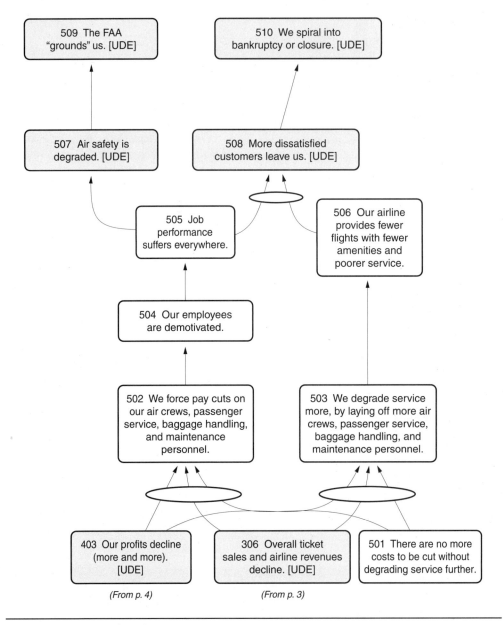

Figure 7.3e Strategic Current Reality Tree—commercial airlines.

The following article indicates that, nine months after the terrorist attacks of September 11, 2001, it's beginning to dawn on the airlines that something more than safety and low prices alone is needed to bring customers back. Wouldn't management have been better served by having been able to anticipate this ahead of time and address it in a structured way—perhaps with a comprehensive Strategic Current Reality Tree—rather than through late recognition followed by trial and error?

Peninsula Daily News, Thursday, June 6, 2002, p. B4

Airlines Turn to Comfort

Yoga, Bagels Added to Draw Riders

The Associated Press (Reprinted with permission.)

In-flight yoga. More legroom. Better food. The airline industry, crippled by the terrorist attacks and a downturn in business travel, spent the past several months trying to convince Americans that flying is safe and affordable. Now, as business slowly recovers, the airlines are trying to make people believe that travel can be enjoyable, too.

"They're trying to get everybody in the mood again," 18-year-old Gloribel Rodriguez, who flies to Puerto Rico once a month to visit family, said on a recent morning at New York's LaGuardia Airport. "They know they need to satisfy the customer. If we're not happy, they have no money."

- JetBlue Airways is encouraging passengers to relax a little with placards in the back of seats that show how to do simple yoga without standing up.

- Continental is serving higher-quality food to coach passengers on trans-Atlantic flights.

- American Airlines is spending millions on advertising to ballyhoo several inches of legroom added on every plane.

The little extras run counter to the ruthless cost-cutting of the past several months. With passenger traffic down 12 percent in April compared with last year, and security costs on the rise, major U.S. airlines have canceled meals on short flights, removed pillows and blankets, and closed airport lounges.

The more recent amenities represent a subtle but significant shift in marketing strategies, said Robert Mann and airline consultant at R. V. Mann & Co. in Port Washington, NY. "It's a return to Marketing 101," Mann said. "The airlines are back to the product differentiation factors to take the edge off this perception that the airports should be avoided."

Continental announced last week that it will serve chicken breasts instead of chicken thighs on trans-Atlantic flights and that breakfast will be upgraded from a cold croissant to a warm bagel with cream cheese. The only catch: Continental will charge $4 for alcoholic drinks on trans-Atlantic flights, an amenity that used to be free.

Low-fare airline JetBlue, which has never served meals, is using quirky humor to try to make its customers happier. "A flight attendant may ask you if you need something," JetBlue's in-flight yoga manual says. "Tell them that we all need inner peace."

Punching Bags

Recognizing the stress involved in going through airports these days JetBlue is also encouraging travelers to release tension before they board the plane: The airline is installing heavyweight punching bags that travelers can take a whack at once they get through security at Kennedy Airport.

$2.4 Billion Industry Losses

The nine largest U.S. airlines lost a combined $2.4 billion during the first three months of the year. Southwest—the only major U.S. airline to record quarterly profits since Sept. 11—is sticking with its low-frill strategy. "When's the last time anyone bragged about an in-flight meal?" spokeswoman Linda Rutherford said. "We'd rather you saved money on the cost of the flight and be able to have a steak dinner when you get to your destination."

Mary Jo DeMartini, 38, who flies once a month as a public relations manager for Parade magazine, said the best way to put a smile on her face would be to reduce the hassles of baggage and passenger screening.

THE BASICS OF CAUSE AND EFFECT

As you look at Figure 7.3, notice that the arrows lead from the bottom of each page to the top. These arrows represent the sequence of logical causal connections. Read each statement with either "if," "and," or "then" preceding it, as appropriate. Taking the bottom layer on the first page as an example:

> *If* (101) airlines are in business primarily to make a profit, *and* (102) expenses are a "drag" on profits, *then* (104) airlines seek to keep expenses as low as possible.

The numbers associated with each block are merely navigation aids that allow us to direct people's attention to the block we're talking about at the moment. 101 and 102 are causes leading to an effect, 104.

Each successive level of effect becomes the cause for the next level. Almost all the blocks have arrows leading into them. Some don't. They only have arrows leading out. We refer to these as *root causes,* even though some of them may appear higher up in the tree. Notice, too, that most causal connections have more than one arrow, enclosed with an ellipse, leading from multiple causes into a single effect. This configuration indicates a mutual dependency between causes; take one away, and the other isn't sufficient alone to produce the effect.

Eventually, the chain of causality leads from the deepest "roots" of the Current Reality Tree to what we call "undesirable effects" near the top. In Figure 7.3, these are indicated by shaded blocks and the acronym "UDE." The undesirable effects represent the gap between current reality and the strategic goal, or one of its supporting necessary conditions. Even though I haven't included a Strategic Intermediate Objectives Map for the airlines, you can be pretty sure that the statements in those shaded UDE blocks would be direct contradictions of those critical success factors. Notice, too, that there are two instances in this tree where an arrow leads from an effect higher in the tree *back down* to a cause lower in the tree. These are "negative reinforcing loops." In other words, the effects exacerbate the cause, either perpetuating the effect or making it worse. Eventually, negative reinforcing loops can be devastating, as page 5 of this tree shows.

In its entirety, the Strategic Current Reality Tree gives us a "snapshot" of existing reality's inner workings—the interdependencies among factors that cause the performance results that we see around us. This "snapshot" is valid as long as the assumptions associated with the causality arrows remain valid. If parts of the environment change, and those assumptions no longer apply, parts of what is expressed in the tree may be invalidated as well. This should be a hint to you that S-CRTs *are not static documents*—they're *dynamic* and must be periodically reviewed and updated if they're to remain useful.

If the tree is properly constructed, meaning that it's logically sound,* we should be able to verify an unbroken chain of cause and effect from the root causes all the way to

---

* There are seven standard rules of logic that each connection in this kind of tree must adhere to. Refer to *Goldratt's Theory of Constraints* (Dettmer, 1996) for an explanation of these rules and how they're applied.

the undesirable effects. The implication of this causality is very important: *if we can interrupt this chain of causality at the lowest point over which we have some influence, we can: (a) eliminate the undesirable effects, and (b) prevent them from happening again in the future* (at least from *these* causes). Moreover, if that lowest root cause is actually a dependent pair of causes joined by an ellipse, we have another unique advantage: *flexibility of action.* We can choose which of the dependent causes to eliminate. One might be technically, economically, or politically easier than the other to change. It's not necessary to eliminate them both.

Think of reality as a chain of dominoes erected on their ends, each positioned so that when it falls, it will knock over the one behind it, until all the dominoes have fallen. If we can interrupt that chain reaction, the last domino in line will never fall—the undesirable effect will never happen. The earlier in the chain we can halt the chain reaction, the fewer dominoes will fall (the fewer negative outcomes we'll have). This concept will have positive implications later, too, as we try to create *future* causality that will give us desirable effects.

The S-CRT identifies for us the chain of negative causality we should destroy in order to get rid of the undesirable effects (UDE). But it does something even more important than that: it keeps us from wasting time "rearranging the deck chairs on the *Titanic.*"

"ARCHIMEDES" POINTS

Why do we care about eliminating root causes? In most cases, you'll find that a Strategic Current Reality Tree will display some convergence toward the bottom. In other words, a wide variety of undesirable effects normally originate from relatively fewer root causes—in rare cases, maybe only one. This implies exceptional potential to exert "leverage" on an organizational system. Change one, or maybe a very few root causes, and we can have a major positive impact on the system. Some have referred to these exceptional leverage factors as "Archimedes points."* Goldratt calls them *system constraints,* because they prevent a complex system from making progress toward its goal.[7] It's for this reason that chapter 4 characterizes this methodology as the *constraint management* model.

Picture a big river. At some point, the course of the river narrows, and the speed of flow increases. Sometimes a log or large rock will lodge itself in the narrow spot, and debris carried by the river will lodge behind it. Eventually, there may be a logjam that causes the water upstream of it to flood over the riverbank. If the logjam isn't cleared, sooner or later the river will "reengineer" its own course to a path of lesser resistance.

The same thing happens in organizations at an Archimedes point. If some policy or practice is rendered invalid by a paradigm shift, or even just a major change in the competitive environment, the organization's progress toward its goal can be "clogged."

---

* In ancient Greece, Archimedes was reputed to have said, "Give me a lever long enough and a place to stand, and I will move the world." (I think there was a small matter of a fulcrum, too.)

Knowing exactly where that Archimedes point is and what to do to clear the logjam can produce benefits to the organization far out of proportion to the efforts applied. The Strategic Current Reality Tree enables senior executives to identify these Archimedes points—the places where a concerted effort can pay back disproportionate rewards.* Appendix C, "Case Study: Wurtzberg Corporation," shows the value of such a tree. All of Wurtzberg's undesirable effects can be traced back along the chains of cause and effect to one critical root cause, which, if fixed, eliminates every one of those undesirable effects.

HOW TO CONSTRUCT A PICTURE OF THE STATUS QUO

The obvious next question is, "How do we construct a Strategic Current Reality Tree?" Figure 7.4 shows an abbreviated checklist of steps for doing so, but if this is your first exposure to the logical *thinking process* developed by Goldratt,[8–10] you'll find that it isn't quite that easy to build a logically sound tree. If you have the luxury of time to go through some trial and error, you might be able to create a passable S-CRT on your own. However, if time is of the essence, or if you just can't afford any mistakes in the first attempt, it would be to your advantage to enlist some qualified outside assistance.

A CONSENSUS PICTURE

Each of us sees the world through our own uniquely colored set of glasses. One person's perception of reality frequently diverges from another's. And even if the perceptions of two people are the same, plurality doesn't necessarily establish validity. For this reason, the best S-CRTs usually result from the inputs of a diverse group of contributors. Remember the story about the five blind people and the elephant? The only way they could "see" the elephant was by touching it. And each one touched a different part: one had the trunk, another the ear, a third the side, the fourth a leg, and the last the tail. Each "saw" and described something different. Individually, their descriptions were all accurate, but suboptimal, impressions. Together, their combined descriptions gave a fairly accurate picture of the whole elephant.

Likewise, knowledgeable people from different functional areas of an organization each have their own perspective on the system's problems. If you can combine these diverse perspectives efficiently and effectively in a Strategic Current Reality Tree, the resulting picture of the whole system, its deficiencies, and their interdependencies will be much "richer," and certainly a more accurate representation of "the whole elephant." Even more important, the process of constructing a unified S-CRT from the contributions of a group of knowledgeable people actually elicits consensus on the problem

---

* On the other hand, you could ignore the root cause and hope it will go away on its own (not likely). More likely, the unaddressed root cause will "reengineer" the system on its own, following a path of least resistance—which you might not like! W. Edwards Deming once said, "Change is not necessary—survival is not mandatory."

1. Define the system boundaries, its goal, and necessary conditions (cr
   success factors)

   • Use the Strategic IO Map (Ch. 5)

2. State the system problem as a question

   • "Why are we not able to achieve [the goal/NC-CSF from the Strategic IO Map]?"

3. List all the indications that the goal/necessary conditions are not being achieved

   • These are the undesirable effects (UDE)

4. Ask "Why do these undesirable effects (UDE) exist?"

   • List at least one reason/cause for each UDE

   • Ask why each reason/cause exists

   • List the second-order causes

5. Convert the listed UDEs and first- and second-order reasons to Post-It notes

   • Stick related Post-It notes together (clusters) for each UDE

6. Arrange the Post-It notes on a large blank surface (paper or whiteboard)

   • Second-order causes below first-order causes

   • First-order causes below UDEs

   • Connect causes to UDEs with arrows in the direction of causality

7. Verify sufficiency, add additional causes

   • Apply the *categories of legitimate reservation* (rules of logic)

   • Add clarification, more causes or assumptions, as needed

   • Result should be a completed causality "cluster"

8. Arrange related UDE clusters near one another

   • Complete vertical or cross-connections

   • Add intermediate causes/effects as required for sufficiency

   • Continue building clusters downward or interpolating until all clusters can be connected into a single tree

9. Look for negative reinforcing loops

10. Identify critical root causes

11. "Scrutinize" the entire tree

    • Enlist help from those who did not participate in tree construction

    • Recruit people with good knowledge of the system

    • Correct the tree as required

Figure 7.4 Strategic Current Reality Tree directions.

Note: These directions are adapted and modified from H. W. Dettmer, *Breaking the Constraints to World-Class Performance* (Milwaukee: ASQ Quality Press, 1998).

statements (root causes) as you go. By the time the tree is finished, everyone is pretty much in agreement about what needs to be changed.

Building an S-CRT by consensus of more than two people can be a slow process. In fact, I've noticed that speed of progress is inversely proportional to the number of people involved, reaching a practical limit ("dead in the water") somewhere between 6 and 8. In some cases, it's better to have one or two people with broad knowledge do the actual construction, then have their work reviewed* by others with more detailed knowledge of parts of the system. The case study in Appendix B, U.S. Transportation Command, provides an example of how this review and verification process works.

The Crawford slip method, described in chapter 6, offers a way to elicit some of the key building blocks for a Strategic Current Reality Tree. With these inputs and some detailed guidance,[11] an S-CRT can be assembled much like a jigsaw puzzle.

REVIEWING THE "BIG PICTURE"

Let's quickly review what we've covered recently. In chapter 5, we saw that developing a Strategic Intermediate Objectives Map forced us to answer three basic questions:

1. What is our system's goal?

2. What are the critical success factors we must have in place to achieve that goal?

3. What is the dependency relationship between the goal and the critical success factors?

Answering these questions fulfills Step 1 of the constraint management model. Then in chapter 6, we discussed the importance of having the right system knowledge and a source of creativity to generate strategic solutions—"breakthroughs," if you will.

In chapter 7, we've seen how to take that knowledge of our system and its environment, combine it with our own experience and intuition, and create from these a Strategic Current Reality Tree that fairly and accurately answers two more basic questions:

1. What is the nature and scope of the mismatch between where we want to be (represented by the Strategic IO Map) and where we currently are?

2. What are the few key issues to work on—among them the system's constraint—in order to eliminate that mismatch as quickly as possible?

Recalling the OODA loop, these three chapters have given us ways to *observe* and *orient* our organization and ourselves in our environment. (See Figure 7.5.) In the chapters that follow, we'll see how the first two steps of the constraint management model lead us to the *decide* and *act* parts of the OODA loop.

---

* We refer to this review as "scrutinizing" the logic. Specific rules of logic are applied to verify that the statements in the tree are valid, that causality is also valid and sufficient, and that no crucial chains of causation have been omitted.

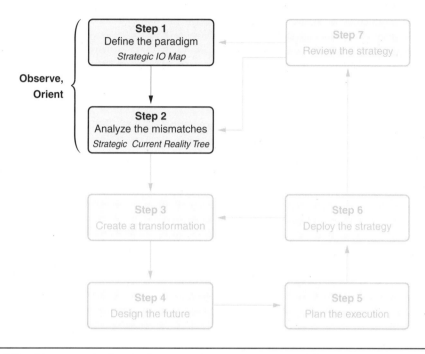

Figure 7.5 *Observe* and *orient* in the constraint management model.

RESISTANCE TO CHANGE

It's been said that one person's "improvement" is another person's change. This is another way of saying that not everybody sees change in a positive way. Many see it as an inconvenience. To the extent that changing or eliminating a critical root cause inconveniences people, or they perceive it as "bad" for them, they may resist it, either openly or covertly. Either way, if their cooperation is essential for strategic success, the required changes may fail.

Resistance to change is an indication of hidden conflict. Such conflicts must be resolved early on for new strategies to succeed. In chapter 8, we'll see how to do this.

> *Unless you know the mountains and forests, the defiles and impasses, and the lay of the marshes and swamps, you cannot maneuver with an armed force. Unless you use local guides, you cannot get the advantages of the land.*
>
> —Master Sun
> *Sun Tzu and the Art of War*

ENDNOTES

1. G. Strauss, "Airlines' Finances Shaken Again," *USA Today* (13 November 2001).
2. M. Adams, "Airport Gridlock," *USA Today* (14 August 2001)
3. M. Trottman, "Antodotes to Airport Rage," *Wall Street Journal* (14 August 2000).
4. M. Adams, "Frequent Fliers Not So Frequent Anymore," *USA Today* (27 November 2001).
5. W. M. Bulkeley, "Travel Fears, Economy Trim Turnout at Corporate Conventions, Meetings," *Wall Street Journal* (11 January 2002).
6. J. Costello, "Alaska Airlines Is Publicly Offering Elite Status to United Frequent Fliers," *Wall Street Journal* (8 January 2002).
7. E. M. Goldratt, *The Haystack Syndrome: Sifting Information Out of the Data Ocean* (Croton-on-Hudson, NY: The North River Press, 1990): 53–59.
8. H. W. Dettmer, *Goldratt's Theory of Constraints: A Systems Approach to Continuous Improvement* (Milwaukee: ASQC Quality Press, 1996).
9. H. W. Dettmer, *Breaking the Constraints to World-Class Performance* (Milwaukee: ASQ Quality Press, 1998).
10. L. J. Scheinkopf, *Thinking for a Change: Putting the TOC Thinking Processes to Work* (Boca Raton, FL: CRC/St. Lucir Press, 1999).
11. See note 9.

8

Creating a Transformation: Resolving Conflict

Therefore those who win every battle are not really skillful—those who render others' armies helpless without fighting at all are the best of all.

—Master Sun
Sun Tzu and the Art of War

One of Sun Tzu's most important precepts was the principle of "winning all without fighting."[1] Though Sun Tzu was speaking of opposing armies—external adversaries—his advice is even more important when considering internal adversaries. The latter might include contemporaries, superiors, or even subordinates. Internal adversaries are the people in any organizational system opposed to changing the status quo. To the extent that they're able to frustrate a strategy, either by direct sabotage or by passive resistance when their willing cooperation is needed, such opponents must be taken into account in the strategy. Forces outside the organization can also thwart strategy, even if they're not direct competitors. Whatever the configuration of resisting forces, the resistance amounts to conflict, even if it isn't overt.

Take a look at Figure 8.1. This is a replication of the "vector analysis" of changing strategic direction that we saw in Figure 7.1, with some minor changes. Vector A represents the path our ship (or organization) is on today in its mission to close the gap on today's deviations. We're making reasonable progress, with no significant obstacles. Now let's assume that we've decided on a strategic change in direction. We want to head in the direction of vector C, to close the gap between ourselves and our expectations of the future. This requires a major turn for the ship. But maybe there are members of the crew who don't like the idea of changing direction. For whatever reason, they're comfortable continuing on the organization's present heading. So they fight for control of

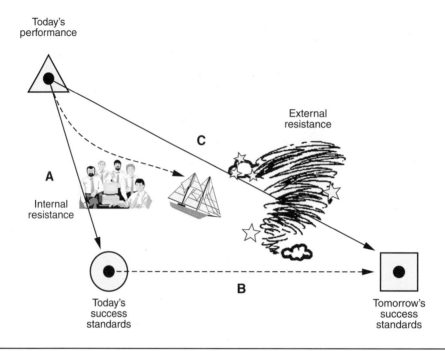

Figure 8.1 Sources of conflict.

the ship's wheel, trying to keep the ship on the original course. Or maybe they adopt a more surreptitious approach: someone stands beside the compass binnacle with a magnet, displacing the compass needle so that the quartermaster *thinks* the ship is steering the proper heading, but in fact it hasn't changed from the original heading at all. These examples are the equivalent of either overt or passive resistance within an organization, and either type of resistance can frustrate a new strategy.

On the other hand, let's assume that there isn't any internal resistance to the change in strategy. We turn the ship to the new heading, and everything seems to be working out well. Then, somewhere along the new course (vector C), we come head-to-head with a storm that forces us to change course again to avoid it, or to seek a safe harbor. The storm isn't really a competitor. It's just an environmental factor that prevents us from following our planned course. Then again, we *might* have to change direction because of the actions of a competitor—in our nautical example, that might be a pirate ship closing on us. In either case, we're likely to encounter resistance—conflict—deliberately trying to thwart our strategy.

THE INHERENT NATURE OF CONFLICT IN CHANGE

We can see conflict in changing strategies graphically represented in Figure 8.2. If this picture looks somewhat familiar, it's because it's a modified version of the conceptual Strategic Current Reality Tree (S-CRT) in Figure 7.2.

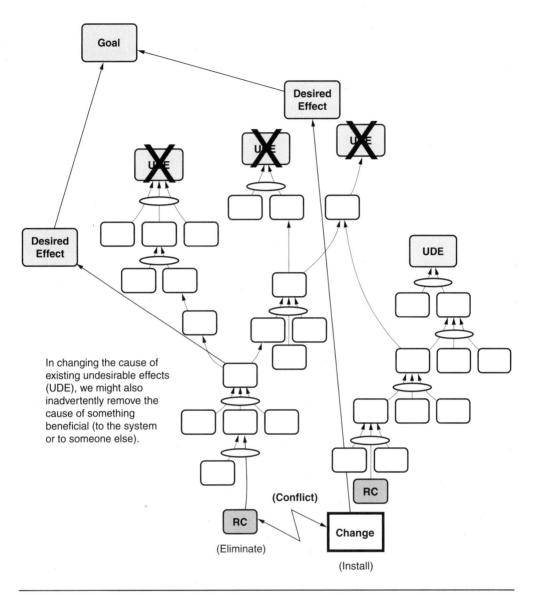

In changing the cause of existing undesirable effects (UDE), we might also inadvertently remove the cause of something beneficial (to the system or to someone else).

Figure 8.2 Conflict inherent in change.

The S-CRT shows a picture of the cause-and-effect relationships that lead to the existence of the gaps between where we are now and where we want to be in the future. These are reflected in the statements of undesirable effects (UDE) in the S-CRT. We know what we must change: one or more of the root causes. Doing so will give us one or more of the desired effects that represent the opposite—or elimination—of the gaps inherent in the UDEs. You can see this represented in Figure 8.2. The change at the bottom leads to the cancellation of the three UDEs at the top of the tree and their replacement by a new desired effect.

But there's a fly in the ointment. The root cause of the S-CRT, perhaps a policy that must be changed, certainly produces the UDEs in that tree. But inevitably, for someone either within the organization or outside of it, that same root cause *also* produces some desired effect. In most cases, that desired effect never shows up in the S-CRT. Why not? Because it's *not negative!*

Remember, the whole concept behind the S-CRT is that it represents gaps between the actual state and the desired state of our system. Because we've focused on what we want to *fix* (the negatives), we haven't paid much attention to—or included in the S-CRT—those things that we're satisfied with. Because of this exclusive focus on the system's negatives, we're at serious risk of throwing somebody's baby out with the bathwater. And people don't *like* having their babies thrown out, with or without bathwater! So, naturally, they resist. If they feel powerful enough, they'll resist openly, maybe even confrontationally. If they don't, they'll resist passively, possibly through quiet sabotage.

ANTICIPATING RESISTANCE TO A CHANGE IN STRATEGY: THREE DIMENSIONS OF FEASIBILITY

Sometimes we can anticipate resistance to a change in strategy; other times, we might not be able to. But if we *can,* doesn't it make sense that we should try to prevent that resistance from arising in the first place? In other words, we'd like to create a strategy that accounts for the sources of resistance and the reasons for resisting.

There are basically only three reasons why people, departments, or whole organizations resist change: technical, economic, and political.[2]* Almost all the rationales for not doing something new can be sorted into one of these three categories. The first two are fairly obvious. People might resist because the technical feasibility of the new strategy is questionable, or because it's not economically feasible (too expensive).

Let's consider the technical roadblocks people might interpose. We're talking here about the legitimate technical reasons why individuals or factions might resist a new strategy. There are six of these *technical feasibility* issues[3]:

1. The problem prompting the strategy change doesn't really exist; or, "It's not *my* problem"; or, "It's not *really* a problem."

2. We have no control over the situation (usually meaning the market or the competitive environment); or, inability to agree on the solution to the problem.

3. The new strategy won't take us where we need to be; or, the proposed solution is incomplete.

4. The new strategy is likely to create more problems than it solves (or new ones we're not experiencing now).

---

* These three categories—technical, economic, and political—are adapted from a discussion of the feasibility of policy changes in R.M. Krone, *Systems Analysis and Policy Sciences* (New York: John Wiley & Sons, 1980).

5. The obstacles to executing the new strategy are insurmountable.

6. We don't know *what* to do about the problem.

If your strategy is properly constructed and verified, and you use the thinking process tools described in this book, you can expect one of two outcomes: either (a) you'll have accounted for all five of these technical objections, in which case you'll be ready to respond to them when they're raised; or (b) you'll find one that is truly and legitimately insurmountable. If you find that "we can't get there from here," it's better to discover this sooner, rather than later, so you can go back and redesign the strategy to completely avoid the technical problems. Far from being a setback, you should thank your lucky stars if the second outcome occurs. By discovering this problem before "forces are engaged" (meaning resources are committed to a new course of action), you can avoid devastating—possibly embarrassing—failure that you might otherwise not have foreseen.

The second significant reason for resisting a strategy change is *economic feasibility:* the strategy can't be executed within the organization's resource or investment constraints. In other words, "We just can't afford it." The thinking process might not tell you that this is a problem. In all likelihood, only a thorough financial analysis based on realistic assumptions can do that. However, knowing ahead of time that there are economic feasibility challenges associated with a strategy, it may be possible to overcome them in the strategy development phase. There are creative ways to overcome resource or investment shortages. Though we won't discuss all of these "creativity engines" in detail, later in this chapter we will identify one useful tool called an Evaporating Cloud that can help break economic or financial constraints. It's not by any means the only way to do so, but it is fairly easy to use.

The last line of resistance to changing a strategy is *political feasibility.* This is also the most insidious one to come to grips with, and it's rooted in both individual and organizational psychology. Significant research has been done in the area of individual motivation. Between 1950 and 1975, several renowned researchers offered theories on the motivations behind human behavior.[4–7] All of these theories except McClelland's centered on individuals' needs for security and satisfaction as motivators of behavior. Only McClelland addressed the issue of people's need for power. Let's first consider security and satisfaction.

PERSONAL RESISTANCE TO CHANGE: "EFRAT'S CLOUD"

In 1995, a PhD student in Israel, Efrat Goldratt, suggested that a common psychological conflict underlay a wide variety of demonstrated behaviors in individuals.* Ms. Goldratt maintained that most people in the world had a common goal: to achieve a

---

* Efrat Goldratt is the daughter of Eliyahu M. Goldratt, who conceived the theory of constraints (Goldratt, 1986, 1990).

degree of happiness in their lives. Obviously, the precise definition of "happiness" will vary from one person to another, but let's accept this premise for a moment.

In order to achieve happiness, people need to feel both secure and satisfied. Ms. Goldratt defined "security" as a level of confidence in the predictability of future events. This is another way of saying people find comfort in the familiar things around them and the consistency with which things happen. In essence, this is the cause and effect in their lives. To the degree that individuals can predict what will happen to them from day to day, even if it isn't always pleasant, they achieve a level of comfort in their situation. This comfort level, in turn, engenders a sense of security. Personal satisfaction, on the other hand, comes from a sense of accomplishment. This sense of accomplishment grows when people are able to achieve challenging objectives, especially when there's some element of doubt about their ability to do so. The more difficult the objective, or the greater the risk—climbing Mount Everest or winning an Olympic gold medal, for example—the higher the degree of satisfaction.

But it's almost a law of nature that achieving challenging, high-risk objectives requires people to do things far out of the ordinary, very possibly things that have never been done before. If this weren't the case, then everybody would be doing these things routinely and achieving lofty goals. Another way to put it is that people must "get out of their comfort zones" to do great deeds and achieve great things. Any way you look at it, this inevitably means changing what they're doing *now*—and not just grudgingly accepting change, but actively seeking it out and embracing it. On the other hand, security implies consistency, or predictability. Realizing a significant degree of security almost freezes out the possibility of changing from the familiar.

Efrat Goldratt created an Evaporating Cloud (Figure 8.3) to succinctly present this conundrum. We'll explore how an Evaporating Cloud is developed later in the chapter, but for the moment let's see what one looks like.

Because the conflict characterized in Figure 8.3 is really generic, it has broad applicability to a wide variety of circumstances. This particular generic conflict has a name—*Efrat's Cloud*. Evaporating Clouds are read from left to right—opposite from the direction of the arrows: "In order to attain [the objective], we must achieve [the requirement]; in order to achieve [the requirement], we must complete [the prerequisite]."

Notice that each connection (arrow) in the cloud has one or more assumption statements beside it. These assumptions represent the rationale behind the connection, or in other words, *why* the connection exists.

The conflict illustrated in this cloud is very real for a lot of people. Can you think of situations in which you or someone you know has been "on the horns of a dilemma," where some kind of change has been required, yet you or they are reluctant to initiate that change? Now translate that tug-of-war to the strategic level: one executive wholeheartedly supports a strategy change, while another opposes it. Beyond the technical and economic issues involved, there's a question of security and satisfaction—the political, or psychological, impact.

The existing ways of doing things provide a sense of security to most people, especially decision makers. Many of them achieved the positions they're in now because they succeeded in tried-and-true patterns of thinking and action. And they're not about

Assumptions:
1. Satisfaction is essential to happiness.
2. Satisfaction is a sense of fulfillment.
3. Satisfaction results from achieving challenging objectives when the risk of failure is significant.

Assumptions:
4. Very few people live (for very long) in a challenging, high-risk environment.
5. The satisfaction achieved by doing the same things over and over decreases over time (the "novelty" wears off).
6. New challenges are needed to sustain satisfaction.
7. Meeting new challenges requires people to do things differently (change).

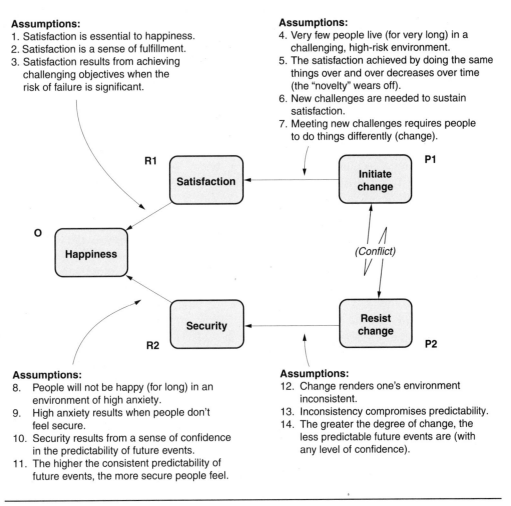

Assumptions:
8. People will not be happy (for long) in an environment of high anxiety.
9. High anxiety results when people don't feel secure.
10. Security results from a sense of confidence in the predictability of future events.
11. The higher the consistent predictability of future events, the more secure people feel.

Assumptions:
12. Change renders one's environment inconsistent.
13. Inconsistency compromises predictability.
14. The greater the degree of change, the less predictable future events are (with any level of confidence).

Figure 8.3 "Efrat's Cloud."
Source: Efrat Goldratt. Used with permission.

to change without a compelling reason to do so.* Ironically, satisfaction can play a part in discouraging change, too. As people succeed in their jobs, they find satisfaction in the things they do well. And the ability to do things well often results not just from sheer personal brilliance, but also from repetitive practice of the same skills. Athletes are a prime example. The really good ones are often both satisfied with their skills and secure in the knowledge that, by diligently practicing them, they can overcome most opponents. "Hey, coach! What do you mean, you want me to change the way I swing at the ball? No way!" Sometimes even coaches are reluctant to tinker with an athlete's technique. However, there comes a time when the tried-and-true ways of doing things just won't get the job done anymore. Change is required if newer and higher objectives are to be realized.

---

* I remember one executive justifying his decision not to change the way things are done by saying, "I'm going to dance with the partner that brought me to the party."

POWER ISSUES

There's another reason that people resist change. It's probably even more prevalent than the security-versus-satisfaction conflict. Political feasibility is wrapped around a real underlying issue: a possible *threat to someone's personal power.* What they're thinking, but won't say, is that a proposed change is likely to compromise their personal power. This is often referred to as "getting into somebody else's rice bowl."

Why won't people talk about such things openly? The principal reason is that it isn't "politically correct" to cite personal loss as a reason for opposing change that's supposed to be good for the organization as a whole. Everyone is supposed to be a "team player," sacrificing personal ambition for the greater good of the organization.

Yet the need for power is an influential driver of people's behavior.[8] Take presidents of the United States, for example. Who would *want* such a job? It doesn't pay very much, relative to the stress and responsibilities. You don't have any privacy, and you're always the target of the political party that's out of power. Take a look at "before-and-after" pictures of every president in recent memory: the job ages them prematurely. Not to mention that it's like living in a fishbowl, and you live your life wondering who's going to take a shot at you, and when. Certainly, there are perquisites ("perks") associated with the job. The neatest house east of Hearst Castle is certainly one of these, and there's nothing like Air Force One to haul you and a hundred of your assistants and the press around. Moreover, it's probably good for the ego to hear them play "Hail to the Chief" just about everywhere you go. But these aren't the reasons people lust after the job: it's *power.** The power to change the course of human events, to make history. People who yearn to be president of the United States have a high, intensive need for power. If people have power—even if it's not quite as much as the president of the United States has—they guard it. They don't want to lose it. They might even want to increase it, and they inevitably do so by "dancing with the partner that brought them to the party."

EIGHT TYPES OF POWER

As you seek to develop and deploy new strategies, you can count on the fact that somewhere, sometime, you're going to run up against someone who sees your efforts as usurping, diminishing, or otherwise compromising their power. And they're going to oppose you, but they're not likely to advertise the fact that they're worried about losing power. In fact, they'll go to great lengths to direct attention anywhere but there. So if you're going to try to do what Sun Tzu recommended—to win all without fighting—you need a way to overcome the resistance of powerful people, and you need a way to see through the "smoke and mirrors" they erect to hide their true concerns. One of the best places to start is to understand the different types of power and to do your best to match

---

* "It's good to be the king!" (Mel Brooks, in the movie *History of the World, Part I*).

them with the powerful people who might oppose a strategy change. Once you know what types of power motivate decision makers, you can create ways to make new strategies while preserving or enhancing existing power bases—or at least not threatening them. If that's not possible, you might be able to substitute new and different possibilities for power.

Eight different types of power have been identified, comprising two categories (refer to Figure 8.4.). One category is *interpersonal power.*[9] This is power closely connected to, or inherent in, the individual. The types of power in this category include *legitimate, reward, coercive, expert,* and *referent.*

Legitimate power. Legitimate power is the ability to influence because of position in the organization. This power flows from formal authority.

Reward power. Reward power is derived from an individual's capability to reward behavior or compliance.

Coercive power. Coercive power is the opposite of reward power—it's the power to punish. Normally, reward power and coercive power are used to back up the use of legitimate power.

Expert power. Expert power isn't related to position in the organization. An expert possesses knowledge or skills that are both essential to the organization and difficult to replace. The greater the difficulty in replacing the person (and the greater their importance to the organization), the higher their level of expert power. So, even someone formally lower in an organization, such as a technical specialist or creative person, can have (and exercise) expert power.

Referent power. Referent power is another way of saying "charisma." It's personality based—the ability to influence or lead people by the sheer force of personality. President John F. Kennedy had it. Generals George S. Patton and Norman Schwarzkopf had it. President Richard Nixon didn't.

Interpersonal	**Positional/Situational**
Legitimate: Derives from formal authority	*Resource:* Control over/special access to resources or information
Reward: Ability to reward behavior or compliance	*Decision-making:* Influence over decisions, or selection of which decisions are made
Coercive: Ability to punish noncompliance	
Expert: Irreplaceable knowledge and/or skills	*Information:* Control over/special access to knowledge or data by virtue of position
Referent: Personality; charisma	

Figure 8.4 Types of power.

Source: Gibson, Ivancevich, and Donnelly, *Organizations: Behavior, Structure, Processes,* 7th ed., 1991.

Power can also accrue to an individual because of their position in the organization. This is the second category. Positional power doesn't care who holds the job; by virtue of occupying the position, the incumbent has power. The types of power most commonly exercised from a situational perspective are *resource, decision-making,* and *information* power. These power types are related to legitimate power, but they aren't in all cases a function of formal authority.

Resource power. Resource power accrues when someone has access to resources, information, and support that others don't and the ability to muster cooperation in doing necessary work.[10]*

Decision-making power. Decision-making power would seem to be related to formal authority, but what this really means is the ability to influence decisions. We see this kind of authority exercised regularly with elected representatives. Former Mayor Richard J. Daley of Chicago was highly renowned as a power broker in the 1960s and 70s. This is because he had the influence not only to affect a decision process in which he didn't have final authority, but even to decide which decisions would be made—or not made.[11]

Information power. Perhaps the most important type of power in today's society is *information power.* People who know the right things often have (and exercise) power far beyond their formal station in life. For example, accountants may not have a great amount of formal power in an organization, but to the extent that their knowledge of a company's financial situation is important to strategic, operational, or tactical decisions, they can exercise exceptional amounts of power at times—maybe even all the time. A person with a well-connected personal communication network among friends, fellow employees, or influential people knows things that aren't obvious to most people. Sometimes investment professionals have "inside knowledge" of corporate plans that give them an edge over other people. These are all examples of information power. In summary, if you know something of importance that nobody else does, you have information power.

Why have we devoted so much time to the discussion of power? Because changes in the alignment of power are often at the root of resistance to change—including new strategy—even when the reasons offered look more like technical or economic feasibility concerns. So, while it might be easy to account for technical and economic obstacles in creating new strategies and tactics, we must never lose sight of the fact that humans are "wanting" animals. They want security and satisfaction, certainly, but most of all they want power. And when they get it, they're not happy about the prospect of losing it. So they may attempt, overtly or covertly, to discourage a particular change or to re-channel it into a different direction—one that better serves their psychological needs. Recognizing that this *will* happen is the first step to accommodating these power/security/satisfaction needs with the organization's needs ahead of time, and precluding the rise of outright resistance or subversion. We call these "win–win" solutions, and the Evaporating Cloud is specifically designed to deliver them.

---

* Always remember the Golden Rule: "The one with all the gold makes the rules."

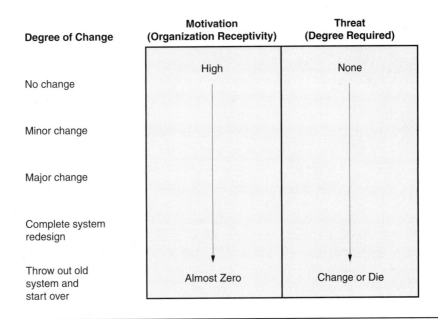

Degree of Change	Motivation (Organization Receptivity)	Threat (Degree Required)
No change	High	None
Minor change		
Major change		
Complete system redesign		
Throw out old system and start over	Almost Zero	Change or Die

Figure 8.5 Motivation to change and threat—an inverse relationship.

THE RELATIONSHIP BETWEEN CHANGE AND POWER

There's a direct relationship between the scale of the change required, the threat giving rise to the need for change, and the motivation of decision makers to embrace the change. Figure 8.5 summarizes this relationship. The degrees of change increase down the left side, from "No change" to "Throw out the old system and start over." Looking first at the right column, you can see that no threat generally means no change is required. Progressively greater threats to survival almost always require progressively larger changes. Only the threat of failing to survive will normally justify throwing out an existing system and completely redesigning it from scratch.

At the same time, management's receptivity to change varies inversely with the degree of change required. Remember our discussion of security, satisfaction, and power? No change at all is highly popular, especially among those who are well off or secure under the status quo. Throwing out the existing system and starting over is so distasteful that there isn't any motivation at all for it under normal conditions. Only a survival threat ("change or die") can overcome resistance like this. Where is your organization on these continua?

SELF-REINVENTION: A MILITARY EXAMPLE

Here's a military example. Since 1945, the U.S. military has been structured to fight large-scale major force battles. The expected scenario for 45 years was an attack by Warsaw

Pact armored divisions and mechanized infantry, through Germany's Fulda Gap, into western Europe. A similar scenario was envisioned for the Korean peninsula. So the U.S. spent trillions of dollars building and maintaining a massed conventional force capability. As nuclear weapons proliferated, strategy and force structure were adjusted to capitalize on the capabilities (and threats) of these weapons, but only within the context of massed force engagements and long-range projection of strategic power. Then the Warsaw Pact folded in the early 1990s with the collapse of the Soviet Union—no more "big enemy" to fight. When Iraq subsequently invaded Kuwait and the U.S.-led coalition responded, the result was comparable to a high school football team challenging the Super Bowl champions: no contest, because that's what American forces were designed and structured to do—fight Soviet-made weapons and doctrine in large-scale land battles.

However, between the early 1980s and the end of the 20th century, factions within the U.S. Department of Defense began to realize that the nature of warfare was changing. Slow, painful steps were taken to begin balancing both force employment doctrine and force structure to fight a different kind of war—one that required light but agile, hard-hitting units to deploy quickly to anywhere in the world and sustain highly focused combat operations in a limited area. As worldwide terrorism increased, special forces assumed a more prominent role than they had ever seen before. The Department of Defense began research and development on an entirely new class of weapon systems, including so-called "smart" bombs, global positioning satellite navigation systems, and night-vision devices.

These changes were not easy, and many were resisted within the traditional war-fighting establishment, which was enamored of long-range strategic bombers, sophisticated tactical fighters, heavy tanks, heavily armed infantry vehicles, aircraft carrier battle groups, and nuclear submarines. But as a new, emerging threat became clearer through limited-scope operation in places like Panama, Somalia, and Bosnia, even the "old guard" recognized a need to find something other than a sledgehammer with which to swat flies. Long-range nuclear bombers were reconfigured to carry a wide variety of the most up-to-date "smart" weapons to the remotest places in the world. New battle-field management aircraft and equipment were developed to find nontraditional enemies in real time, target-designate them for incoming aircraft, and even deliver weapons by remote control.* More money and effort were allocated to developing highly-trained special forces capable of waging unconventional war effectively at night on short notice anywhere in the world. The ultimate result was that the kind of irregular enemy capable of completely thwarting large-scale Soviet conventional forces in Afghanistan between 1980 and 1988 was quickly and efficiently neutralized in a few months by U.S. forces in late 2001 and early 2002.

However, the true measure of the success of this transformation became dramatically clear in April 2003 with the stunning collapse of the entire Iraqi military at the hands of a force one-quarter the size of the coalition of 1991.

---

* During Operation Enduring Freedom in Afghanistan, within minutes after detecting enemy movements *in the dark*, Hellfire missiles were launched with deadly accuracy in eastern Afghanistan from unmanned Predator drones controlled by operators half a world away at the U.S. Central Command Headquarters in Tampa, Florida.

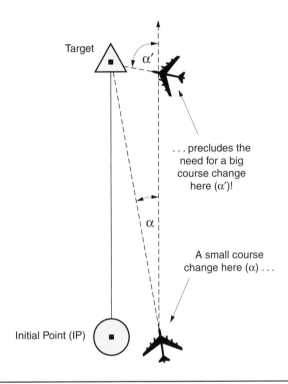

Target

α'

... precludes the
need for a big
course change
here (α')!

α

A small course
change here (α) ...

Initial Point (IP)

Figure 8.6 Course changes over time—an inverse relationship.

To ensure that this capability was ready when needed, changes required in force structure, strategy, and tactics were required. These changes were not easy to make. Relating this level of change to Figure 8.5, it would qualify somewhere between "major change" and "complete system redesign." Only the acceptance of "the handwriting on the wall"—the gravity of the change in the threat—could overcome the traditional inertia that is unique to superpower military establishments.*

There's also an inverse relationship between time and the severity of change. When I was in the Air Force, we used to say, "A one-degree heading change at the initial point of a bomb run is better than a 90-degree heading change near bomb-release." Figure 8.6 illustrates this concept. What it means is that in an organization's journey toward its goal, the earlier you detect a deviation from planned course and act on it, the smaller the required changes are. The longer you wait, the more difficult it will be to make the change, and the larger the change required. This is a powerful argument against deferring decisions, waiting to see if things will get better on their own.

---

* All is not sweetness and light in this regard. Even as this is written, the secretary of defense is locked in a political battle with the U.S. Army leadership and supporters in Congress over the cancellation of a multibillion dollar next-generation mobile artillery system, which the secretary contends is not needed for the kinds of battles envisioned in the future, but which Army generals and the secretary of the Army insist is critical to the Army mission.

To summarize:

- There are potentially powerful motivations to resist a change in strategy: security, satisfaction, and power.

- There is an inverse relationship between the willingness to change strategies and the scope of the change in most organizations.

- The longer decisions for necessary changes are delayed, the more painful (that is, difficult, expensive) it will be to make the changes. Moreover, delaying a change decision can increase the magnitude of change required.

The fastest way to get past the psychological or political obstacles to change is to (a) recognize the conflict between individuals' and the organization's needs as quickly as possible, and (b) accommodate those needs in the strategy to the extent possible. In other words, construct a "win–win" solution: the organization gets what it needs (a new strategy), and the people with the power to frustrate the change get what they need, even if their personal goals are not congruent with the organization's. How can we possibly do this?

THE EVAPORATING CLOUD

The Evaporating Cloud (EC) is a simple tool conceived by Eliyahu M. Goldratt to resolve conflicts or dilemmas in a way that satisfies people's nonnegotiable needs—those that they're willing to fall on their swords to protect or to satisfy—while simultaneously satisfying the needs of the larger system. The EC is a five-element diagram that enables us to surface and evaluate underlying, often unstated, assumptions entrenching each side of the dilemma. The articulation of these assumptions is the key to resolving the dilemma in a way that both sides can truly achieve a win. This resolution is considered "breakthrough," because creating it challenges us to consider new ways to achieve the same ends.

Here's an example of a strategic dilemma structured as an EC. (See Figure 8.7.) Notice the five elements: one objective (O), two requirements (R1 and R2), and two prerequisites (P1 and P2). The two requirements are necessary conditions for attaining the objective. The two prerequisites are *assumed* to be necessary in order to satisfy the two requirements. The conflict resides between the prerequisites. This particular EC represents a problem common to publicly-held original equipment manufacturers (OEM).

Shareholders expect their stock value to increase over time, so their ultimate goal is beyond even the objective reflected in Figure 8.7. Profitability, both now and in the future, is widely accepted as the most influential factor in assuring that stock prices continue to appreciate, so the company's senior executives bend every effort to improving profitability. Earnings are usually reported quarterly, even though stock prices change daily (even hourly!), but when quarterly earning reports come out, stock prices often take their biggest jump (or make their biggest slide). Clearly, executives want the change to be a jump, not a slide, so they normally do whatever they can to make profits improve each quarter. But notwithstanding Alfred Sloan's opinion, companies must be profitable over time as well

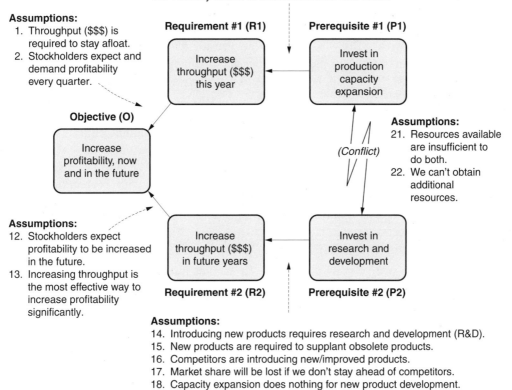

Assumptions:
3. Capacity expansion is the *fastest* way to increase throughput ($$$).
4. Capacity can be effectively expanded in the short term (1–2 quarters).
5. Capacity expansion is the *only* way to increase throughput ($$$).
6. Capacity expansion is the *best* way to increase throughput ($$$).
7. Capacity expansion won't cost more than throughput ($$$) generated in the short term.
8. Product demand will be sufficient to fill most of the expanded capacity.
9. R&D investment will not increase throughput ($$$) this year.
10. The only way capacity can expand is if we invest in our own facilities.
11. The only source of investment is our own funds.

Assumptions:
1. Throughput ($$$) is required to stay afloat.
2. Stockholders expect and demand profitability every quarter.

Requirement #1 (R1)

Increase throughput ($$$) this year

Prerequisite #1 (P1)

Invest in production capacity expansion

Objective (O)

Increase profitability, now and in the future

Assumptions:
21. Resources available are insufficient to do both.
22. We can't obtain additional resources.

(Conflict)

Assumptions:
12. Stockholders expect profitability to be increased in the future.
13. Increasing throughput is the most effective way to increase profitability significantly.

Requirement #2 (R2)

Increase throughput ($$$) in future years

Prerequisite #2 (P2)

Invest in research and development

Assumptions:
14. Introducing new products requires research and development (R&D).
15. New products are required to supplant obsolete products.
16. Competitors are introducing new/improved products.
17. Market share will be lost if we don't stay ahead of competitors.
18. Capacity expansion does nothing for new product development.
19. The only source of new product engineering is our own staff/laboratories.
20. The only source of investment is our own funds.

Figure 8.7   A strategic conflict.

as quarterly.* So the overall objective (O) in Figure 8.7 is to increase profitability, both immediately (this quarter, if possible) and in the future.

There are several ways to improve profits, both short term and long term, but increasing throughput (marginal contribution to profit) is probably the best way for most companies to do so. In the end, this means increasing sales revenue. So, in order

---

* Alfred P. Sloan, former chairman of General Motors, was reputed to have said, "We haven't been in business for 50 years—we've been in business for 200 quarters."

to attain the objective (O), executives must ensure that sales revenue improves continuously this year (R1). At the same time, they can't leave the future to chance, so they must also ensure that sales revenue continues to increase *beyond* just this year (R2).

Now, good leaders are usually very effective at instilling in their subordinates an understanding of the overall objective (O) and its supporting high-level requirements (R1 and R2). But by the nature of hierarchical organizations, these subordinates are usually more narrowly focused—probably on a single necessary condition. In this example, we have the vice president for operations aiming for production increases this year, maybe even this quarter. And we have the vice president for engineering concentrating on the new product development that will keep the company competitive well beyond this year. Both of these vice presidents aggressively seek budget increases, but for different reasons. Operations wants to buy more plant equipment and hire more operators (P1). Engineering wants to hire more engineers and open new laboratories to increase new product development projects (P2). And therein lies the dilemma for the president: there's not enough cash in the bank to do both at the same time, and paying for both out of cash flow will kill throughput (and profitability) in the short term. In other words, this conflict reflects a resource shortage—not an uncommon situation for most companies.

Notice in Figure 8.7 that there are 22 assumptions associated with this conflict. Four of them (1, 2, 12, and 13) are the underlying reasons why throughput increases are required to improve profitability. If R1 and R2 have been verified as truly necessary conditions, it's highly probable that these are valid assumptions. Assumptions 3 through 11 and 14 through 20 are the underlying reasons the vice presidents for operations and engineering use to justify their arguments for budget increases (P1 and P2, respectively). But are *these* assumptions all likely to be valid?

We all know how complex organizations work. Because they're functionally organized, they tend to suboptimize: functional departments tend to maximize their own performance, often at the expense of other departments or the organization as a whole. So the vice president for manufacturing will make his case for capturing the limited funds available, and so will the vice president for engineering. And the arguments of each will contain only the assumptions that support their respective positions. They may even stretch the validity of their arguments by citing assumptions that are questionable.*

So for the president to resolve this dilemma in a way that doesn't promote (or add to) friction between departments, he or she needs a "win–win" solution: a breakthrough that will allow both vice presidents to reasonably satisfy their requirements, even if only one (or maybe neither) gets exactly what they're demanding (P1 or P2). To do this, the president must identify viable alternatives to one or both of the prerequisites. Maybe another alternative can be found that satisfies one of the paired requirements (R1 or R2), yet is not in direct conflict with the remaining prerequisite.

---

* No! Executives don't *really* do this . . . do they??!!

But how can we find such an alternative? There's a wide variety of creative idea generation techniques available, for example, Delphi method, brainstorming, nominal group technique, Crawford slip method, and, for technical problems, TRIZ.[12]* However, most of these methods either depend on, or capitalize on, identifying the questionable underlying assumptions each side uses to support its own side of the dilemma. Take a look at the assumptions in Figure 8.7, specifically numbers 3 through 11 and 14 through 22. Can you see any that jump out at you as being questionable?

Let me draw your attention specifically to numbers 10, 11, 19, 20, and 22. Do these suggest alternatives to P1 or P2? What might those alternatives be? How about a combination of one or more of the following:

- Contract out workload to other businesses working at less than full capacity

- Obtain cost-plus government production contracts

- Obtain government grants (or grants from other industries) for R&D

- Contract out R&D work to specialized laboratories

Any of these may (or may not) work in a particular circumstance. Or you might think of others not listed here. The point is that resolving the dilemma in a win–win manner requires identifying the true necessary condition each side is trying to satisfy and creating alternatives to the obvious ways of satisfying them. The Evaporating Cloud provides a means to quickly and succinctly frame the essence of the dilemma and expose the questionable assumptions that are crucial to creating breakthrough solutions to "war-stopping" conflicts. Maybe in your situation there are no strategic, operational, or tactical conflicts. Perhaps everyone intellectually and emotionally supports the proposed strategy. In that case, you might not experience any conflict. There may be no dilemma to resolve. But if you think there's the slightest chance that someone in the organization has the capability to derail the strategy, especially through silent, passive resistance, you'd better seriously consider the idea that you have a hidden conflict embedded in your organization. And you'd better not shrink from dealing with it. An Evaporating Cloud can help to visualize the dilemma and point you toward possible ways to resolve it.

THE STRATEGIC EVAPORATING CLOUD

Let's see how the Evaporating Cloud might be applied to a strategic-level conflict. Suppose we're faced with a dilemma of some kind: *changing the status quo versus leaving the status quo alone.* When it comes right down to it, this is the essence of almost all organizational conflict. The first thing we would do is to represent the conflict in an

---

* TRIZ is the Russian acronym for *theory of inventive problem solving.* Refer to Altov (1992) and Terninko (1997) for more on TRIZ.

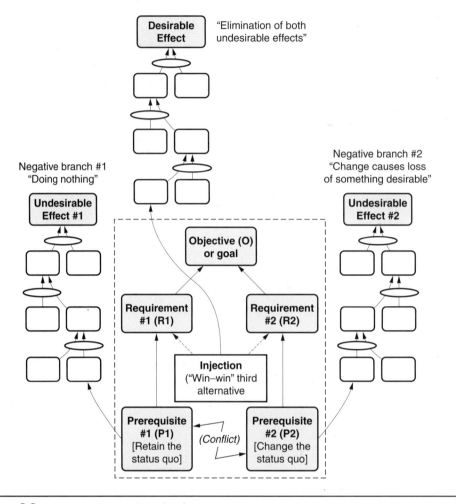

Figure 8.8 Strategic Evaporating Cloud.

Evaporating Cloud (See Figure 8.8). Even though they aren't shown, the assumptions underlying each side of the cloud are an essential part of it.

The next thing to do is to develop the chain of cause and effect that leads from the first prerequisite (P1)—doing nothing about the problem—to the unavoidable undesirable outcome of failing to act (Undesirable Effect #1). Chapter 10 addresses the concept of these "negative branches" in more detail, but essentially they're intended to show the possible unfavorable outcomes of a particular decision, or, in this case, a failure to act.

Another negative branch is then developed from the second prerequisite (P2)—changing the status quo. Since a change to the status quo often involves the power issues we talked about earlier in the chapter, the unfavorable outcome (Undesirable Effect #2) of making the change is likely to be the degradation of somebody's power.

Finally, as we saw earlier, the resolution of the conflict requires the creation of some third alternative (injection) that is likely to satisfy one or both requirements (R1 and/or R2) while simultaneously neutralizing—in other words, not leading to—the two undesirable effects. This injection may turn out to be a hybrid of the change (P2) and some new element. Or it might be a separate additional decision that replaces only P1 (the status quo) but does so in a way that doesn't produce Undesirable Effect #2.

Of course, as the renowned journalist Eric Sevareid once observed, "The chief cause of problems is solutions." So before assuming that the injection is really what we want to do, we should construct at least one more logic branch. This one should show an unbroken chain of cause and effect confirming that the two undesirable effects are truly neutralized.

Appendix E provides additional examples, showing how an Evaporating Cloud might be used to resolve both a military dilemma and an organizational power struggle.

CONSTRUCTING AN EVAPORATING CLOUD

Representing a dilemma in an Evaporating Cloud (EC) doesn't have to be a difficult exercise. While it might at first take a little self-study[13–15] or perhaps a little supervised assistance, constructing an EC can be done in six steps (see Figure 8.9). Try framing a simple dilemma on your own using these steps.* With practice, it should be possible to build an EC that accurately represents your conflict or dilemma in no more than an hour, and perhaps as little as 15 minutes. This is true even for big, strategic-level dilemmas.

BREAKTHROUGH STRATEGIES

In chapter 9, we'll talk more about "breakthrough" strategies—solutions to the kinds of dilemmas we've discussed in this chapter. You'll see what kinds of characteristics effective strategies and operational or tactical problem solutions should have. In chapter 10, you'll see how these solutions all fit together into the "big picture": a Strategic Future Reality Tree.

---

* It's beyond the scope of this book to explain the process in detail, so if you find yourself bogged down, you may want to read either Dettmer (1996) or Scheinkopf (1999). Or you can contact the author for assistance at gsi@goalsys.com.

1. Articulate the conflicting positions (prerequisites)

   • Write them in boxes as P1 and P2

   • Connect the boxes with a zig-zag arrow

2. Articulate the strategic necessary condition each prerequisite satisfies

   • "We must do this [prerequisite] in order to . . . [fill in]"

   • Write them in boxes as R1 and R2

   • Connect the P1 to R2 and P2 to R2 with an arrow

3. Articulate the common strategic objective of both necessary conditions requirements)

   • Objective (O) must be common to both sides of the dilemma

   • Requirements (R1 and R2) must be truly necessary to attaining the objective (O)

   • Write the objective in a box (O)

   • Connect R1 and R2 to O with arrows

4. Verify true necessity of all connections

   • Ensure that R1 and R2 are truly necessary to attain O

   • Verify the perceptions of each stakeholder in the dilemma that P1 is required to achieve R1 and P2 to achieve R2

5. Articulate *all* assumptions related to each arrow (including the zig-zag arrow)

   • Ask *why* R1 and R2 are necessary to attain O

   • Ask *why* P1 and P2 are necessary to achieve R1 and R2

   • The answers (" . . . because . . .") are the assumptions

   • Write and number the assumptions beside the connections (arrows) they pertain to

6. Identify the questionable or faulty assumptions; use these as the basis for creating alternatives

   • "We don't have to do P1 (or P2), instead we can . . . [fill in]"

   • List *all* alternatives. These are the "breakthroughs". Defer value judgments until late

Figure 8.9 How to construct an Evaporating Cloud.

Adaptation means not clinging to fixed methods, but changing appropriately according to events.

—Zhang Yu
Sun Tzu and the Art of War

ENDNOTES

1. M. McNeilly, *Sun Tzu and the Art of Business: Six Strategic Principles for Managers* (New York: Oxford University Press, 1996): 18.
2. R. M. Krone, *Systems Analysis and Policy Sciences* (New York: John Wiley & Sons, 1980).
3. D. Lepore and O. Cohen, *Deming and Goldratt: The Theory of Constraints and te System of Profund Knowledge* (Great Barrington, MA: The North River Press, 1999): 83–87.
4. A. H. Maslow, *Motivation and Personality* (New York: Harper and Row, 1954).
5. F. Herzberg, B. Mausner, and B. Snyderman, *The Motivation to Work* (New York: John Wiley & Sons, 1959).
6. D. C. McClelland, "Business Drive and National Achievement," *Harvard Business Review* (July–August 1962).
7. C. P. Alderfer, *Existence, Relatedness, and Growth: Human Needs in Organizational Settings* (New York: The Free Press, 1972).
8. See note 6.
9. J. R. P. French and B. Raven, "The Basis of Social Power," in *Studies in Social Power*, ed. D. Cartwright (University of Michigan: Ann Arbor Institute for Social Research, 1959).
10. R. M. Kanter, "Power Failures in Management Circuits," *Harvard Business Review* (July–August 1979).
11. M. Royko, *Boss: Richard J. Daley of Chicago* (New York: E. P. Dutton, 1971).
12. H. Altov (pseudonym for Genrich Altshuller), trans. by L. Shuulyak, *And Suddenly the Inventor Appeared* (Technical Innovation Center, 1992).
13. H. W. Dettmer, *Goldratt's Theory of Constraints: A Systems Approach to Contiuous Improvement* (Milwaukee: ASQC Quality Press, 1996).
14. H. W. Dettmer, *Breaking the Constraints to World-Class Performance* (Milwaukee: ASQ Quality Press, 1998).
15. L. J. Scheinkopf, *Thinking for a Change: Putting the TOC Thinking Processes to Work* (Boca Raton, FL: CRC/St. Lucir Press, 1999).

9

Sun Tzu and the Art of Modern Combat

The one who figures on victory at headquarters before even doing battle is the one who has the most strategic factors on his side. The one who figures on inability to prevail at headquarters before doing battle is the one who has the least strategic factors on his side. The one with many strategic factors in his favors wins, the one with few strategic factors in his favor loses—how much the more so for one with no strategic factors in his favor. Observing the matter in this way, I can see who will win and who will lose.

—Master Sun
Sun Tzu and the Art of War

In chapter 8, we examined the ideas of resolving dilemmas and "breakthrough" strategies or tactics. In the first part of this chapter we'll investigate in more detail the translation of military strategy, operations, and tactics to the business world. Then we'll see how you can use the principles of war to create sound "breakthrough" business strategies and tactics.

TRANSLATING MILITARY CONCEPTS TO BUSINESS

Sun Tzu was a Chinese general who first conceived of the principles of land warfare in the fifth century BC. His writings on military strategy and tactics were expanded and interpreted by various other Chinese generals between the second and 13th centuries AD and consolidated into *The Art of War*.[1] These precepts form the basis of modern military thought from Clausewitz to Guderian, and from Washington to Schwarzkopf.

By now, almost everybody in the business world knows about Sun Tzu, because modern business thinkers have suggested that these timeless principles of military combat translate to "business combat" as well. In fact, *The Art of War* is required reading in many graduate business schools.

However, those seeking to transfer the principles of war to the competitive commercial environment would be better served by studying U.S. Army Field Manual (FM) 3-0, "Operations." This manual is a distillation of both the prescriptions of Sun Tzu and the lessons learned by generations of military practitioners and scholars throughout the second half of the 20th century. In reviewing its detailed, structured approach to planning and executing military operations, potential business applications become quite clear—many more so, in fact, than one finds in the writings of Sun Tzu. A few of the "high points" of FM 3-0 follow (those most obviously transferable to the business world). Bear in mind, however, that these excerpts are no substitute for reading the original, in context.*

LEVELS OF ENGAGEMENT

The military recognizes three levels of combat engagement, based on their contributions to achieving different kinds of objectives. These levels are *strategic, operational,* and *tactical.* It should come as no surprise that this same classification applies to the business environment. For now, though, we'll confine our attention to the military perspective and only relate it, briefly, in general terms to the business world. Let's start by defining some terms.

Strategy

For the military, *strategy* is the art and science of developing and employing armed forces and other instruments of national power in a synchronized fashion to secure national or multinational objectives.[2] The emphasis in this definition is on integrating efforts of different instruments of power (military, political, economic, and psychosocial) to achieve the highest-level objectives. When Iraq invaded Kuwait in 1990, America's strategic objectives were the ejection of Iraqi forces from Kuwait and the long-term security of Western access to Middle Eastern oil. Let's see how this definition might be translated for business:

> Strategy is the art and science of developing and employing skilled people, technology, marketing and sales, and other instruments of organizational power in a synchronized fashion to achieve the corporate goal and objectives.

---

* Surprisingly, this isn't as difficult to do as many people might think. This "bible" of force employment doctrine is available to the public (downloadable as Adobe Acrobat files) at http://www.adtdl.army.mil/cgi-bin/atdl.dll/fm/3-0/toc.htm.

A corporate strategy might be a unified effort to penetrate a new international market. McDonald's Corporation's expansion of fast-food franchises outside of North America would be an example of a corporate strategy. Lexmark Corporation's reinvention of itself from a spin-off of IBM's electric typewriter business to a computer printer company would be another.

Operations

A major *operation* is a series of tactical actions (battles, engagements, strikes) conducted by various combat forces of a single or several services, coordinated in time and place, to accomplish operational, and sometimes strategic, objectives in an operational area.[3] Operation Desert Storm is the classic example in recent military history. The operational area was the Arabian peninsula in southwest Asia. The operational objective was the destruction of the Iraqi Republican Guard. The tactical actions of U.S. Army, Navy, Marine, and Air Force units, along with those of multinational coalition partners, were coordinated and synchronized in a unified operation that lasted only six weeks.*

Translated for business, the definition of *operation* might look like this:

> A major operation is a series of short-term activities, which collectively might constitute a project, conducted by various company divisions, departments, or functions, coordinated in time and place, to accomplish significant medium-term objectives, and sometimes the corporate goal.

An example of a major corporate operation might be a new product introduction, requiring the coordination of engineering, production, distribution, marketing, and sales. Microsoft's introduction of Windows XP would qualify as a major operation, because it required the coordination of the tactical efforts of engineering (programming), production, marketing, distribution, and customer support.

Tactics

The military defines *tactics* as the employment of units in combat. It includes the ordered arrangement and maneuver of units in relation to each other, the terrain, and the enemy to translate potential combat power into victorious battles and engagements.[4] In Operation Desert Storm, the U.S. Army's VII and XVIII Corps executed a lightning advance into Kuwait, maneuvering individual units to encircle and destroy most of the Iraqi Republican Guard.**

---

* In actuality, the ground combat part of Operation Desert Storm was decisively concluded in about 96 hours. One Iraqi general said afterward, "I started with 39 tanks and lost seven in six weeks of air attacks. I lost the other 32 in 20 minutes after engaging the American tanks."

** This tactical maneuver was no small undertaking. General Fred Franks, VII Corps commander, directed more than 146,000 soldiers comprising three heavy armored divisions, four artillery brigades, a cavalry division, an armored cavalry regiment, and an aviation brigade—50,000 vehicles in all. They advanced more than 400 kilometers in less than four days, flanking the Republican Guard and decimating it before it could retreat back to the Euphrates River. (Clancy and Franks, 1995, p. 176)

Translated for business application, the definition of *tactics* might look like this:

Tactics refers to the employment of skilled people, technology, and information in direct contention with competitors. It includes the disciplined completion of production, marketing, sales, and distribution functions and their assignment to specific short-term activities in order to achieve limited company objectives.

Though the definition refers to discipline, this is not to suggest that creative problem solving and decisive initiative in unexpected situations are discouraged. On the contrary, they are expected, as we'll see in a few moments when we examine commander's intent and initiative.

One example of tactics might be installing a new production management methodology that significantly improves manufacturing lead time or reliability. Another might be a unique marketing campaign or sales offer that competitors would have a difficult time matching. Figure 9.1 summarizes the relationship between the levels of military engagement and their respective business-related counterparts.

Military	**Business**

Strategic
    War at national level
    Engagement over broad
       geographic area
    Geopolitical factors are important
	Strategic
	    Penetration of new markets
	    Portfolio diversification
	    Capture of major/dominant
	       market share

Operational
    Combat engagement of a large unit
       (corps, numbered air force, fleet)
    Significant medium-term objective
	Operational
	    Introduction of new products/service
	       lines
	    Adoption of ERP system
	    Major marketing campaign
	    Ongoing systemwide improvement
	       (adoption of new large-scale
	       methodologies)

Tactical
    Force engagement at small-to-
       medium size unit level (company,
       brigade, air wing, squadron, naval
       battle group)
    Limited objectives
    Limited geographic area
	Tactical
	    Installation of new hardware
	    Direct customer engagement
	    Continuous process improvement

Figure 9.1 Strategy, operations, and tactics.

ATTRIBUTES OF STRATEGICALLY RESPONSIVE FORCES

Now we know what strategy, operations, and tactics are. But a plan is no better than the people called upon to execute it. Let's see what the military considers important in executing strategy. The U.S. Army values seven critical attributes in its forces. (See Figure 9.2.) These attributes are *so* important that the Army is redesigning the entire force (structure, equipment, training, deployment doctrine, power projection platforms, command and control, intelligence, surveillance, reconnaissance, and joint transportation) based upon them. These attributes are *responsiveness, deployability, agility, versatility, lethality, survivability,* and *sustainability.*[5]

Now, not all of these necessarily apply to all kinds of businesses, but all systems need at least some of these attributes in varying degrees. Imagine redesigning *your* system with these attributes driving the design. . . .

Responsiveness

Responsiveness means "it happens quickly." In other words, you don't have to wait around for a reaction to a crisis. Perhaps the best example of responsiveness occurred after the terrorist attacks on the World Trade Center and the Pentagon on September 11, 2001. Within minutes—as soon as the nature of the threat became clear—the president grounded all commercial air traffic within or entering the United States. Within an hour after that, the skies over the entire nation were clear of all nonmilitary aircraft. Information later proved that this fast response prevented at least one additional airliner hijacking, and saved hundreds—maybe thousands—of lives. *That's* responsive.

Responsiveness spans operational planning, preparation, execution, and assessment. In the military context, it's more than just the ability to deploy forces quickly. It encompasses training, planning, and preparation as well. Crises rarely allow enough time to correct training deficiencies. It's a common axiom among military people that

+ Responsiveness
+ Deployability
+ Agility
+ Versatility
+ Lethality
+ Survivability
+ Sustainability

Figure 9.2 Attributes of strategically responsive forces.
Source: U.S. Army Field Manual 3-0, *Operations,* June 2001.

"no plan survives first contact with the enemy intact." (See appendix F, Strategic Wisdom, "Murphy's Laws of Combat," number 8.) This is another way of saying, "You'd better be ready to respond to changes in the battlefield environment quickly."

Likewise, responsive businesses *expect* short notice changes in requirements, and they prepare their people accordingly. They plan for the most likely contingencies, and they might even practice (train) responding to a crisis. Most important of all, the leaders of a responsive business think through their priorities before the chaos and stress of a crisis occurs, and they communicate these priorities clearly and regularly to their employees. If you expect people to exercise good judgment and initiative in a crisis, you *must* do this.

Deployability

Deployment is much more than just getting people and equipment to combat theaters on ships and airplanes. Good commanders visualize the entire process, starting with the end condition: a unit fully deployed and ready to commence operations in theater. Then they reverse-plan everything back to the unit's normal location and alert condition. As much as possible is prepositioned, prepackaged, and preplanned so that when the actual deployment order is given, everybody knows exactly what to do, in what sequence, and how to do it fast and with minimum mistakes. It's this kind of thinking that enabled the Department of Defense to complete a movement of forces equivalent in size to the city of Des Moines, Iowa—people, equipment, living facilities, and all the support required to sustain them there—halfway around the world and have them ready to fight in less than four months. Try to imagine your organization doing something like that. . . .

Deployability doesn't relate much to many commercial businesses, or even most government agencies. Manufacturing plants and insurance companies never really need to think about moving their operations lock-stock-and-barrel over long distances. Neither would the Department of Agriculture or a county clerk's office. But the Federal Emergency Management Agency, the Red Cross, National Forest Service firefighters, or a city disaster response team might have to be deployable. Transportation companies or on-site service companies might, too. In all of these cases, deployability could be critical to success.

Agility

An agile military force can go from a dead stop to full motion very quickly. It can also change direction almost instantaneously. To be responsive, a force must be agile, too. *Agility* requires a trade-off between mobility and sustainability. If you want to be able to move quickly, you can't bring everything including the kitchen sink with you. A responsive, agile force can pack its bags quickly with the minimum "stuff" it needs to accomplish the mission, yet sustain itself until it can be resupplied. To assure agility, mission commanders must balance competing mission requirements, and in some cases create innovative solutions. Agile forces are mentally and physically able to transition within or between types of operations without losing momentum.

In August 1990, Iraq's invasion of Kuwait was so fast and so overpowering that Western strategists were afraid the Iraqis would roll into, and over, Saudi Arabia as well. The 1st Tactical Fighter Wing at Langley Air Force Base was alerted to deploy with the unenviable mission of helping naval carrier air to delay any possible invasion of Saudi Arabia until substantial ground forces could be moved into place. Within 48 hours after the deployment order was issued, the 1st Tactical Fighter Wing had 75 F-15E Strike Eagle fighters on five-minute alert at Saudi airfields. *That's* agility!

Agility in business is related to responsiveness as well. While responsiveness might be likened to how quickly a person can wake up, agility is equivalent to how quickly that person can get moving once awakened. For example, when Amazon.com caught on as a new way to transact business (e-commerce), its only service was selling books online. Once online bookselling competition appeared from Barnes and Noble and Borders, Amazon.com quickly added other types of products to their line as well, so as to be able to distinguish themselves from similar competitors. Now they offer more than 20 different kinds of products and services, from music of all types to toys, computers, electronics, cameras and photo supplies, tools and hardware, and a travel service. Amazon quickly "morphed" itself from an online bookstore to an online department store.

Versatility

Versatility is the characteristic of being able to do many different things well. Military forces have historically been one-dimensional. Armies were created to fight pitched land battles on well-defined battlefields, using frontal assaults. In fact, American forces went to Vietnam thinking that way, only to find themselves engaged in a type of combat for which they were not prepared: broad-based guerrilla warfare. The lessons of that experience were not lost on the Department of Defense. Between 1976 and 1996, the face of the Army changed to accommodate a much wider variety of conflicts. Operation Desert Storm, in 1991, was still a traditional set-piece conflict, but it was probably the last such engagement we'll ever see. In a world with only one superpower, not many opponents are likely to challenge American military power directly. Consequently, we can expect to see more conflicts such as Bosnia, or the war on terrorism, which is, itself, a completely new experience for American military forces. Thirty years ago, the American military establishment would have been totally out of its depth in responding to a terrorist war. Now it's creating new kinds of tactics as the situation demands, employing conventional forces where they can be used, but thinking and acting unconventionally most of the time. This is versatility: *the ability to be able to do many things well.*

Versatility is no less important in business. In the early 1980s, a long recession hit the American automobile industry very hard. Auto dealers found their new car and used car sales almost drying up. One dealer in Dayton, Ohio, recognized that this situation wasn't likely to change soon, yet like other car dealers he wanted to survive. So for about two years, he converted his business from an auto sales firm that provided warranty service on what it sold to an auto repair business that serviced all makes of vehicles, and sold a few new cars on the side as opportunities presented themselves. His advertising even emphasized the repair side of his business. And for two years until the economy recovered, his service department carried his business completely.

Lethality

Lethality is important to armies. Battles are a matter of life and death. As General Franks once said, "This isn't football. We can't afford a 24 to 21 victory. We have to plan for and expect 100-to-nothing." Everything from tactics to force structure and equipment is designed to produce overwhelming victory.

This concept is somewhat less useful to businesses. After all, killing and destroying competitors is *not* the objective of most businesses. Yet the concept of overwhelming victory does apply in a somewhat more genteel way. The U.S. Department of Justice's Anti-Trust Division might not look kindly on a "100-to-nothing" score, but it would certainly tolerate 75-to-25 (and has!). Thus, most companies strive for decisive shares of their chosen markets, whether this is local, regional, national, or international. Balancing the need for overwhelming business "firepower" with the need for agility and versatility can be a challenge, especially for big businesses. One company that has managed this type of "lethality" exceptionally well is Microsoft. It has either absorbed or driven out of business every significant competitor in the computer operating system field, and it's expanding its reach to applications and the Internet as well. In fact, it's done so well in being "lethal" to its competition that it's had to defend itself in court against the government's attempt to break the company up.

Survivability

In the military context, *survivability* has two components. In one respect, it implies "do unto others *before* they do it unto you." In other words, "the best defense is a good offense." But the second component is the ability to withstand a surprise attack, recover, retaliate, and achieve victory. Between 1960 and 1990, the Mutual Assured Destruction concept was designed to guarantee survivability of nuclear forces against a first strike. As unpleasant as it was to live under the constant possibility of a nuclear war, the strategy *did* work: neither the Soviet Union nor the U.S. attacked each other with nuclear weapons. The strategy did, however, result in a very expensive arms race—which ultimately broke the Soviet Union both economically and politically, though this was not the way the arms race was intended or expected to play out.

In business, survivability is the characteristic of being able to absorb an unexpected move by your competitors that leaves you on the defensive.

Sustainability

It's rare to see major operations, either military or business, initiated and prosecuted to conclusion in a short period of time. That's not the way we'd *like* it to be. In fact, Sun Tzu himself observed that the most effective military operations are quick and decisive, even if they're less than completely efficient. Speed and decisiveness are admirable objectives, but sometimes the strategic situation dictates otherwise.

This immediately implies that either military forces or businesses should be prepared to sustain their activities, both in time and in depth. For a military force, it means having enough resources (troops, equipment, supplies, and so on) to continue fighting at an intensive level until resupply can be established. During the cold war, the United States maintained deployed forces worldwide. The U.S. European Command had substantial army, navy, and air force units already positioned close to the Iron Curtain, ready to engage any incursion into West Germany by Warsaw Pact forces.

The concept of *sustainability* had several levels. First, it meant that the forces in place in Europe could fight successfully until deployment of reinforcements from the continental U.S. could be completed. Second, it meant that those reinforcements would, themselves, bring enough supplies in addition to their equipment to enable them to fight for 30 days without further resupply.* Finally, it meant that the U.S.-based logistical commands from each of the military services would, within 30 days, mount a continuous airlift, sealift, and ground resupply of *all* the forces (both prepositioned and deployed) in place in Europe, so that combat operations could continue at the same levels, and perhaps even increase in intensity. This is what sustainability is all about: the ability to continue an intensive level of engagement with an enemy over time and in depth, until decisive victory is achieved.

In business, the most common failing is not planning for the long haul. Small businesses are particularly susceptible to this pitfall. They fail to consider that it might take time to build a decisive—or even survivable—market share, and they run out of cash before they can establish a firm foothold in the market. The major reason why most small businesses fail is insufficient capitalization: not enough money to sustain them through their formative period. In other words, they didn't plan to carry the fight to their competition without "resupply" (that is, strong positive cash flow) for a long enough time. Failure to be sustainable, for most businesses, means underestimating how long it will take to get a start-up company "into the black," or for an established company to win a decisive market share over its competitors.

These seven attributes—*responsive, deployable, agile, versatile, lethal, survivable*, and *sustainable*—are characteristics. In other words, if one were to describe how the U.S. Army conducted its mission, these are the adjectives that would be desired. Everything the Army does in peacetime to prepare for war is aimed at maximizing these characteristics. As we've seen, these same characteristics could be considered worthy attributes for businesses as well.

---

* The U.S. military refers to these "bring-your-own-lunch" supplies as *war reserve supply kits* (WRSK, pronounced "risk"). WRSK is designed to sustain a deploying force until heavy resupply can be established.

EVALUATING YOUR STRATEGY USING THE SEVEN ATTRIBUTES

So, as you formulate strategy for your organization, before you begin deployment of that strategy, ask yourself these questions:

- *Is our strategy responsive?* Will it allow us to change gears quickly, if needed, or are we locked into it once we begin? Do we have a contingency plan?

- *Is our strategy deployable?* Can we actually do the things we've decided to do, or is the strategy too ponderous? Do we have enough of the right people, skills, resources, and assets to get the job done?

- *Does our strategy demand agility?* Does it require us to maneuver in ways we might not be able to do quickly enough? Is the agility required more or less than that required for our competitors to respond?

- *Are we versatile enough?* Does our strategy depend too heavily on specialists, or can people do more than one kind of task effectively and efficiently?

- *Will our strategy be "lethal" to our competition?* Can we realistically expect our actions to be decisive, or might they "bounce off" our competitors?

- *Does our strategy provide for us to survive an unexpected counterattack by our competitors?* What will we do when *they* respond to our offensive?

- *Can we sustain our offensive long enough to ensure victory?* Do we have the willpower for protracted engagement? Do we have the resources to persist if it turns out to take longer than we expected?

How many businesses do you know that consciously apply these success criteria to themselves before they begin an operation? Though these attributes were intended to define successful military forces, they can comprise a checklist for successful businesses, too. Use them to test and evaluate your strategy and your organization's capability to execute before you "engage the enemy." Now it's time to examine the fundamentals of military operations and see how they apply to business operations, too.

THE FUNDAMENTALS OF MILITARY OPERATIONS

Military operations are based on a conceptual foundation known as the *fundamentals of full spectrum operations.* These fundamentals are, in turn, composed of three parts: the *elements* of combat power, the *principles* of war, and the *tenets* of operations. Refer to Figure 9.3 to see how these parts relate to one another. The elements of combat power are applied according to the principles of war, keeping in mind the tenets of operations. Together, these parts form the *operational framework* for achieving decisive operations to support the objectives of offense, defense, support, and stability. Let's consider each of the three parts individually.

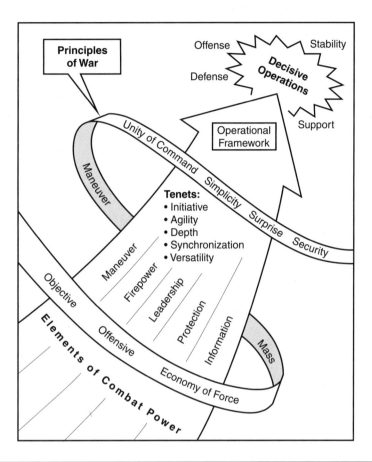

Figure 9.3 Fundamentals of full spectrum operations.
Source: U.S. Army Field Manual 3-0, *Operations,* June 2001.

Elements of Combat Power

The elements of combat power include *maneuver, firepower, leadership, protection,* and *information.* (See Figure 9.4.) They are interrelated.

• *Maneuver.* Maneuver is the movement of forces, combined with fire or potential fire, to achieve a position of advantage over the enemy. It's the means by which commanders concentrate combat power in the right place, at the right time, to achieve surprise, shock, momentum, and dominance. In Operation Desert Storm, the undetected movement of VII Corps and XVIII Corps in the desert to the west of Kuwait positioned them to envelop and turn the strongest Iraqi defenses in a direction that created a disadvantage for them in battle.

• *Firepower.* Firepower is the volume and intensity of the effect of weapons that can be directed on enemy targets (forces or vital infrastructure). Simply put, it's how much hellfire and brimstone you can rain down on your opponents. Your firepower is decisive when it forces your enemy to keep his head down and not move or offer effective return fire.

• *Leadership.* This is the most dynamic element of combat power. Outstanding leadership turns battles, secures victory against superior opposing forces, and serves as the catalyst creating the conditions for success. Confidence, audacity, purpose, direction, motivation, and discipline are all characteristics of good leadership. This is true in both war and business.

• *Protection.* Protection is the preservation of the fighting potential of a force, so the commander can apply maximum force at a decisive time and place.

• *Information.* Information enhances leadership and magnifies the effects of maneuver, firepower, and protection. In other words, it's the fuel that powers the other four. Games of chance become less of a game and less chancy when the player has excellent information about what is likely to happen. The same is true of both war and business.

In Operation Desert Storm, the coalition forces went to great lengths during the first six weeks of aerial bombardment to destroy the Iraqi command, control, communication, and intelligence networks. Deceptive psychological operations were also used to achieve information supremacy, primarily by confusing the enemy about our own intentions. At the same time, American satellites, unmanned reconnaissance aircraft, night vision devices, and other forms of technology were employed to give coalition commanders as close to real-time intelligence on the position and activities of the Iraqis as possible. All of these efforts were designed to stack the "information war" in favor of the coalition.

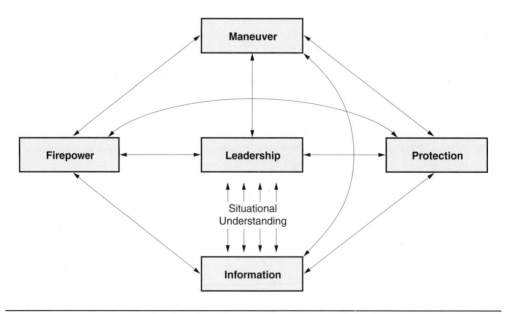

Figure 9.4 The elements of combat power.
Source: U.S. Army Field Manual 3-0, *Operations,* June 2001.

Evaluating Your Capability to Execute Strategy

The elements of combat power can serve as a kind of checklist to help you determine whether your assets and resources will be effective enough to successfully execute your strategy. We used the seven attributes to evaluate our strategy. Now we use the five elements of combat power to evaluate our capability to *execute* that strategy.

• *Maneuver.* Can we recognize unexpected threats quickly? Is our decision process fast enough to respond quickly? Once a change decision is made, can we *move* quickly to redirect our efforts? If it's not able to change quickly, what will you have to do to enhance that capability?

• *Firepower.* Do we have the preponderance of forces (that is, resources) needed to execute the strategy? If not, what more do we need?

• *Leadership.* Are our leaders capable of independent, effective execution of their parts of the strategy? Do they have the skills, both technical and people-related, to extract maximum performance from their people and resources? Can we depend on them as "wingmen?" (See accompanying sidebar.)

• *Protection.* Do we have the proper resources to protect ourselves from counterattack? Or from preemptive attack?

• *Information.* Are our intelligence sources adequate to the task of validating our strategy and collecting updated information once we've begun to execute? Is our information system capable of sorting, storing, and retrieving the information we need, when we need it, for decision making?

The Wingman

The wingman concept is used by the U.S. Air Force to help ensure mutual protection. A formation of combat aircraft consists of a minimum of two, though sometimes more. The leader is primarily responsible for navigating to the target and leading the attack. The wingman is primarily responsible for ensuring that the formation is not successfully attacked from the side or the rear while the leader focuses on the primary mission.

After the leader has delivered his ordinance on target, the wingman rolls in on the target, while the leader temporarily assumes the protection for the wingman. The relationship between the flight leader and the wingman is unique in that it requires absolute trust between the two. Whichever one is in the lead at the moment puts his life in the hands of the other, trusting that the wingman will not permit an attack from the side or the rear. This is sometimes referred to as "covering your six o'clock," meaning, "Don't worry, I won't let anybody sneak up on you from behind." The leader–wingman relationship is a life-and-death trust issue. Many a military commander has chosen officers or NCOs to fill subordinate positions using a single final criterion: *Would I want to go into combat with this person on my wing?*

In executing a broader strategy involving a number of divisions, departments, or branches of a company, the executive should have the same level of confidence in the leaders of these subordinate departments that the flight leader has in his or her wingman: "I can trust them to get the job done independently, the way I would have done it myself, without having to check up on them continually.

Principles of War

The principles of war (see Figure 9.5) provide general guidance for conducting war at all levels—strategic, operational, and tactical:

• *Objective.* Every military operation should be directed toward a clearly defined, decisive, and attainable objective. This was a principle completely ignored in the Vietnam War, but most carefully observed in the Gulf War. President Bush and the Department of Defense went to great pains to make clear what constituted victory, so that there would be no doubt about what was required to achieve it and when it had been achieved.

• *Offensive.* The best defense is a good offense. To stay on the offensive, military commanders must seize, retain, and exploit the initiative. In other words, make the enemy continually react to you and what you do. Don't let the opposite happen. This is second nature to combat commanders. In business, however, it usually requires leaders to consciously think about what they can do to keep their competitors continually off-balance.

• *Mass.* Concentrate the effects of combat power at the decisive place and time. Massing in time means hitting multiple targets simultaneously. Massing in space is equivalent to using a single overwhelming blow from a pile driver, rather than a dozen strokes from a sledgehammer. (Remember: the final score we're looking for is 100-to-nothing, not 24-to-21!)

• *Economy of force.* This is the reciprocal of mass. You allocate the minimum essential combat power to secondary efforts. When you concentrate your force at the decisive place and time, you may have to accept prudent risk in other areas by distributing less-than-decisive numbers there—maybe only enough to fight a "holding" or protective action. A good commander economizes by allocating just enough force in noncritical areas to ensure acceptable risk, so that the rest of the combat power can be applied to the critical places. In business, this would mean that you don't intentionally run "lean" (that is, maximum efficiency) everywhere. Rather, you apportion effort to match the risk of disruption in secondary areas, but no more than that.

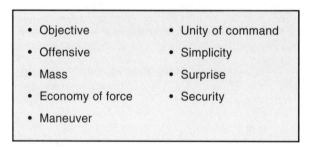

Figure 9.5   Principles of war.
Source: U.S. Army Field Manual 3-0, *Operations,* June 2001.

- *Maneuver.* Combat commanders always strive to place the enemy in a disadvantageous position. They do this through the flexible application of combat power. You keep your enemy off balance by confronting them with new problems and dangers faster than they can deal with them. Just consider the benefits to a business of being able to do this to a competitor!

- *Unity of command.* There's an old saying that goes, "You might not know who's right, but you always know who's in charge." This epitomizes unity of command: for every objective, ensure unity of effort under one responsible commander. Businesses frequently fail at this by assigning tasks to groups or teams, rather than to accountable individuals.

- *Simplicity.* This is the "KISS" principle: "Keep it simple, stupid!" Prepare clear, uncomplicated plans, and issue clear, concise orders to ensure thorough understanding. Simple plans, executed on time, are better than detailed plans executed late. Commanders at all levels must weigh the apparent benefits of a complex concept of operations against the risk that subordinates will not be able to understand or follow it.*

- *Surprise.* This comes right out of Sun Tzu's writings: Strike the enemy at a time or place or in a manner for which he is unprepared. Do the unexpected. In war or in business, this requires speed, information superiority, and asymmetry (force superiority). It's not necessary that the opponent be completely unaware, only that he become aware too late to react effectively. Picture the defensive back on a football team, watching the opposing team quarterback handoff to a wide receiver on a reverse, thinking that a running play is underway, only to see—too late to react—the wide receiver pulling up to heave the ball downfield to the other receiver who has just run past the defensive back. This epitomizes surprise, and it's all the sweeter when your competitor can see what's about to happen, but knows it's too late to do anything about it.

- *Security.* This is the reciprocal of surprise. Never permit the enemy to acquire an unexpected advantage. In other words, don't let them catch you with your pants down around your ankles. Don't be excessively cautious—calculated risk is inherent in business as well as in combat operations. Security results from measures taken to ensure against reasonable risk of surprise. Trying to protect everything from all risks violates the economy of force principle. But don't fail to consider your vulnerabilities and take reasonable precautions to ensure that your competitors don't exploit them faster than you can react to their attempt to do so.

Evaluating Strategy Using the Principles of War

The principles of war, too, can be used as a kind of "business checklist" to ensure that you're doing everything you ought to be doing, and that you haven't missed

---

* I remember a time when one employee of a company I consulted with told me, with tongue firmly planted in cheek, "*We* can't even figure out what we're doing—there's no way our *competitors* will be able to figure it out!" This might be considered the ultimate in deceiving one's enemy!

anything vital. Use it as a kind of "micrometer" against your strategic, operational, and tactical plans:

- *Objective.* Are our objectives clear? Do we have a firm understanding of what the end state should look like, so we'll know when we can declare victory?

- *Offensive.* Are we proactive, rather than reactive? Does our plan keep the pressure on our competitors? Do we give them no time to think or react?

- *Mass.* Do we have enough resources to apply to the decisive activities? Are we planning to attack at more than one point simultaneously?

- *Economy of force.* Are we assigning too much effort to secondary activities? Do we know where the system constraint lies and are we subordinating nonconstraints appropriately?

- *Maneuver.* Does our plan keep them from focusing an effective response to our initial efforts? Are we distracting them enough to slow down their response?

- *Unity of command.* Are the lines of responsibility and authority clear? Does everyone know who's boss of each part of the operation? Are communication lines clear and unambiguous to facilitate fast decision making?

- *Simplicity.* Is the plan relatively simple and capable of being executed on time by all departments, teams, or task forces?

- *Surprise.* Do we know what the competition expects us to do? Does our plan do the unexpected?

- *Security.* Do we know what our competitors are planning to do? Can we find out? Does our plan safeguard our own vulnerabilities while we plot our attack on the competition? Can we keep our own secrets?!

How many companies do you know that consciously consider these factors when they design their own strategies? The chances are not many do. If you do, you're likely to have a competitive advantage even before forces are engaged. Remember the admonition of Master Sun at the beginning of this chapter: "The one who figures on victory at headquarters before even doing battle is the one who has the most strategic factors on his side."

Tenets of Military Operations

The tenets of military operations build on the aforementioned principles and describe the characteristics of successful operations. (See Figure 9.6.) They don't guarantee success, but their absence risks failure. To that extent, they might be considered necessary conditions. You'll notice some overlap with the aforementioned attributes of strategically responsive forces, the elements of combat power, and the principles of war. These tenets are:

> - Initiative
> - Agility
> - Depth
> - Synchronization
> - Versatility

Figure 9.6 Tenets of successful operations.
Source: U.S. Army Field Manual 3-0, *Operations,* June 2001.

- *Initiative.* Set or dictate the terms of action throughout the battle by maintaining an offensive spirit and reduce your enemy's options. Compel the enemy to conform to your purposes and tempo, while you retain your own freedom of action.

- *Agility.* Configure your own forces to be able to move and adjust quickly and easily.

- *Depth.* Attack the enemy throughout the area of operations, simultaneously when possible, sequentially when necessary, to deny him freedom to maneuver.* In other words, keep your competitors as busy as possible in as many places as possible. This carries the added benefit of confusing them about your real intentions.

- *Synchronization.* Synchronization means you arrange activities in time, space, and purpose to mass maximum relative combat power at a decisive place and time. In the Vietnam War, Operation Linebacker II was designed with maximum synchronicity. Each day for 12 days, American airpower struck at the heart of North Vietnamese political, economic, and military support power—Hanoi and Haiphong. These attacks were concentrated in time, usually less than an hour. But they synchronized the strikes of Naval carrier aircraft, Air Force air defense suppression fighters and combat air patrol, and massive but highly accurate bombing by over 100 B-52s from six different directions in a 15-minute period. The effects of this application of offensive, mass, maneuver, and synchronization had the North Vietnamese suing for peace (temporarily, anyway) in less than two weeks.**

Note: Recall from the discussion of Boyd's theory of maneuver warfare in chapters 2 and 4 that there is some disagreement about the value of synchronization. In fact, Boyd castigated the U.S. Army's doctrine rather severely about it. He suggested that the VII Corps' delay in "closing the loop" on fleeing Iraqi forces in Operation Desert

---

* "When he's up to his neck in alligators, it's exceedingly hard for him to think about anything else except being chomped!"

** This experience also emphasizes what happens when other important principles and tenets of war are ignored. The U.S. spent the preceding seven years mired in an unwinnable conflict. Operation Linebacker II demonstrated that a resolution could have been achieved much faster had those principles not been ignored.

Storm—up to 24 hours during which the corps stopped completely—was directly attributable to efforts to synchronize the attack of all armored divisions. Instead, Boyd maintained, an immediate, violent attack by whatever forces were available would have wreaked havoc on an already disorganized enemy, confused by the multiplicity of fronts and actions. As a result of the delay, some four and a half Republican Guard divisions escaped the envelopment maneuver and lived to fight another day.

- *Versatility.* This is the ability to be ready for hostile engagement across the entire spectrum of combat operations. It means being equally prepared to engage terrorists in the mountains of Afghanistan with special forces teams, or to destroy Saddam Hussein's Republican Guard with VII Corps tanks, artillery, helicopters, and infantry.

Evaluating Operations Using the Tenets of Military Operations

At some point, strategies must be operationalized. This means converting the high-level strategy into discrete, detailed operations supporting strategic objectives. Recall in chapter 2 we discussed that the Joint Strategic Planning System (JSPS) established the overall strategy for the Department of Defense, and the Joint Operation Planning and Execution System (JOPES) used that strategy to design combat operation plans to win wars in specific geographic theaters. In the same way that we used the attributes of responsive forces and the principles of war to evaluate our strategy, the tenets of military operations can be used to evaluate operation plans.

If your business or operation plan embodies these characteristics, your chances of success are multiplied. Again, use these tenets as a checklist to determine whether you're doing the right things, and whether you might be overlooking something critical.

- *Initiative.* Does our plan preserve our control of the competition between ourselves and our competitors? Do we keep *them* always reacting to what we do, rather than the other way around?

- *Agility.* Is our plan and our internal organization for executing it ponderous or nimble? Can we adjust rapidly to unexpected changes in the competitive business environment (for example, the terror attacks of September 11, 2001)?

- *Depth.* Is our competitive engagement only at the "forward edge of the battle area" (FEBA)—for example, a direct, head-to-head sales campaign for the same customers, or do we engage him "behind the lines" as well (for example, developing a fast new-product introduction capability, or impossibly short manufacturing lead times)?

- *Synchronization.* Does our plan attract our competitor's attention to just one point of focus, or do we force him to consider multiple competitive issues at the same time?

- *Versatility.* Are we equally able to take on competitors in a variety of areas having to do with product and service features?

OPERATIONAL FRAMEWORK

All of the preceding parts—the elements of combat power, the principles of war, and the tenets of successful military operations—determine success or failure *before* forces are even engaged, or, as Sun Tzu observed, "at the headquarters," during the planning of a campaign. They constitute the operational framework in which good combat leaders conduct the military operations they've planned. The operational framework relates the activities of forces in time, space, and purpose, with respect to each other, the enemy, and the situation. It consists of the area of operations, battle space, and battlefield organization. These are advanced concepts that space doesn't permit us to explore here in detail. When you've become confident that you can translate the principles/tenets of war and the elements of combat power to your business environment, you might think about learning in more detail about operational framework. For that, I'll suggest you read the original source: U.S. Army Field Manual 3-0.

But there are two messages I want to convey unequivocally: (1) The application of military principles in complex operations and their support is effective in the extreme (see accompanying sidebar, *A Desert Storm "Scorecard,"* page 154); and (2) These principles are most assuredly transferable to the civilian world.

CONCLUSION

This chapter had been a little bit heavy on military flavor, but with good purpose. The factors, principles, and other aspects of military strategy and operations discussed here are probably more applicable to "business combat" than any other aspect of the military paradigm except leadership. If you can adopt and internalize the art of war to your business, even if only the minimal facets of it described in this chapter, you can put your organization in a position of unquestionable strength when dealing with competitors and the external environment.

In chapter 8, we talked about the idea of resolving conflict, both internal and external, associated with change. The solutions we create to resolve such conflicts become discrete tactics or operational tasks in our strategy for the future. To these dilemma-resolvers, we'll "inject" other tactics and tasks in chapter 10 to make the future unfold as we want it to. As we evaluate the value of these injections, we can measure them against the benchmarks provided by the principles of war, the tenets of operations, and the elements of combat power. Does our proposed project clearly advance us toward our objective? Does it keep us "on the offensive?" Does it put our resources where they will have the highest impact (mass)? Are we practicing effective economy of force in our nonconstrained activities? Is our plan simple, and will it surprise our competition? Are we agile enough to change what we're doing, should the need arise? If not, what do we need to do to become more agile? The applications of military thinking to business activities are almost endless.

Now it's time to move on to the real fun—developing a strategy that will take us to our goal.

A Desert Storm "Scorecard"

How effective can the application of military principles, tenets, and planning be? General Fred Franks, USA, Commander of the VII Corps tallied the scorecard of a mere 89 hours of successfully executed strategy against Iraqi forces during Operation Desert Storm.

IRAQ	U.S. VII Corps
Destroyed: • 11 Iraqi divisions, including the Tawalkana and Medina Divisions of the Republican Guard • 1,350 Iraqi tanks • 1,224 personnel carriers of all types • 285 artillery pieces • 105 air defense pieces • 1,229 trucks Casualties and prisoners: • Combat fatalities: unknown, estimated in the tens of thousands • 22,000 confirmed Iraqi prisoners of war taken (estimates go twice that high, as VII Corps lost count midway through the engagement)	• 55,000 artillery rounds fired • 10,500 multiple launch rocket system (MLRS) rockets fired • (ATACM) fired in 21 missions • 348 close air support strikes (mostly by Air Force A-10s) • 46 soldiers killed in action • 196 soldiers wounded • 11 MA1A tanks damaged, 4 destroyed • 16 M2 Bradley fighting vehicles damaged, 9 destroyed • 1 Apache attack helicopter damaged, 1 destroyed Logistic Support (moved 250 miles in less than 4 days) • 2.6 million meals transported • 6.2 million gallons of diesel fuel • 2.2 million gallons of aviation fuel • 327 major assemblies (e.g., tank engines, etc.) • 4,900 tons of ammunition per day . . . . . . using . . . • 1,385 tractor trucks • 608 fuel tankers • 1,604 trailers • 377 5-ton trucks . . . augumented by . . . • CH-47 helicopters • C-130 airlift drops

    The combat and logistic figures are only for the U.S. VII Corps. The U.S. XVIII Corps and other coalition forces are not included in these figures.

    A combat operation and the logistics to support it don't happen as flawlessly as this without a robust, rigorous planning process. You can't "make it up as you go along." This victory was the product of years of strategic planning, intensive training, concerted efforts to learn and incorporate lessons (both from training and unforeseen contingencies), and flexibility to adjust as necessary when the actual situation didn't conform to the planning assumptions.

Source: T. Clancy and General F. Franks, Jr. (Ret.) *Into the Storm: A Study in Command.*

Therefore measure in terms of five things, use these assessments to make comparisons, and thus find out what conditions are. The five things are the way, the weather, the terrain, the leadership, and the discipline. The way means inducing people to have the same aim as the leadership, so that they will share death and share life, without fear of danger. The weather means the seasons. Terrain is to be assessed in terms of distance, difficulty or ease of travel, dimension, and safety. Leadership is a matter of intelligence, trustworthiness, humaneness, courage, and sternness. Discipline means organization, chain of command, and logistics.

—Master Sun
Sun Tzu and the Art of War

ENDNOTES

1. Sun Tzu, *The Art of War,* translated by Thomas Cleary (Boston, MA: Shambhala, 1988).
2. U.S. Army Field Manual 3-0, *Operations* (June 2001): 2-2.
3. Ibid, 2-3.
4. Ibid, 2-5.
5. Ibid, 3-1–3-4.

10

Designing the Future: Laying Out Strategy

So the rule of military operations is not to count on opponents not coming, but to rely on having ways of dealing with them; not to count on opponents not attacking, but to rely on having what cannot be attacked.

—Master Sun
Sun Tzu and the Art of War

In earlier chapters, we defined our system and introduced the idea of a Strategic Intermediate Objectives (IO) Map to express a dependent hierarchy of the system's critical success factors. We also created a picture of the status quo—a Strategic Current Reality Tree (S-CRT)—to define the size of the gap between where we are now, and where we want to be at the limits of the planning horizon. And, recognizing that any change in direction can foment resistance, we examined the potential for resolving change dilemmas using a Strategic Evaporating Cloud (S-EC). All of these tools provide the logical means to identify the scope and nature of the strategic problem: *Where do we want to be, and what challenges must we overcome to get there?* Now it's time to answer the ultimate question: How will we travel between where we are now, and the end state that we desire in the future?

THE FRAME AND THE PICTURE

I'd like you to envision strategy in your mind as being composed of two key components: a picture and its frame. The picture is the content; the frame represents the way the content is structured—a template, if you will. Like a picture and its frame, the template is largely independent of the content. In much the same way that you can put any picture into the same frame, you can "load" almost any strategy content into the same general template.

Our template is going to be a Strategic Future Reality Tree (S-FRT). The content will be specific details about our business environment, our competitors, our assumptions about our situation, and our organization. The structure will provide a clear picture of the cause-and-effect relationships between the content details.

Until now, I've deliberately refrained from including too many "how to" details where the Strategic IO Map, the Strategic Current Reality Tree, and the Strategic Evaporating Clouds were concerned. There were two reasons for this. First, it's not productive to "reinvent the wheel"—to go into detail on subjects that are covered more thoroughly in other books. Second, I intend for this book to maintain its focus on the *application* of these tools to strategy, not on a description of how they work. But that approach must change here. This chapter, and this tool—the Strategic Future Reality Tree—are the foundation and motivation for this book. It's critical that you know how the strategy development phase of the constraint management model works. So there will be considerably more detail on how to build an S-FRT in this chapter than you saw on the other tools in earlier chapters. We'll start with the frame, then we'll talk about the picture that goes into it.

FRAMING STRATEGY

The S-FRT looks a lot like the S-CRT. In the same way that the S-CRT was a cause-and-effect picture of the past and present, the S-FRT is a representation of future causality. It presumes that if we make the right changes in what we're doing now, we can trace an unbroken chain of cause and effect to our desired ends: the satisfaction of our critical success factors and our goal. By laying out that step-by-step logic for all to see, we realize three invaluable benefits.

First, we satisfy ourselves that what we plan to do will actually bring us to our desired future. We find any "holes" in our logic long before we run the risk of falling into them. Second, we afford ourselves the opportunity to discover that we might be jumping from the frying pan into the fire before we're in mid-air between the two. Knowing this, we can either jump in a different direction or put on our "fireproof suits" ahead of time. Finally, we open the door to the possibility that we've got blind spots— that we're not seeing pitfalls or disconnects that others might readily see. I call this "bulletproofing" the strategy, and we'll talk more about it later.

The S-FRT looks something like the conceptual diagram in Figure 10.1. The first and most obvious thing that you should notice is the relationship between the S-FRT and the Strategic IO Map. The organization's goal and necessary conditions are transferred intact from the Strategic IO Map to the upper part of the S-FRT. The goal and necessary conditions become statements of *desired effect*—the strategic outcome—of the actions we'll take to change course.

Notice in Figure 10.1 that there are many more elements in the S-FRT than there are in the Strategic IO Map. That's because the Strategic IO Map was more of an outline, while the S-FRT is a detailed, fully "fleshed out" road map. Think of the Strategic IO

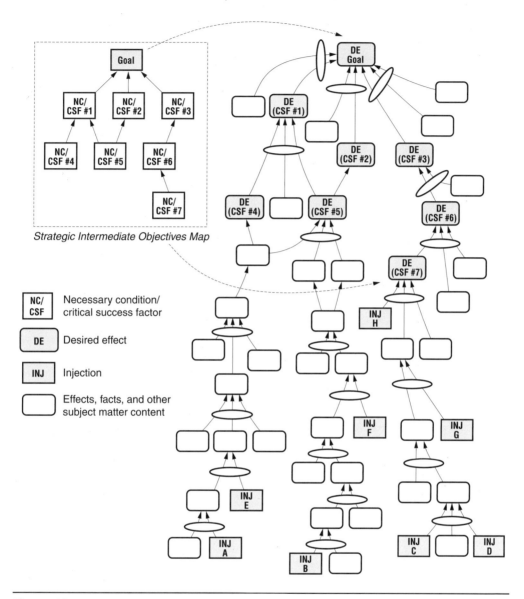

Figure 10.1   Strategic Future Reality Tree (S-FRT).

Map as a "stick figure." (See Figure 10.2.) A stick figure is easily recognizable as a person, but there's not enough detail in it to know much more than generalities about the person. It's only after we put in the details that we have a clear understanding of what the person looks like. The S-FRT provides those details.

Notice, too, that there are different kinds of elements in the S-FRT that don't appear in the Strategic IO Map. The empty (blank) boxes represent intermediate effects and contributing causes. Some of these may be facts about existing reality. Others may be assumptions about events or behaviors. What goes into these boxes is the content mentioned

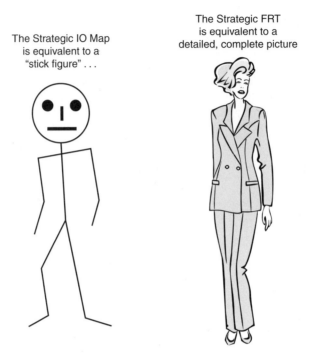

The Strategic IO Map
is equivalent to a
"stick figure" . . .

The Strategic FRT
is equivalent to a
detailed, complete picture

Figure 10.2 Difference between the Strategic IO Map and the Strategic FRT.

earlier. These are the "rich" details that make the difference between the stick figure and the complete person.

There are also ellipses, which indicate dependency. Where future causality is concerned, these ellipses are critical. They indicate that *all* causes whose arrows pass through the ellipse are required to produce the indicated effect—absence of any one of them destroys all the causality that follows. The last type of element is an injection, indicated by the heavy-bordered, shaded rectangle. These injections are the "initiators" of our strategy.

INJECTIONS: THE INITIATORS OF STRATEGY EXECUTION

Clearly, the future won't unfold as we'd like it to if we don't *do* something to change what's happening now. The changes we make will usually take the form of policies, actions, programs, or projects. We'll refer to any such changes as "injections," meaning something new that we must inject into our existing situation to make change happen. We have to "inject" these actions or conditions, because they aren't already happening now. But how do we decide what the injections will be?

We can either create injections "from scratch," or we can derive them from two other sources: Strategic Evaporating Clouds (chapter 8) and the Strategic Current Reality Tree (chapter 7). If we had strategic conflicts to resolve, we probably developed injections to break those conflicts. Those injections would become entry points into the chain of cause and effect of the S-FRT.

Remember, too, that the Strategic Current Reality Tree (S-CRT) showed us root causes of undesirable effects that the organization is experiencing now. Changing some of these root causes may not pose conflicts, either internal or external. But, other injections will also be needed to eliminate the root causes of some of these undesirable effects. These injections will probably result from creative thought.[*]

However, keep in mind that the S-CRT only deals with deviations of the moment—discrepancies between what *should be* happening now and what *is* happening now. It doesn't really address at all the necessary conditions crucial for future success, those which don't pose problems at the moment but might be considered strategic divergences. So at some point, we may also have to include injections in the S-FRT that will lead to the satisfaction of future critical success factors, but which don't pose a problem for the organization at the moment. Again, this is a creative exercise. Figure 10.3 shows how injections might be created under these three circumstances.

HOW TO CONSTRUCT A STRATEGIC FUTURE REALITY TREE

Okay, we have the desired outcome—the necessary conditions and the goal we want to achieve. And we have the injections we plan to begin with (most of them, anyway). How do we put this S-FRT together? Figure 10.4 shows the general guidelines for assembling a Strategic Future Reality Tree. Other sources provide much more detailed instructions.[**]

1. *Determine desired strategic effects.* Convert each of the necessary conditions and the goal into a complete sentence that describes the successful achievement of the goals and necessary conditions. For example, one necessary condition might be "Competitive advantage." That's not a complete sentence. So rephrase it to read, "We have a significant advantage over our key competitors." Write it on a 3" × 3" Post-It note,[‡] and mark it with a large "DE," for "desired effect."

Do the same with all the other necessary conditions and the goal. Then position them on a large sheet of paper or a whiteboard in the same respective configuration as the necessary conditions in the Strategic IO Map. You can see this arrangement of the desired effects in Figure 10.1.

Your S-CRT will have statements of undesirable effect in it. These were all constructed as statements of variance using the goal and necessary conditions to begin with.

---

[*] We have already mentioned different kinds of idea-generation techniques, such as TRIZ, Delphi method, brainstorming, Crawford Slip Method, and so on. Any of these can be effective "injection generators."

[**] For more on constructing Future Reality Trees, see *Goldratt's Theory of Constraints* (Dettmer, 1997), *Breaking the Constraints to World-Class Performance* (Dettmer, 1998), or *Thinking for a Change* (Scheinkopf, 1999).

[‡] Post-It is a registered trademark of the 3M Corporation.

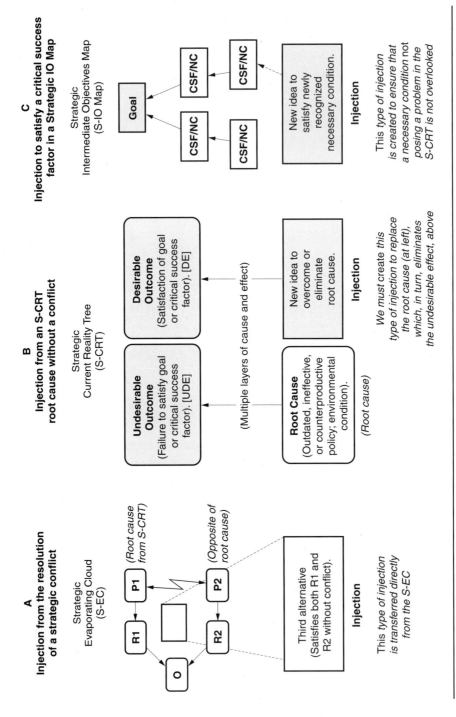

Figure 10.3   How injections originate.

1. Determine desired strategic effects

   - Goal (from Strategic IO Map)
   - Necessary conditions (from Strategic IO Map, opposites of undesirable effects in Strategic Current Reality Tree)

2. Articulate injections

   - From Strategic Current Reality Tree root causes
   - From Strategic Evaporating Cloud(s)
   - From Strategic IO Map necessary conditions

3. Compile other elements for the body of the S-FRT

   - METT-TC elements
   - Research facts
   - Assumptions about future reality

4. Assemble the S-FRT

   - Build cause-and-effect layers between injections and desired effects
   - Fill in logical gaps as required with items from step 3

5. Look for opportunities to incorporate positive reinforcing loops

   - Try to make desired effects self-sustaining

6. Search for possible negative branches

   - Besides the desired effects, what unfavorable side effects can be anticipated?
   - Develop the logical connections
   - Create new injections to preclude the new undesirable effects from developing

7. Verify and validate the Strategic Future Reality Tree

   - Rigorously apply the categories of legitimate reservation (CLR) to validate the logic
   - Obtain third-party review (scrutiny) to:
     - Verify the logic
     - Verify factual accuracy (where possible)
     - Identify possible missing Injections
     - Identify any missing negative branches

Figure 10.4   Strategic Future Reality Tree directions.

Note: These directions modified and adapted from H. W. Dettmer, *Breaking the Constraints to World-Class Performance* (Milwaukee: ASQ Quality Press, 1998).

Be sure that every one of these undesirable effects (UDE) from the S-CRT is accounted for by a desired effect in the S-FRT. We don't want to overlook anything important. In fact, you could convert the wording of the UDEs to "positives" to create your desired effects.

2. *Articulate injections.* Go back, first, to your Strategic Evaporating Clouds (S-EC). These are the critical dilemmas that frustrated any previous efforts to change the course of the company. The injections you developed to resolve these conflicts are, by definition, the foundation of your S-FRT, because they are the most important things you must do to overcome inertia. (See Figure 10.3, part A.) Replicate these injections on Post-It notes, and distinguish them, perhaps with a different color sticky note. Be sure to write "Injection" and a number clearly on each one (for example, "Injection #1"). Place all these injections down near the bottom of the paper or whiteboard.

Now review your S-CRT again. Can you find any important root causes—things that you know you must change—that don't have conflicts associated with them? These would be changes that have the consensus of the management team, and no overt opposition from outside the organization (for example, legal or political). If you find such root causes, you must now create injections that represent the opposite conditions of the root cause. (See Figure 10.3, part B.) For example, if the root cause in your S-CRT reads, "Our production process is not fast enough to build to customer demand," the injection might read, "We streamline and accelerate our production process by a factor of two."* Put these injections on Post-It notes, too, and position them near the bottom of the tree close to the others.

Finally, take another look at your desired effects. Did any of them come from necessary conditions that were *not* reflected in your S-CRT? In other words, they might not present a problem now, but they are still necessary for success in the future. If you find any such desired effects, make sure that you have an injection written that will lead to their achievement as well. (See Figure 10.3, part C.) Add these injections to the bottom of the tree, too. When you've finished step two, you should have a configuration that looks something like Figure 10.5.

3. *Compile the other elements for the body of the S-FRT.* This is the content of the tree that I mentioned earlier. Content comes from data, facts, or research about the company, competitors, and the business environment. Relevant facts are extracted from this broad body of knowledge and rendered as statements on Post-It notes for inclusion at the appropriate places between the injections and the desired effects.

A useful tool for collecting and compiling this information is referred to as "METT-TC," which is obviously an acronym. It originates from the military environment, and it stands for *mission, enemy, terrain and weather, troops and available support, time,* and *civil considerations.* METT-TC is discussed in more detail shortly, in the content part of our S-FRT discussion.

---

* Don't become distracted at this point by the question of how you're going to make that happen. As long as you have a reasonable suspicion that others can do it, or have done it, or that there are methods for doing so, leave it at a general statement that says it's been done. The details of how will follow in the chapter on Prerequisite Trees.

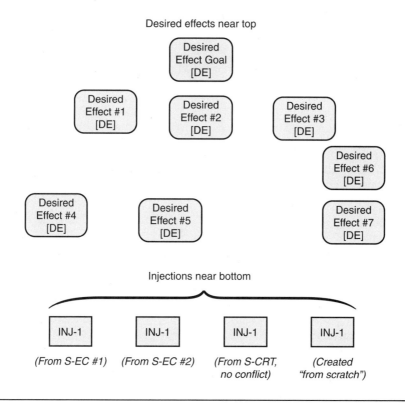

Figure 10.5 S-FRT—initial configuration.

---

4. *Assemble the S-FRT.* We're now ready to construct the S-FRT. We do this much as you would a jigsaw puzzle, starting from known points—the injections and the desired effects—and working upward from the former until the connections are complete.

Cause and effect is structured in layers of boxes with statements in them, connected by arrows in the direction of causality. The arrows are enclosed as needed by ellipses signaling dependency. Once past the injections at the bottom, each successive layer of effect constitutes the cause of the next layer. The impression I want to convey is a set of dominoes stood on their ends, positioned so close together in causality that knocking one over inevitably "drops" the one beyond it.

The content of the S-FRT—the boxes between the injections and the desired effects—comes from the Post-It notes written on the business situation, the company itself, and competitors. Constructing the connections between layers of cause and effect requires you to ask: "If [Injection #1], what is the direct and unavoidable outcome?", followed by, "Is [Injection #1] alone enough to produce the next outcome? If not, what's missing?" You then add the missing element to make the connection sufficient.* That

---

* For a more detailed explanation of the process of building these cause–effect connections, refer to *Goldratt's Theory of Constraints* (Dettmer, 1997).

missing element may come from the content Post-It notes or from your own intuitive knowledge of the situation.

A picture is worth a thousand words. Look at Figure 10.6. This is part of an S-FRT for a medical equipment company. The first injection (#1) calls for an infusion of new

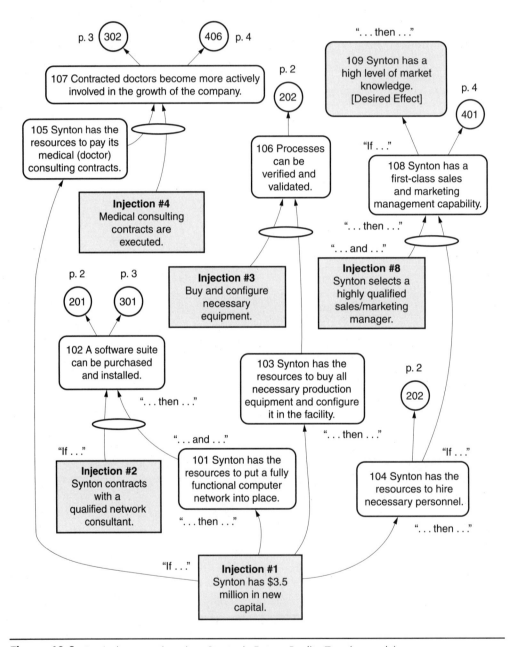

Figure 10.6   Logical connections in a Strategic Future Reality Tree (example).

capital. This leads directly and unavoidably to two effects: the ability to buy a needed computer network (101) and the ability to hire new employees (104). Another injection (#8) requires hiring a sales and marketing manager. Combined with the preceding effect (104), this injection leads to a first-class sales and marketing capability (108), which, in turn produces a desired effect (109)—a high level of knowledge in the company's chosen market.

Figure 10.6 is, of course, only a part of an S-FRT. You can see that it continues onto other panels. Refer to Dettmer[1] or Scheinkopf[2] for a more complete description of how logical connections are constructed.

5. *Look for opportunities to incorporate positive reinforcing loops.* An important consideration in strategy development is how to make it self-sustaining. Life is much easier for managers when they don't have to keep prodding an initiative along. One way to do this is through the use of *positive reinforcing loops.* A positive reinforcing loop is a situation in which a desired effect higher in the tree can be used to perpetuate, or reinforce, one of its causes lower in the tree. Profit-sharing would be an example. The employee behaviors lower in a tree that produce profits are reinforced when they are rewarded with a share of the profits generated. Figure 10.7 illustrates a positive reinforcing loop.

6. *Search for possible negative branches.* The law of unintended consequences suggests that our actions can give us results we hadn't anticipated. In some cases, these results can be highly undesirable, and if they unfold faster than the chain of causality that was supposed to produce our desired effect, that effect may never happen. Even if it does, the price in the form of a new problem might be more than we're willing to bear. This unintended consequence is called a negative branch. Once we finish the S-FRT, we must examine each of the injections in it very carefully and ask ourselves, "Besides our desired effect, what other outcome that we can't tolerate might result from this injection?" We then develop the chain of cause and effect leading to this intolerable outcome, and create a means of preventing it from occurring in the first place—an additional injection.

Take a look at Figure 10.8. It shows the S-FRT of an electronics manufacturer. The original injection (#1) is to invest $2 million in capital equipment to relieve a production bottleneck. The expected desired effect is an increase in speed of the manufacturing process (110). However, adding a surface-mount machine pushes the bottleneck about eight steps downstream to the automated test equipment section (ATE). This section has only marginally more capacity than the original single surface-mount machine, so the increase in workflow is minimal. The first undesirable effect is that return on the investment was terrible (NB-7). The second undesirable effect is that it will cost much more money, and probably be more difficult, to cure the ATE bottleneck. Because the constraint management model anticipates this problem, senior management can prevent the negative branch from happening by adding another injection (NB-A)—subcontracting some of the testing workload to keep ATE from becoming the new bottleneck.

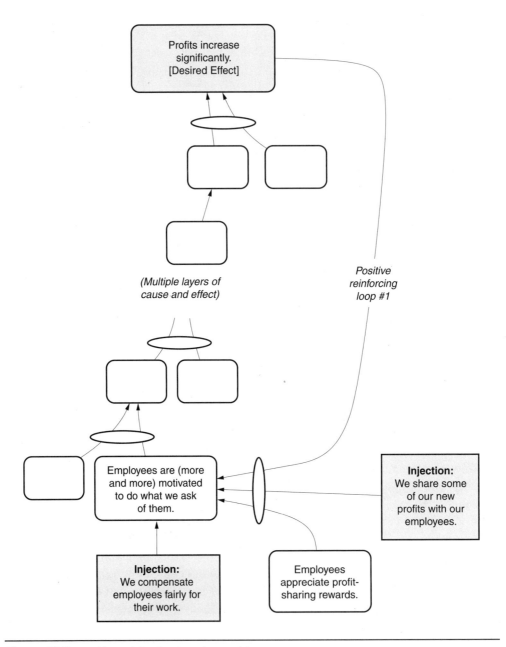

Profits increase
significantly.
[Desired Effect]

*(Multiple layers of
cause and effect)*

*Positive
reinforcing
loop #1*

Employees are (more
and more) motivated
to do what we ask
of them.

Injection:
We share some
of our new
profits with our
employees.

Injection:
We compensate
employees fairly for
their work.

Employees
appreciate profit-
sharing rewards.

Figure 10.7 Positive reinforcing loop (example).

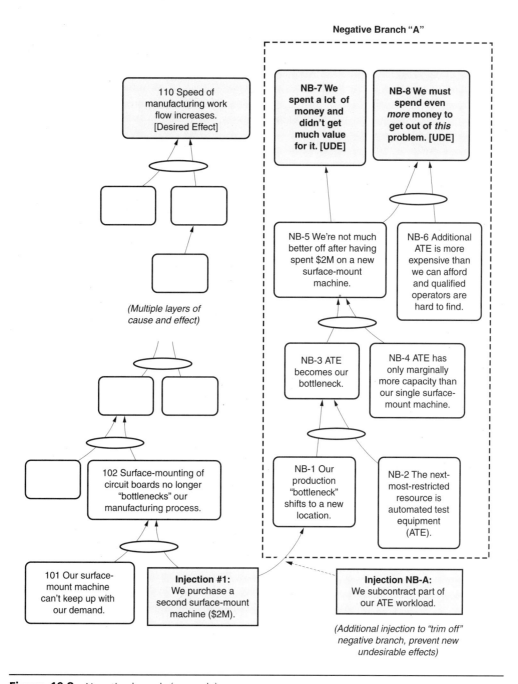

Figure 10.8 Negative branch (example).

7. *Verify and validate the Strategic Future Reality Tree.* There are well-defined rules of logic for validating the thinking process cause-and-effect trees. These rules are called the *categories of legitimate reservation* (CLR). Figure 10.9 summarizes the CLR.

When constructing the S-FRT, you should apply these rules in building each upward connection. After the tree is completed, you should have someone else review both the content and the connections to ensure they make sense and are logically sound.

---

1. Clarity

   - Are the ideas/statements in the tree unambiguous?

   - Do the entities in the tree communicate accurately?

2. Entity existence

   - Are the statements factual?

   - Are the facts verifiable?

   - Is *just one* idea completely conveyed in each entity?

3. Causality existence

   - Does each cause lead directly and unavoidably to the next effect?

   - Is causality verified, rather than just correlation?

4. Cause insufficiency

   - Are all contributing/dependent causes identified?

   - Is sufficiency verified?

5. Additional cause

   - Are all other independent causes of each effect identified?

   - Is each independent cause realistic and probable?

6. Cause–effect reversal

   - Are any cause–effect connections reversed?

7. Predicted effect existence

   - Are intangible/unmeasurable causes verifiable?

   - Is another tangible/measurable effect of the same cause verifiable?

8. Tautology

   - Is any logic in the tree "circular?"

   - Is any effect offered as the rationale for assuming a cause?

Figure 10.9 Categories of legitimate reservation.

Note: These directions modified and adapted from H. W. Dettmer, *Breaking the Constraints to World-Class Performance* (Milwaukee: ASQ Quality Press, 1998).

This is referred to as logical scrutiny. The more different people you can find to help with this, the better—especially if they aren't biased by having participated in the construction of the S-FRT.

CREATING THE PICTURE TO PUT INTO THE FRAME

In chapter 9, we saw the contributions several military concepts can offer in defining the content of these trees. A little later in this chapter, we'll address the use of those concepts to verify business strategy, too. But first there's another military tool that is particularly useful in defining specific, important issues to consider in developing the content of our strategy.

When the military is alerted for a major combat operation—for example, something on the order of Desert Storm—senior battlefield commanders will prepare a document for their subordinate unit leaders called the *commander's intent*. In many respects, it resembles the output of the *thinking process* steps we've already discussed (though the thinking process hasn't actually been used for this purpose). In other words, the commander's intent describes the desired ending condition of the combat operation in general terms. In the business world, this might be called a "vision." It also lays out the major operational objectives in reaching that desired state.

The commander's intent is not a "micromanagement" document. Much like the Joint Strategic Planning System (JSPS, chapter 3), it's intended to set the overall direction of the operation. It tells division commanders, "Here are the military objectives we expect you to attain, here are the circumstances and limitations we face, and here are forces you have to do it with—now go plan your own combat engagements." The commander's intent takes into account the capabilities of available units, intelligence information, and guidance of the theater commander.

Development of the commander's intent is serious business. Unlike the business world, the Army often works under conditions where communication with higher authority is externally constrained, sometimes nonexistent. Subordinate division commanders can expect to be faced with unique or unforeseen circumstances on the battlefield, and it might not be possible (or desirable) to obtain guidance from higher headquarters in the rear echelons. Knowing this, good senior field commanders want their subordinate unit commanders "inside their heads," knowing the "big picture," and able to make the right decisions for the maximum benefit of the whole operation at all times, even when the unforeseen occurs and no communication is possible.[*]

Despite the fact that the commander's intent is a uniquely military concept, it has potentially powerful implications for the business world as well. Imagine how much more effective senior executives could be if they knew to a near certainty that their subordinates understood exactly what their intent was—perhaps even had it in writing before them to refer to when needed. There would rarely be any doubt in the executive's

---

[*] In my military days, we had a saying: "When in doubt, ask yourself what John Wayne would do!" The commander's intent helps isolated subordinates to answer the question, "What would the corps commander want me to do?"

mind that everyone in the organization was "on the same page," and knew the right thing to do in order to advance the organization's goal.

In the military, commanders' intents don't just spring fully formed from their minds. Neither are they the result of "free association" or "stream of consciousness" thinking. The commander's intent follows a general framework that allows for differences between situations, but consistency in results.

METT-TC

U.S. Army combat commanders use a technique called METT-TC to help them develop the commander's intent (that is, define operational challenges and to develop the strategies, design the operations, and select the tactics needed to meet those challenges). METT-TC is, of course, an acronym.* It stands for:

• *Mission (M).* The mission, of course, is characterized in the military unit's objectives. These are usually assigned by higher authority than the battlefield commander. For example, in Operation Desert Storm, the mission of the U.S. VII Corps was to engage and destroy (not just defeat) the Iraqi Republican Guard Forces Command and all of its component units. In a commercial setting, a company's mission is embodied in the achievement of its goal and necessary conditions (refer to chapter 5), which we've seen represented in the Strategic Intermediate Objectives Map.

• *Enemy (E).* Obviously, for the U.S. VII Corps, the enemy was the Republican Guard. But it's not sufficient to know merely *who* the enemy is. Detailed intelligence on the character of the enemy force is also essential: strength, weapons available, deployment, leadership capabilities, doctrine, level of skill (which is a function of training), and possible intentions.** Likewise, in a business situation comparable information about competitors is equally important, both in assessing the current situation and in designing strategy for the future. This kind of information is useful content for both the Strategic Current Reality Tree and the Strategic Future Reality Tree.

• *Terrain and weather (T).* In combat, the terrain and weather are the environmental conditions in which war is waged. They define both hardship and opportunity for each side. In a comparable business situation, "terrain" might be equivalent to the characteristics of the geographic market territory or the market segments at issue between competitors. "Weather" might be compared to general economic conditions. These factors, too, are useful inputs for both the S-CRT and S-FRT.

---

* The U.S. Army, like all the other services, has no shortage of these, and the Department of Defense as a whole has even more. Of course, private industry has its own unique acronyms.

** Failure to consider these factors can be fatal. General George A. Custer, upon sighting a party of Sioux near the Little Bighorn River on June 25, 1876, is widely rumored to have said, "We've got them!" How anyone would know that he said this is a mystery, since Custer's force was killed to the last man, but the rumored quotation reflects Custer's prevailing attitude at the time, and his incomplete appreciation for the capabilities of his enemy, to his (and their) ultimate regret.

- *Troops and support available (T).* To a military commander, a complete under-standing of the capabilities of his own troops and their logistical support is even more important than knowing enemy capabilities. While a military commander must often operate with incomplete knowledge of the enemy, to do so with incomplete knowledge of his own forces' capabilities is pure folly. Good military leaders are intimately famil-iar with what their subordinates can and can't do. Life or death depends on it. The same is not always true in the civilian sector. Senior executives are sometimes isolated from the working level to such an extent that they don't really know what their organization is capable of doing and what it isn't. Yet this knowledge is as important in business competition as it is in combat. The life or death of the business could depend upon it. Explicit, objective information on one's own resources and capabilities is a useful input, primarily for S-FRTs and the Prerequisite Trees (PRT) needed to execute the strategy.*

- *Time available (T).* For both military and civilian leaders, an essential input to any strategy is a clear understanding of the time available to achieve intermediate objectives or to complete the mission. Time available is a prominent planning consideration pri-marily in the S-FRT, and to some extent in PRTs as well.

- *Civil considerations (C).* In a military context, civil considerations would be the collateral impact of combat on indigenous civilian populations. Avoidance of civilian casualties is the most prominent civil consideration in planning combat operations. In Operation Desert Storm, it didn't pose quite as much of a problem as it did in Operation Enduring Freedom (Afghanistan), and to an even greater extent in Operation Iraqi Freedom. In a business scenario, civil considerations might be interpreted to include environmental, economic, or social impacts in the company's area of activities or influ-ence. Civil considerations usually figure most prominently in the operational PRTs required to execute the strategy embodied in the S-FRT.

Figure 10.10 illustrates the various METT-TC inputs into the different logic trees. The easiest way to apply this technique in gathering information is to develop a series of discrete questions pertaining to each category. By answering these questions with as much verifiable data as possible, the content of the various trees becomes easier to develop, and the biggest challenge to the strategic planner is then constructing valid causal connections. Figure 10.10 also illustrates some typical METT-TC questions that might apply to a commercial business situation. Noncommercial or government agencies could develop similar questions pertaining to their own unique METT-TC.

GATHERING INPUTS FOR METT-TC

Right now, you might be saying, "This METT-TC idea could be useful, but how do I gen-erate the inputs for each of its components?" The short answer is "brainpower network-ing." It's highly unlikely that the required knowledge in each of the METT-TC topics will

---

* We'll see how Prerequisite Trees are developed and what purpose they serve in chapter 11.

Factor	Information Required	Used In
Mission	1. What is the desired ending state of affairs? (That is, describe the final outcome in specific terms.) 2. What are the critical success factors in achieving the end state? (That is, not doing *what* will cause failure to reach the desired end state?)	Strategic IO Map
Enemy	3. What are the key capabilities and skills of our major competitors? (That is, what do *they* do well? What are they not particularly good at? What advantages do they have? What liabilities do they have? What is their objective/strategy?)	Strategic CRT/FRT
Terrain and Weather	4. What are the key characteristics of the market, or our potential clients? (That is, What are their likes/dislikes, expectations? What are they willing to accept? What will they *not* accept?) 5. What critical economic conditions or assumptions must be made to favor us? What critical economic conditions or assumptions would hamper or neutralize us? What steps can we take to mitigate risk in these areas?	Strategic CRT/FRT
Troops and Support Available	6. What advantageous capabilities do we have? (That is, strengths, skills, technologies, or other assets that work to our advantage?) What do we do well? What research, logistical support, or information do we need?	Strategic FRT/PRT
Time Available	7. What is the time horizon for the execution of our strategy? By what deadline will we risk mission failure if we are not complete? What is the lead time we enjoy over our competitors? How long before external environmental changes (for example, market, economy) render our strategy ineffective?	Strategic FRT/PRT
Civil Considerations	8. What key environmental, political, or social factors bear on our success? In what ways might they limit our latitude for action? (That is, what we *must* do or *cannot* do.)	Strategic FRT/PRT

Figure 10.10 METT-TC—nonmilitary application.

be resident in any one place, or in any single individual's head. The challenge is to collect valid information from as many knowledgeable people as possible. Brainpower networking is nothing more than a label to describe the pooling of many people's expertise. The trick is to do it completely, effectively, and efficiently.

You might use any number of ways to pool the combined brainpower of different people. One means is the Delphi method, which is no more than interviewing true subject matter experts. This can be both expensive and time-consuming, as it's unlikely that you'll be able to gather all the experts you need at one time and in one place. Another means is brainstorming.[3] But brainstorming is a verbal method, which makes information flow sequentially rather than in parallel. Moreover, the verbal nature of brainstorming can hold it hostage to assertive personalities and other group dynamic and psychological factors.

My preferred technique, which I mentioned earlier and describe in more detail in appendix A, is the Crawford slip method. This is probably the fastest, most efficient group survey method ever devised. All it requires, besides someone with a good working knowledge of the procedure, is that you convene as many people as you can with the requisite knowledge of the subject—people who really *know*. The subject, in this case, is your organization's METT-TC factors. You need not even have them all together at the same place and time. Soliciting their knowledge can be done in small groups, in different locations, either simultaneously or sequentially.

You can pose questions to focus people's thinking on METT-TC and have them "data dump" everything they know about the topic onto slips that you can consolidate and categorize under the headings of *mission, enemy, terrain/weather, troops and support available, time available,* and *civil considerations.*

The METT-TC data constitute only a part of the strategy. Along with various assumptions about the future and other statements of conclusions (outcomes or effects of actions), these data will form the body of the Strategic Future Reality Tree (S-FRT). That tree will begin at the bottom with major policies, actions, or programs (injections) that you initiate to start the cause and effect of the strategy rolling. The S-FRT comes to life as you logically develop the direct and unavoidable effects of these injections on your environment. The injections, combined with statements pertaining to the METT-TC, produce new conditions that don't exist now. As you subsequently add more injections to the new outcomes, reality unfolds toward the desired effects (mission completion), much as a chain of dominoes falls following the tipping of the first one.

Figure 10.11 shows how the sorted, consolidated output of Crawford slips written about METT-TC can form part of the content of a Strategic Future Reality Tree (S-FRT). It's possible that many of the slips written won't be incorporated into the S-FRT, but having them all available enables you to select which ones are relevant.

The slips written on the mission are essentially the same as those written to develop the goal and critical success factors (necessary conditions) for the Strategic Intermediate Objectives Map (chapter 5). These slips become statements of desired effect—the culmination of the tree.

Now that we have all the elements in hand, it's time to begin actually constructing our strategy.

SEQUENCE, NOT TIME

Once our strategy is fully developed into a Strategic Future Reality Tree (S-FRT), we should have a clear, unified picture of the end results we expect to achieve, the injections we must put into place to realize them, and the cause-and-effect paths that connect them. Having this picture enables us to see definable intermediate conditions, or effects, whose presence can be observed—an instantaneous check on how far along we are to achieving our strategy.

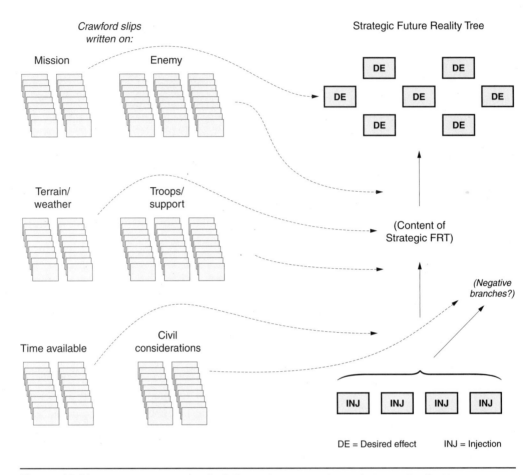

Figure 10.11   Using METT-TC Crawford slips as inputs to a Strategic Future Reality Tree.

Please note, however, that the causality represented in the S-FRT reflects *sequence, not time*. In other words, there may be 20 levels of cause and effect in an S-FRT, yet the first three or four levels may take many months to unfold—perhaps even years—while the last 16 or 17 layers may play out in a very short time, perhaps only days or weeks. It's helpful to keep that in mind as you're using the S-FRT to assess progress in strategy execution.

For example, consider the S-FRT represented in Figure 10.12. You can see that three independent branches converge in the middle of the tree before the cause-and-effect chain leads to the desired effects. It may be that you fully expect the center and right branches to be completed right up to the convergence point in a very short time—months or weeks—but the left branch may take many a year to play out. You can be assured, however, that once that left branch is completed to the convergence point, the outcomes of the other two branches will be already waiting and ready to produce the next level of effect when the left branch catches up.

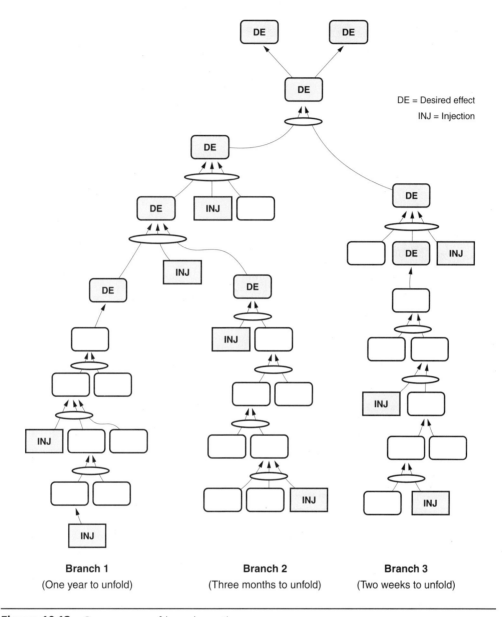

Figure 10.12   Convergence of branches—time versus sequence.

"BULLETPROOFING" THE STRATEGIC FUTURE REALITY TREE

Before we can begin to execute the strategy embodied in the completed S-FRT, it would be a good idea to be sure that there are no weaknesses in it—in other words, we should minimize the risk of failure. We might call this "bulletproofing" the strategy.* Bullet-proofing has two characteristics: *content* and *logic*. Bulletproofing the content ensures that the subject matter in the tree is robust. Bulletproofing the logic ensures that it's sufficient and expresses valid causality.

Let's briefly talk about logical sufficiency first. There are two key questions we must answer to ensure that our S-FRT is logically sufficient:

1. *Will the injections we've chosen lead directly and unavoidably to the desired effects?*

2. *Will the injections cause new problems that we might find unacceptable?*

The first question is answered by applying the categories of legitimate reservation (Figure 10.9)—to every causal connection in our S-FRT. We accomplished this in Figure 10.4, step 7. The second question is resolved by searching out negative branches (Figure 10.4, step 6).

Now let's talk about content. The overriding question about the chosen actions in the strategy is: "Are they robust?" In other words, do they represent the most effective way to do the job with the resources and time available?

Remember the military operations concepts we discussed in chapter 9? (See Figure 10.13.) We translated those military concepts into business strategy. Now's the time to use them to assess and strengthen the content of our strategy.

These attributes, principles, elements, and tenets can be used as a checklist to test the robustness of the chosen injections and identify "holes" in the strategy that might need to be plugged. Figure 10.14 reduces the military principles to a "robust injection" checklist that can be applied as acceptability criteria to both the forces and strategy represented in the S-FRT.

By the time you've vetted your Strategic Future Reality Tree against all of these criteria, you should be supremely confident in your new strategy.

Now let's see how applying this checklist might strengthen an S-FRT. Figure 10.15 shows one cause–effect connection in a hypothetical S-FRT. The immediate outcome we want is a manufacturing production capability somewhere near the West Coast markets for our products. The original injection might read: "We establish a new production facility in the Southwest." After applying the principles of war, we find that this injection leaves something to be desired in several key areas: *mass, time available,* and

---

* Realistically, it's not possible to make any strategy completely "bulletproof." This is really an informal way of saying that we're going to mitigate the risk of failure by strengthening weak spots and plugging possible holes in the strategy.

Attributes of Strategically Responsive Forces	Principles of War
1. Responsiveness	1. Objective
2. Deployability	2. Offensive
3. Agility	3. Mass
4. Versatility	4. Economy of force
5. Lethality	5. Maneuver
6. Survivability	6. Unity of command
7. Sustainability	7. Simplicity
	8. Surprise
	9. Security
Elements of Combat Power	**Tenets of Military Operations**
1. Maneuver	1. Initiative
2. Firepower	2. Agility
3. Leadership	3. Depth
4. Protection	4. Synchronization
5. Information	5. Versatility

Figure 10.13 Military operations concepts.

unity of command.* Mass and unity of command come from the 11 principles of war. Time available comes from METT-TC. So, how do we fix these shortcomings? The original injection is replaced by two injections that provide substantially better descriptions of expectations without being too prescriptive or detailed.

THE DYNAMIC NATURE OF STRATEGY

It's an axiom of military faith that no plan survives contact with the enemy intact. Things change. "Stuff happens." Even the most carefully thought-out plan can become irrelevant if the assumptions that underlie it are invalidated by a change in the direction of human events. That's why it's critical to realize that the strategy embodied in the S-FRT isn't engraved in stone.

---

* There are undoubtedly other shortcomings to be found here, but these are sufficient to illustrate content "bulletproofing."

Strategic Responsiveness

- *Is our strategy responsive?* Will our S-FRT allow us to change gears quickly, if needed, or are we locked into it once we begin? Do we have a contingency plan (i.e., have we identified and "trimmed" negative branches)?

- *Is our strategy deployable?* Can we actually do the things we've decided to do? Do we have enough of the right people, skills, resources, and assets to get the job done?

- *Are we agile enough* to respond to the unexpected? Will our S-FRT allow us to recognize unexpected competitive threats quickly? Is our decision process fast enough to respond quickly? Once a change decision is made, can we move quickly to redirect our efforts?

- *Are we versatile enough?* Do we depend too heavily on specialists, or can people do more than one kind of task effectively and efficiently?

- *Will our efforts be "lethal" to our competition?* Can we realistically expect our injections to be decisive, or might they "bounce off" our competitors?

- *Can we survive* an unexpected counterattack by our competitors? What will we do when they respond to our offensive? Have we developed enough negative branches to anticipate and respond to the full spectrum of possible competitor responses? Can we sustain ourselves long enough to respond?

- *Can we sustain* our offensive long enough to ensure victory? Do we have the willpower for protracted engagement? Do we have the resources to persist if it turns out to take longer than we expected?

Tenets of Competition

- *Initiative.* Does our S-FRT preserve our control of the engagement between ourselves and our competitors? Do we keep *them* always reacting to what we do, rather than the other way around?

- *Agility.* Are our S-FRT and our internal organization for executing it ponderous or nimble? Can we adjust rapidly to unexpected changes in the competitive business environment (for example, the terror attacks of September 11, 2001)?

- *Depth.* Is our competitive engagement only at the "forward edge of the battle area" (FEBA)—for example, a direct, head-to-head sales campaign for the same customers, or do we engage him "behind the lines" as well (for example, developing a fast new product introduction capability, or impossibly short manufacturing lead times)? Do we need additional injections to carry the battle to the competition's rear echelons?

- *Synchronization.* Do our injections attract our competitors' attention to just one point of focus, or do we force them to consider multiple competitive issues at the same time?

- *Versatility.* Are we equally able to take on competitors in a variety of areas having to do with product and service features?

Elements of Competitive Power

- *Maneuver.* Do our injections allow us to change direction quickly, or are we locked into a course of action, once committed? Similarly, do our people and resources have the flexibility to maneuver according to the conditions of the engagement? If not, what additional injections will be necessary to give them that maneuver capability?

- *Firepower.* Have we assigned sufficient resources of the right kind (skills, technology, supporting equipment, facilities) to do the job quickly and effectively? Are we employing the right tools, techniques, policies, and procedures to realize overwhelming advantage?

- *Leadership.* Do we have the right leaders in place to execute the strategy represented in the S-FRT? Are they experienced or thoroughly knowledgeable in the tasks to be performed? Do they command the respect of their subordinates?

- *Protection.* Can we leave the people assigned to the project or operation in place for the duration? Have we anticipated competitors' actions well enough (that is, using negative branches) to avoid having to redirect our efforts in response to their tactics?

- *Information.* Have we identified all the things we need to know about the competitive environment, the market, and our own capabilities? Is this information accurate, current, and readily available?

Principles of Competitive Engagement

- *Objective.* Are our objectives (desired effects) clear? Do we have a firm understanding of what the end state should look like, so we'll know when we can declare victory?

- *Offensive.* Are we proactive, rather than reactive? Does our S-FRT keep the pressure on our competitors? Do we give them no time to think or react?

- *Mass.* Do we have enough resources to apply to the decisive injections? Are we planning to attack at more than one point simultaneously?

- *Economy of force.* Are we assigning too much effort to secondary injections? Do we know where our system constraint lies and are we subordinating nonconstraints appropriately?

- *Maneuver.* Does our S-FRT keep the competition from focusing on an effective response to our initial efforts? Are we distracting them enough to slow down their response?

- *Unity of command.* Are the lines of responsibility and authority clear? Does everyone know who's boss of each part of the operation? Are communication lines clear and unambiguous to facilitate fast decision making?

- *Simplicity.* Is the S-FRT relatively simple and capable of being executed on time by all departments, teams, or task forces?

- *Surprise.* Do we know what the competition expects us to do? Does our S-FRT do the unexpected?

- *Security.* Do we know what our competitors are planning to do? Can we find out? Does our S-FRT safeguard our own vulnerabilities while we plot our attack on the competition? Can we keep our own secrets?!

Figure 10.14 Using military concepts to verify business strategy.

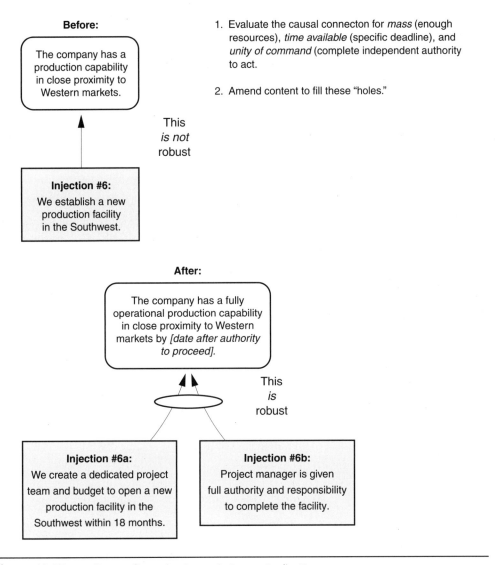

Before:

The company has a production capability in close proximity to Western markets.

This *is not* robust

Injection #6:
We establish a new production facility in the Southwest.

1. Evaluate the causal connecton for *mass* (enough resources), *time available* (specific deadline), and *unity of command* (complete independent authority to act.

2. Amend content to fill these "holes."

After:

The company has a fully operational production capability in close proximity to Western markets by *[date after authority to proceed]*.

This *is* robust

Injection #6a:
We create a dedicated project team and budget to open a new production facility in the Southwest within 18 months.

Injection #6b:
Project manager is given full authority and responsibility to complete the facility.

Figure 10.15 "Bulletproofing" the Strategic Future Reality Tree.

The S-FRT is supposed to be a dynamic document. At periodic intervals, it should be reviewed to determine whether the original assumptions are still valid, and whether events are really unfolding the way they're depicted in the tree. If divergences are detected, the tree should be reevaluated and modified as required, or corrective action taken to resume the planned course (that is, the original S-FRT). Think back to the strategic navigation exercise described in chapter 4. This is equivalent to our ship fixing its position at periodic intervals during the ocean crossing and making corrections to return to course when crosswinds prove stronger or weaker than anticipated.

This review and correction is not difficult to do. The whole constraint management strategy model can be completed in about two weeks.* An S-FRT can be completely constructed in about a week. Making corrections shouldn't take a few knowledgeable people more than a few days, probably less.

The organization should make a concerted effort to monitor the progress of strategy execution as well and recognize when adjustments are required. It would even be advisable to assign this strategy review responsibility to a senior executive.

SUMMARY AND CONCLUSION

The essence of good strategy is taking the actions to cure today's deficiencies, achieve the objectives needed for tomorrow's success, and prevent problems that don't exist now from cropping up. A Strategic Future Reality Tree provides a means to develop such strategy. Using METT-TC to guide content development minimizes the chances of overlooking critical factors. Applying the attributes, principles, elements and tenets of effective military operations can further minimize the risk of "holes" or weak spots in the content of the strategy.

Appendices C and D provide real-world examples of Strategic Future Reality Trees developed using these concepts. Printed on plotter-sized paper and posted on a wall, the S-FRT puts the company's strategy right in front of everyone's eyes every day. Everyone knows where the organization is going and what's required to get there without the need for a doorstop-sized document that sits on the shelf, where few people ever read it. And because it's visible to everyone all the time, it's far less likely that changes in the competitive environment that might obviate parts (or all) of the strategy would be overlooked.

Now let's move on and see how our new strategy is actually executed.

> *Master Guan said, "Go forth armed without determining strategy, and you will destroy yourself in battle."*
>
> —Du You
> *Sun Tzu and the Art of War*

ENDNOTES

1. H. W. Dettmer, *Goldratt's Theory of Constraints* (Milwaukee: ASQ Quality Press, 1996).
2. L. J. Scheinkopf, *Thinking for a Change: Putting the TOC Thinking Processes to Work* (Boca Raton, FL: CRC/St. Lucie Press, 1999).
3. C. Clark, *Brainstorming: How to Create Successful Ideas* (CA: Melvin Powers Wilshire, 1958).

---

* Compare that to traditional strategic planning processes, which can take months.

11

Planning the Execution

*Military formation is like water—the form of water is to avoid
the high and go to the low, the form of a military force is to avoid the
full and attack the empty; the flow of water is determined by the
earth, the victory of a military force is determined by the opponent.*

*So a military force has no constant formation, water has no constant
shape: the ability to gain victory by changing and adapting according
to the opponent is called genius.*

—Master Sun
Sun Tzu and the Art of War

"Take what the defense gives you." This is an expression commonly heard in American football, which, though a sport, is as close to military combat as leisure time entertainment can be.* Another way to say it is, "When it comes to tactical engagements, hit 'em where they ain't." This can apply to the execution of any kind of strategy. Once you've decided to do this, however, you must decide on the details of execution—the "how to."

Effective execution—the "how to"—requires four essential factors:

- Strong leadership

- Competent, skillful troops

---

* Who would have thought that the National Football League would be practicing Sun Tzu's principles, first articulated so long ago?

- Sufficient resources

- A daring but executable plan

Strong leadership is sometimes a matter of chance, though it shouldn't be that way. Resource sufficiency and the competence of the troops usually depend on the quality of leadership. *Mediocre leaders don't invest much time, effort, or resources in developing the capabilities of their people.* Excellent ones know that it makes all the difference when combat (military or business) is engaged. Resources are obviously essential; the best leadership and the most competent people can't win a battle empty-handed. And without a daring, executable plan, the potential of leadership, troops, and resources will never be realized.

There are plenty of books on leadership and employee development. And obtaining adequate resources is beyond the scope of this book, too. This chapter will focus on the creation of a daring, executable plan to implement the strategy.

In the preceding chapter, we introduced the idea of the commander's intent. The commander paints a verbal picture of what he wants to accomplish and provides the major factors and situational considerations that bear on the effort through the METT-TC (mission, enemy, terrain and weather, troops and support available, time available, and civil considerations). This constitutes the strategic guidance to subordinate unit commanders, who then apply the principles of war, tenets of operations, and so on, in designing their tactical engagements.

In chapter 10 we also saw how to develop a Strategic Future Reality Tree (S-FRT). The S-FRT is actually the strategy itself. We might liken it to the commander's intent, but applied to business it's actually a bit more detailed. However, strategy alone isn't much use if it isn't executed. For execution in the constraint management model, we move on to the Prerequisite Tree (PRT).

THE PREREQUISITE TREE

In the S-FRT, the injections are the major strategic initiatives that we must accomplish to make the strategy unfold the way we want it to. Each of these injections is a complex condition of future reality, the summation of many discrete tasks and events. The PRT structures those tasks and events into a logical sequence that culminates in the achievement of the injection. (See Figure 11.1.)

Normally, there will likely be one Prerequisite Tree for each injection in the S-FRT. It's possible that a particular injection would be so simple and straightforward that it wouldn't require a PRT. However, if you've kept the focus of your S-FRT at the strategic level, where it should be, you won't see many injections that don't require PRTs.

Conceptually, the PRT is "appended" from the S-FRT, with the common connector being the injection. (See Figure 11.2.) In fact, the PRT can actually be displayed this way. A large diagram can be posted on each department's wall showing the Prerequisite

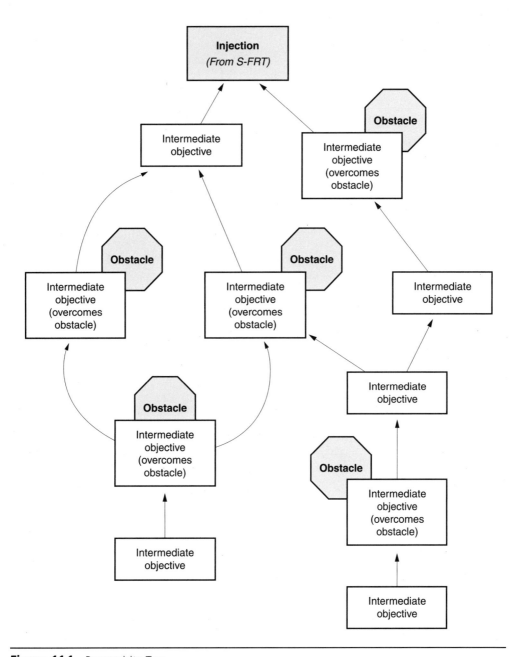

Figure 11.1   Prerequisite Tree.

Trees for which the department is responsible appended to the S-FRT. (See Figure 11.3) This is a good way to make sure that every department in the organization recognizes the importance of its role in the overall strategy.

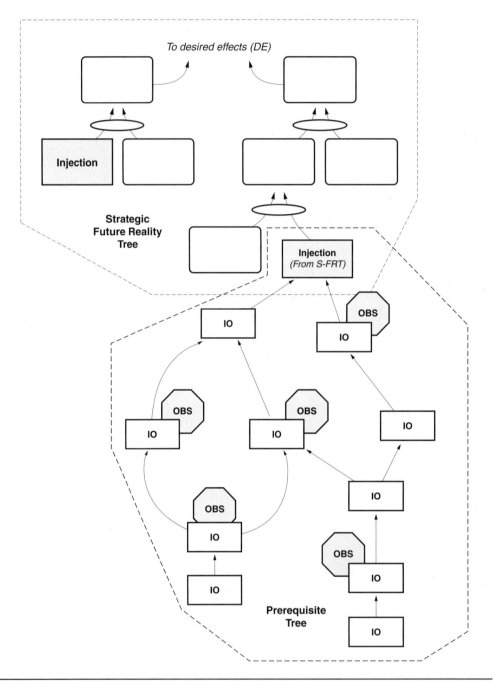

Figure 11.2 Prerequisite Tree and the Strategic Future Reality Tree.

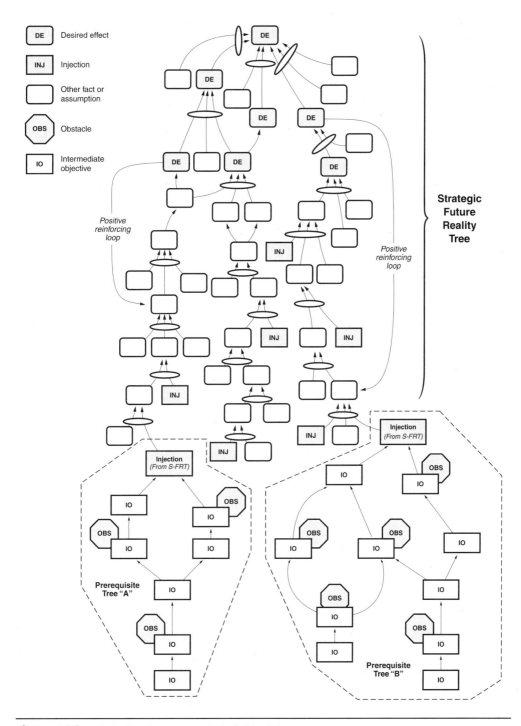

Figure 11.3 Displaying the strategy in individual departments.

AN EXAMPLE

Let's take a look at an example of a PRT. (See Figure 11.4.) This tree culminates in an injection that's part of a larger S-FRT. It describes the major tasks involved in acquiring and preparing to use a new information system. Notice that there are only seven obstacles, but there are 14 intermediate objectives (IO) in the network leading to the achievement of the injection. The IOs paired with obstacles are there specifically to overcome those obstacles. The IOs *without* obstacles are major tasks or milestones that must not be overlooked if the injection is to be achieved.

Notice, too, that there are no ellipses or other supporting statements, as there are in an S-FRT or S-CRT. That's because, like the Strategic Intermediate Objectives Map, the Prerequisite Tree shows only the minimum required tasks—the "showstoppers"—without which the injection surely will not be achieved. Figure 11.5, a variation on Figure 10.2, illustrates this relationship. In the S-FRT, all the contributing causes required to produce an effect are included, and an ellipse is used to indicate causal dependency. In a PRT, you don't see any ellipses, because not all the causality is shown. In fact, each successively higher level is *enabled,* not actually produced, by the lower level.

For example, look at the lower left part of Figure 11.4. The very first task in the PRT is the identification of someone to be the administrator for the system to be acquired. It's a good idea to have this person involved in the acquisition from the beginning. In most cases, system administrators are experienced information systems professionals. By appointing the system administrator at the beginning of the acquisition process, the organization has the benefit of this experience in avoiding mistakes in acquiring the new system. Moreover, the system administrator takes "ownership" of the system for which he or she will be held accountable as early as possible in the process.

The IO that calls for identifying a system administrator was created specifically to overcome the paired obstacle, which reads: "A system administrator has not been identified." Without doing so, the acquisition effort can't proceed. However, even if we *do* identify a system administrator, that doesn't mean we automatically have a project team to complete the implementation. It means only that *nothing stands in the way* of selecting a project team anymore. In other words, project team selection is *enabled,* but not necessarily completed yet. Likewise, selection of a project team means that now high-level system needs can be determined.

When the PRT is complete, anyone who has a reasonable understanding of the purpose of the tree should be able to examine it and say, "Yes, all the necessary tasks have been accounted for, and they're sequenced in the proper order." Alternatively, if something critical has been overlooked, careful scrutiny by a third party should reveal that, too.

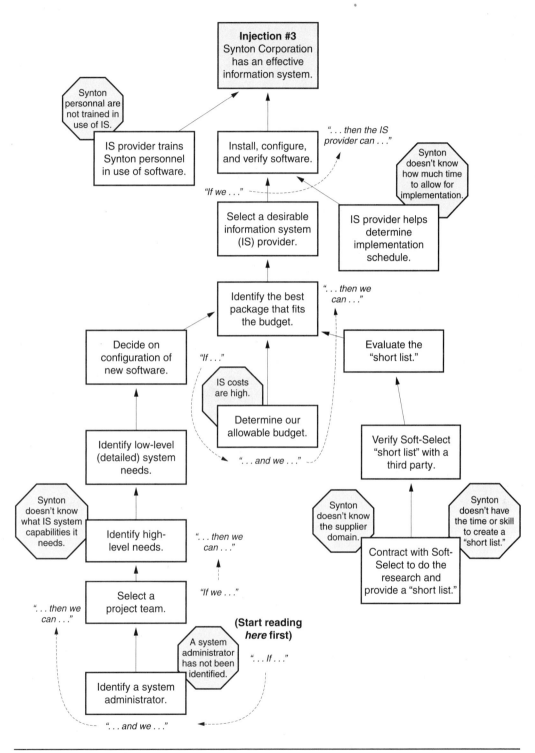

Figure 11.4 Prerequisite Tree (example)—acquisition and installation of an information system.

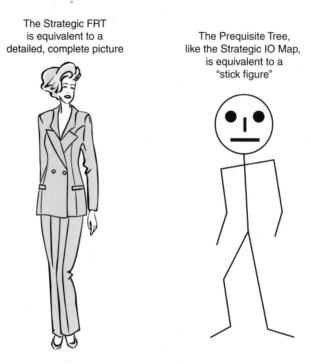

The Strategic FRT
is equivalent to a
detailed, complete picture

The Prequisite Tree,
like the Strategic IO Map,
is equivalent to a
"stick figure"

Figure 11.5   Relation between the Strategic FRT and the Prerequisite Tree.

HOW TO CONSTRUCT A PREREQUISITE TREE

The PRT is fairly easy to build. The following steps should suffice to get you to an acceptable first draft for others to review.* Figure 11.6 summarizes these procedures.

1. *Formulate the objective.* This is the injection you want to implement. Write it on a Post-It note and place it at the top of a whiteboard or flip-chart page.

2. *Identify obstacles.* Write on Post-It notes all obstacles that you or anyone else can think of that would prevent attaining the injection.

3. *Identify intermediate objectives (IO).* Think of as many ways as possible to overcome each obstacle. Write these on Post-It notes, too. Eliminate duplications. Select one or more of the best IOs to be paired with the obstacle. NOTE: More than one IO may be necessary to overcome an obstacle.

---

* As with the other logic trees, the more you understand about how to build a PRT, the faster it will come together and the better quality product you'll have. Again, Dettmer (1997, 1998) and Scheinkopf (1999) provide detailed guidance on how to create PRTs.

1. Formulate the objective.
   - The injection from the Strategic Future Reality Tree
   - Write it on a Post-It note
2. Identify obstacles.
   - Think of all obstacles that would prevent attaining the injection
   - Write on Post-It notes
3. Identify intermediate objectives (IO).
   - Think of as many ways as possible to overcome each obstacle
   - Write on Post-It notes
   - Eliminate duplications
   - Select one or more of the best IOs and pair them with the obstacle
4. Identify all other tasks.
   - Articulate all other required actions for which there are no obstacles
   - Write on Post-It notes
5. Sequence all the intermediate objectives.
   - Place the later IOs nearer the top of the tree
   - Place the earlier ones closer to the bottom
   - Refine the sequence so that all IOs occur in the right order
   - Look for opportunities to do things in parallel, rather than in sequence
6. Connect the intermediate objectives.
   - Link the IOs, *not* the obstacles
7. Review the completed tree.
   - Enlist other knowledgeable people
   - Select those who were not involved in building the PRT
   - Solicit constructive comment

Figure 11.6 How to construct a Prerequisite Tree.

Note: These directions modified and adapted from H. W. Dettmer, *Breaking the Constraints to World-Class Performance* (Milwaukee: ASQ Quality Press, 1998).

4. *Identify all other tasks.* These are other actions that must be accomplished, but don't have any obstacles preventing their completion. Write these on Post-It notes, too.

5. *Sequence all the intermediate objectives.* Using your personal judgment (and that of others), decide which IOs must be completed early in the sequence, and which must be completed closer to attainment of the injection.

   • Place the later IOs nearer the top of the tree

   • Place the earlier ones closer to the bottom

   • Refine the sequence so that all IOs occur in the right order

   • Look for opportunities to do things in parallel, rather than in sequence.

6. *Connect the intermediate objectives.* The arrow connections link the IOs, *not* the obstacles.

7. *Review the completed tree.* Have others who are knowledgeable about the situation, but who were not involved in building the PRT, offer constructive comment.

"FLESHING OUT" THE PREREQUISITE TREE

At this point you might be thinking, "We converted the stick-figure Strategic IO Map into a 'filled-out' Strategic Future Reality Tree. Aren't we going to do the same with the stick-figure Prerequisite Tree?"

The short answer is "no." We *could* do that. There is another logical tool in the *thinking process,* called a *transition tree,* designed to do just that—to "flesh out" the skeleton that is the Prerequisite Tree into step-by-step guidance on achieving each individual intermediate objective and linking them all to the injection in an unbroken chain of sufficiency logic. However, I'm going to leave it to you to decide how much detail you consider necessary to go into.

If the Prerequisite Tree represented an engineering project, for example, I would not presume to give engineers, or other technical professionals, step-by-step instructions on how to do their jobs. Good leaders provide just enough guidance to ensure that their objectives are achieved, while still enabling their subordinates to exercise their own creativity in how to achieve them. In many respects, this is somewhat like the "commander's intent" that we discussed in chapter 9. In most cases, the people at the tactical level know how to do the job. Excessively detailed instructions can be as detrimental as overspecification. I personally prefer to specify the outcomes (injection, intermediate objectives) and let those responsible for them figure out how they want to do the job.

That said, however, if those assigned accountability for delivering an injection are in a complete quandary about how to fulfill some of the intermediate objectives, you can refer them to other sources on the preparation of transition trees.[1-3]

Once the PRT is completed, "projectize" it. Assign someone to be accountable for the execution of the PRT. Set a standard of performance for the attainment and a deadline for completion of the injection. And be sure that those responsible have adequate resources to do the job.

"PROJECTIZING" THE PREREQUISITE TREES

Now that we have a complete PRT, what do we do with it? In reality, each of the PRTs needed to execute a complete strategy can be considered a discrete project. On an even larger scale, all of the PRTs together can be considered a single implementation project. The information system acquisition in Figure 11.4 has a system administrator assigned as the very first step. For all intents and purposes, that system administrator can be considered the "project manager" for the acquisition and implementation of the information system. Other PRTs would require that responsible individuals be assigned to assume accountability for their completion as well.

However, since each PRT supports the achievement of an injection in a larger organizational strategy, the CEO could consider the implementation of that entire strategy to be a "mega-project," or a program, perhaps under the leadership of a vice president. As usual, there are parallels in the military environment. The Department of Defense awards contracts for major weapon system development programs to aerospace and defense contractors. These systems are so complex that each major component is a complex project in and of itself. In fact, even major components are composed of numerous subassemblies so complicated that they might qualify as projects themselves. The entire development effort for a new weapon system is considered a program composed of many coordinated projects.

Take, for example, the development of a new kind of combat (or even commercial) aircraft. The design and fabrication of the airframe is a major project in and of itself. So is the design of new engines for the plane, and the avionics, the fuel system, the hydraulic system, and so on. The integration of all of these is done on a time schedule, and represents the program as a whole. Each major system is a project in itself. Within the avionics package, for example, there are even more subprojects, each of which is managed as an independent effort. Subordinate to him, the avionics project manager may have a weapons subproject, with its own manager, and a different subproject to create a fly-by-wire flight control system. Within the flight control system, the development of new-technology pilot displays might be still another project. Taken all together, the airplane development program is a large program made up of several "nested" vertical layers of projects and subprojects—a "hierarchy," if you will, not unlike the "family of plans" concept in the Joint Strategic Planning System (JSPS) and the Joint Operation Planning and Execution System (JOPES).

The mention of the JSPS and JOPES is deliberate. While they're intended to produce a hierarchy of strategic, operational, and tactical plans, each of these levels is, in essence, the execution of a project—a one-time effort of resources and people to produce a single deliverable in a specified period of time. Unlike projects in the civilian world, however, lives depend on the timely, successful execution of these "projects." But we don't have to stop there, either. The concept of managing strategy execution as a project can be translated to the nonmilitary world as well. All that's required are four things:

1. Assignment of accountability for completion of the strategy (or injection) execution

2. A standard of performance

3. Establishment of a time for completion of the project

4. Adequate resources to complete the job

In the case of the project embodied in Figure 11.4, the system administrator is the accountable person—the project manager. The standard of performance is the implementation of an information system that meets the needs of the organization, and in which all users are trained. More precise performance standards may be established, if required. The promised delivery date is represented in the schedule for completion. And the project team and some level of funding constitute the resources required to execute the PRT. All that is needed now is a way of making sure the "train stays on the track."

CRITICAL CHAIN PROJECT SCHEDULING

As mentioned earlier, the implementation of an organizational strategy, or even just an individual PRT within that strategy, needs a daring but executable plan to succeed. The most robust, reliable way to plan the execution of one or more PRTs is to convert them into *critical chain* project schedules.

Critical chain is a constraint-based methodology for ensuring that projects are completed in the shortest practical time with the highest probability of on-time delivery. It's beyond the scope of this book to address the specifics of critical chain in detail. Other sources do a much better job of that in any event.* Suffice it to say that with relatively little effort, a PRT can be rotated 90 degrees clockwise and represent a decent project activity network. (See Figure 11.7a.) From there, it's a matter of translating each individual intermediate objective into a task of average duration and connecting them into a critical chain chart. (See Figure 11.7b.)** Once this is done, the parallel tracks in the project can be seen.

Responsibilities for individual project tasks (intermediate objectives) can then be assigned, and resource contentions (different tasks scheduled to be done at the same time, by the same resource) can be identified and deconflicted. Time buffers can be

---

* The two most comprehensive books on critical chain are *Critical Chain,* by Lawrence P. Leach, and *Project Management in the Fast Lane,* by Robert C. Newbold. Complete citations for both can be found in the bibliography of this book.

** The critical chain chart pictured in Figure 11.7b is not, strictly speaking, either a Gantt or a PERT chart, though it has characteristics of both.

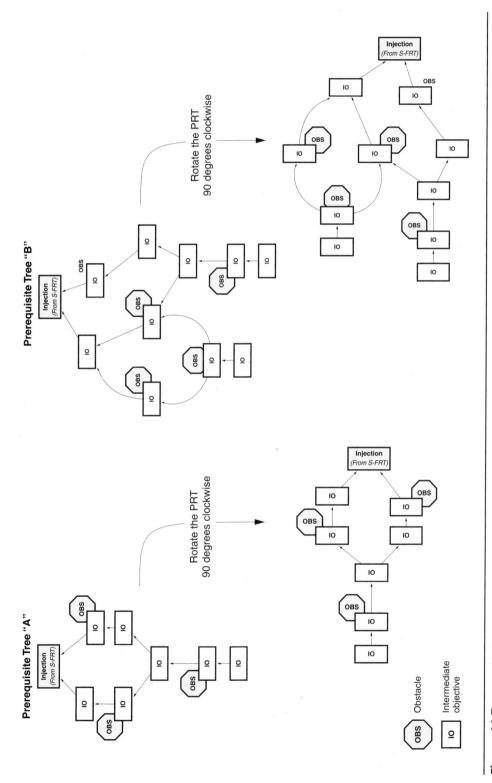

Figure 11.7a "Projectizing" Prerequisite Trees.

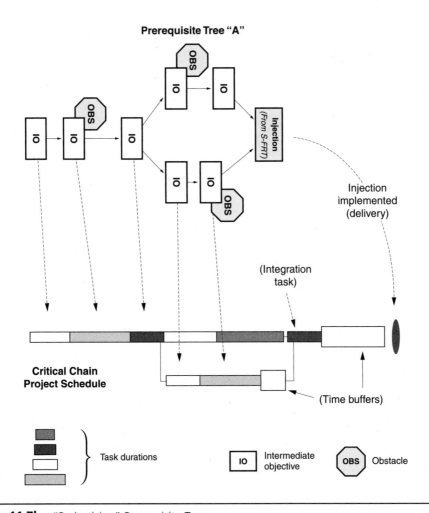

Figure 11.7b "Projectizing" Prerequisite Trees.

inserted and managed to protect integration steps and completion of the injection (that is, project delivery).*

There are documented cases in which critical chain has produced project deliver date reliability in excess of 90 percent confidence, in about half the duration of comparable traditional PERT/CPM schedules. I don't expect you to take my word for this—research it for yourself. I only want to emphasize that the combination of two proven constraint-management methods, the logical thinking process and critical chain, offer a way of developing and executing strategy with maximum effectiveness in minimum time.

---

* Please be aware that I've just done the critical chain methodology a gross injustice by reducing it to two paragraphs. I did so only because two other superior sources (Leach and Newbold) describe critical chain far better than I have space to do here.

THE "META-PROJECT"

Earlier, I suggested that the multiple projects embodied in the execution of individual Prerequisite Trees could be combined into a broader "strategy execution" project, probably headed by a senior executive. Figure 11.8 is a graphic representation showing how various projects to accomplish discrete injections could be integrated into such a meta-project.

What's the value of doing something like this? In short, performance visibility for executives. With the execution of the entire organizational strategy for the next two to five years reduced to a meta-project schedule, a chief executive officer—not to mention the board of directors—would have almost instantaneous visibility on how well strategy deployment is happening. Unanticipated problems[*] can be identified sooner, tactics for dealing with them developed, and less drastic corrective actions are more likely to be sufficient.[**] Moreover, with a single executive-level project manager responsible for monitoring the meta-project (and applying "horsepower" where and when needed), the odds of successful strategy execution increase significantly.

SUMMARY AND CONCLUSION

With the completion of the Prerequisite Trees, the first pass through the constraint management model for strategy development is largely complete. All that remains is to execute those PRTs and to continually monitor progress until the owners of your system are ready to declare victory.

> *So skillful military operation should be like a swift snake that counters with its tail when someone strikes at its head, counters with its head when someone strikes at its tail, and counters with both its head and tail when someone strikes at its middle.*
>
> —Master Sun
> *Sun Tzu and the Art of War*

---

[*] Remember, no plan survives initial contact with the enemy completely intact.

[**] Remember Figure 8.6. A one-degree heading change 60 miles from the target is better than a 90-degree heading change 10 seconds from bomb release.

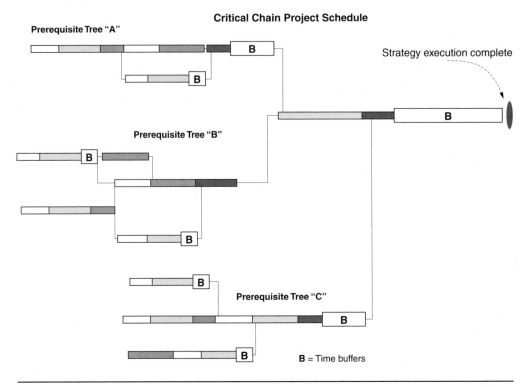

Figure 11.8 "Projectizing" the whole strategy.

ENDNOTES

1. H. W. Dettmer, *Goldratt's Theory of Constraints* (Milwaukee: ASQ Quality Press, 1996).
2. H. W. Dettmer, *Breaking the Constraints to World-Class Performance* (Milwaukee: ASQ Quality Press, 1998).
3. L. J. Scheinkopf, *Thinking for a Change: Putting the TOC Thinking Processes to Work* (Boca Raton, FL: CRC/St. Lucie Press, 1999).

12

Putting It All Together

*Therefore those who skillfully move opponents make formations
that opponents are sure to follow, give what opponents are sure to
take. They move opponents with the prospect of gain, waiting for
them in ambush.*

—Master Sun
Sun Tzu and the Art of War

The constraint management model for strategy development differs from most
strategic planning processes. Notice the distinction in wording: "strategy development" versus "strategic planning." Throughout this book, I've emphasized the
term *strategy development* and avoided the words "strategic planning." Why? Because
strategic planning has for too long been associated with structured, rigid, inflexible, and
often ponderous *form*. The outcome of such processes is often "doorstop-sized" documents that eventually sit on a shelf, gathering dust. Once they're done, nobody reads
these documents, much less strives to follow them, except in the most perfunctory way.
They're almost impossible to communicate throughout an organization.* When they're
updated—which isn't often—it can be a painful exercise, even if it's done conscien-
tiously and done right.

The constraint management model is *designed* to be the diametric opposite of most
strategic planning processes. It's intended to be flexible and relatively streamlined. It's
specifically designed *not* to result in a doorstop-sized document, but instead be a

---

* If you doubt this, and if your organization has a strategic plan, try a little unscientific poll: Ask several people at
  subordinate levels of the organization whether they've ever actually read the strategic plan. If you're fortunate to
  find a few that have, then ask them to describe how what they do day-to-day advances the success of that strategy.
  The results might surprise you—or maybe not.

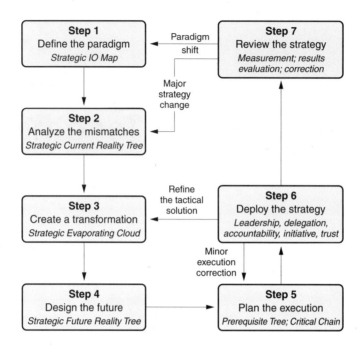

Figure 12.1   The constraint management model.

graphic representation of the organization's "roadmap to the future," logically proven, with everyone's part and responsibilities clearly indicated for all to see. It follows a simple framework—seven basic steps that can easily be tailored to the needs of different organizations. (The only parts we haven't talked about yet are Steps 6 and 7, and we'll get to those in a moment.) The constraint management model also provides the tools to complete the steps, and those tools themselves become the visible expression of the strategy and the operations required to execute it. Let's review the first five steps and tools for a moment. (See Figure 12.1.)

STEP 1: DEFINE THE PARADIGM

In chapter 5, we discussed the importance of defining the boundary of the system for which the strategy will be developed—in other words, just *whose strategy is this?* We talked about how crucial it is to define clearly the system's goal and critical success factors (necessary conditions) for the future—the planning horizon. The Strategic Intermediate Objectives (IO) Map provided a means to express visually the relationship between the goal and necessary conditions in a simple, logical way.

STEP 2: ANALYZE THE MISMATCHES

In chapter 7, we learned how to define the status quo—the system's existing situation—in relation to the goal and necessary conditions defined in the first step. We defined the mismatches between the system's current performance and the standards for success in the future, as expressed in the Strategic IO Map. We called these individual mismatches undesirable effects (UDE), and we saw how a Strategic Current Reality Tree (S-CRT) is used to expose all the logical cause-and-effect connections between those UDEs and their (usually) buried root causes. Since these root causes are normally relatively few in number, our attention can be focused on the minimum changes needed to produce the maximum positive benefit for the system. One of these root causes is invariably the *system constraint:* the factor that most limits the organization's ability to improve itself. The constraint management model takes it name from this concept of identifying and eliminating constraints to improved organizational performance.

STEP 3: CREATE A TRANSFORMATION

The next step is the first of two that help us to design a new road map to our desired future. In chapter 8, we discussed the role of conflict resolution in creating a transformation. We saw the difficulty in effecting system-impacting change, particularly those problems associated with human behavior and threats to power. We discussed the reasons behind the cogent words of Machiavelli.* Chapter 8 also introduced the Evaporating Cloud as a means of ferreting out hidden conflict and structuring it in a way that makes it easier to find "win–win" solutions (that is, avoid compromise). The outcome of the conflict resolution process is breakthrough ideas, or *injections* that we must introduce into existing reality. These form the basis for our "roadmap to the future."

STEP 4: DESIGN THE FUTURE

The injections produced by successful conflict resolution are the entry points into a Strategic Future Reality Tree (S-FRT), a visual depiction of all the layers of cause and effect leading from these injections to our desired effects: *the satisfaction of all future necessary conditions leading to the system's goal.* Chapter 10 described in detail the role of the S-FRT—which itself constitutes the organization's strategic road map.

Our S-FRT road map provides two absolutely indispensable benefits in our strategy development efforts. First, it provides the comfort of knowing that the actions we anticipate taking will, in fact, lead to the results we want, and it does so with lock-step "if–then" logic. It affords us the opportunity to have that logic critically examined, the

---

* "He who innovates will have for his enemies all those who are well off under the existing order of things, and only lukewarm supporters in those who might be better off under the new."—Niccolò Machiavelli

weak spots identified, and the "holes plugged." Second, it allows us to anticipate where and when any of our proposed new actions might produce new, devastating results that don't currently exist. In other words, it keeps us from jumping out of the frying pan and into the fire.

STEP 5: PLAN THE EXECUTION

Once the strategy is fully developed, logically verified, and potential negative outcomes identified and prevented, it's time to plan how to execute it. The particulars of executing each individual injection can be complicated. Because the S-FRT represents a fairly "high level" strategy, it won't show this level of detail. Furthermore, the S-FRT represents the strategy of the whole organization, but the details of executing discrete injections are usually delegated to parts of the organization that specialize in their content matter. For example, an injection that directed the opening of a new market would not include the discrete steps for doing so. Those steps would be left to the marketing department to determine.

However, if an injection is at all complicated, the marketing department, or other functional area, might need to arrange component tasks in some coherent sequence. In chapter 11, we saw how the Prerequisite Tree can be used to identify all the discrete necessary conditions needed to overcome obstacles and to otherwise accomplish the injection. We also broached the idea that functional departments might manage the execution of individual injections as projects. At a higher level, a senior executive might manage execution of the entire strategy as a complex project. Critical chain project scheduling and buffer management were offered as a high-percentage way to complete these projects reliably in the shortest possible time.

STRATEGY "ON THE WALL"

During my career in the Air Force, I never really saw "the big picture," even though I knew it existed. Like most people, even fairly senior ones, I usually saw the parts I was most closely connected with, or responsible for. I took it on faith that my part of the puzzle would fit snugly with all the other parts to form a coherent whole. Even though I was fully knowledgeable in the Joint Strategic Planning System (JSPS) and the Joint Operation Planning and Execution System (JOPES), I never actually *saw* many of the actual documents that made up the military strategy of the United States—the joint vision, national military strategy, joint strategic capabilities plan, joint planning document, and so on. For one thing, at my level I didn't have a "need to know."* For another, the overall strategy embodied in these documents was too broad and complex for one person to absorb in detail.

---

* "Need to know" is one of the criteria used to compartmentalize highly classified information (Secret and Top Secret) for the sake of security.

Figure 12.2 Strategy on the wall.

But commercial businesses, not-for-profit organizations, or other government agencies aren't nearly as complex as the Department of Defense, nor do their strategies need to be. It should be possible for the senior executive in such systems to reduce the organization's strategy to a Strategic Future Reality Tree that can be printed on plotter-sized paper and mounted on the wall of every office in the organization for all to see. Figure 12.2 shows a typical example of such a visual strategy, displayed for those concerned with its execution to see. The simplicity of representing strategy in an S-FRT also gives it the necessary flexibility to permit updating and adjusting as needed without much aggravation.

Moreover, this common "road map to the future" could be customized for each department. Each department's Prerequisite Trees could be appended to its copy of the S-FRT, so that everyone could understand their roles in turning the strategy into reality. (See Figure 12.3) It should be possible for anyone in a department to look up on the wall and know "how goes it" today. Project schedules, with due dates and accountabilities for component tasks assigned, can be created from the Prerequisite Trees and progress monitored and corrected as required—daily, if necessary.*

---

* The theory of constraints (TOC) provides a tool called *buffer management* that is designed for early detection of deviations from planned schedules—early enough to correct the problem, if required, with a minimum expenditure of time and resources. It provides the daily monitoring tool that makes critical chain such an effective way to manage projects. Buffer management in project execution is described in detail in Leach (2000) and Newbold (1998).

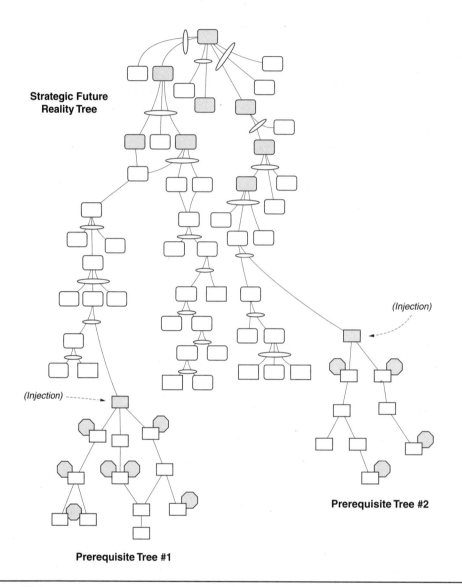

Figure 12.3 Strategy on the wall—individual department's Prerequisite Trees.

STEP 6: DEPLOY THE STRATEGY

In the military, it's almost axiomatic that no plan survives initial contact with the enemy intact. This is true in business as well. The reason is that all plans are based on assumptions, whether explicitly stated or not. These assumptions tend to point us in the direction of certain expected scenarios or events. To the extent that these assumptions are valid, reality is likely to be much closer to what was planned for. When reality doesn't unfold according to the assumptions, our plans must necessarily be adjusted to accommodate those changes.

For example, during the cold war, NATO planners based their operation plans on various assumptions about the capabilities and intentions of the Warsaw Pact forces. They assumed that any attack on western Europe would follow traditional Soviet land battle doctrine, which called for successive waves or echelons of attacking armor and mechanized units. Furthermore, owing to the geography of central Europe, NATO intelligence expected any attack to begin with a swift penetration into West Germany through the Fulda Gap. Other assumptions had to do with the numbers and types of weapon systems the Warsaw Pact would use, and their command-and-control doctrine.* Individually and in total, these assumptions pointed NATO planners toward certain strategies and tactics.

Yet experience almost always shows that things don't always work as planned. What if the Warsaw Pact hadn't initiated its attack through the Fulda Gap? What if they had decided on a North Sea beach landing instead, something similar to the Normandy invasion in June 1944? I know . . . it's not even remotely possible in these days of satellite reconnaissance that a significant seaborne invasion force could sneak up on western Europe. The point is that when the assumptions turn out not to be valid, the plan won't work as originally conceived. So if success is to be achieved, adjustments must be made.

It's no different in strategic planning for business. Competitors don't always do the things we expect them to do. The economic environment doesn't always behave the way we think it will. Customers don't always think the way we do. In other words, the assumptions about what we have to do and how we ought to do it change. When this happens, we must adjust our strategies, operations, and tactics accordingly.

How does the constraint management model provide for this? Take a look at Figure 12.4. After Step 6, Deploy the strategy, is begun, and probably before it's entirely completed, we begin to monitor the progress of deployment activities. This is the step in which the effectiveness of two aspects of our strategy is evaluated and adjusted as necessary.

The most immediate of these adjustments is in the execution of the Prerequisite Trees constructed in Step 5. Since this is where the action is happening, we want to be sure that we're actually making progress. This monitoring and adjustment of strategy execution as it's happening is, in effect, a mini–OODA loop (*observe–orient–decide–act*). In Figure 12.4, it's reflected in the feedback arrow leading out of Step 6, back to Step 5.

The second aspect is the Strategic Future Reality Tree—our strategy itself. In Step 3, we created a transformation, and built our new strategy on it. That strategy was expressed in the S-FRT. However, in the same way that execution of military operations

---

* For example, it was well known that Soviet field commanders didn't have the decision latitude that western commanders did when it came to deviating from plans. They were known to train not to operate autonomously, that is, without higher headquarters direction. Consequently, much focus among western forces was directed toward interrupting the lines of communication that would isolate field commanders from guidance from above.

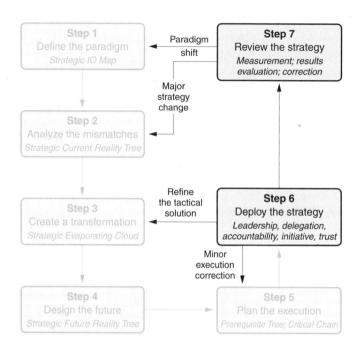

Figure 12.4 Refining the results.

doesn't always follow the predetermined plan, usually because reality invalidated some of the planning assumptions, so, too, must we be ready to adjust our own strategy—and change the S-FRT accordingly—to accommodate unforeseen events. This, in turn, may require that we revise existing Prerequisite Trees or create new ones. This monitoring and adjustment is another mini–OODA loop. In Figure 12.4, it shows up as a feedback arrow leading out of Step 6, back to Step 3.

As Boyd suggested, the organization that can cycle through these mini-OODA loops faster than their opponents "gets inside their opponents' decision cycles." Doing so causes panic and confusion in the ranks of the opponents, and eventual collapse— "unraveling," as Boyd called it.[1]

A final comment about Step 6. Notice that there are no theory of constraints (TOC) tools to support this step. That's because TOC tools are designed primarily for analysis and planning functions. They may provide the means to *help* assess success, but the tools themselves don't *do* the work of strategy execution. That's strictly a function of leadership: inspiring people to pursue the organization's goal single-mindedly, delegating the authority to do the job, holding them accountable for getting the job done, enabling them to exercise their own initiative, and trusting that they'll do the right thing. *The failure of strategy in the real world is, in most cases, as much a failure in leadership as it is in strategy development.*

STEP 7: REVIEW THE STRATEGY

Step 7 is a periodic strategy review. This is a higher-level, longer-term reexamination of our corporate ship's direction. Is our goal still the same? Are our critical success factors still valid, or have technology changes, economic conditions, or other environmental factors rendered some of them moot? Remember the Mothers' March of Dimes? This is the step in the constraint management model where we ask ourselves, "Are we still in the right business?" Maybe, like Toyota, we shouldn't be in the textile machine business anymore. Maybe the time is right to transition into a whole new set of core competencies.

This level of evaluation and adjustment is definitely the purview of senior leadership. It will result in modifications to Step 1, Define the paradigm—the Strategic Intermediate Objectives Map. It might even result in an entirely new Strategic IO Map, which, in turn prompts us to a new mismatch analysis (Step 2). That, in turn, would likely drive us toward a new strategy for the future—a new Strategic Future Reality Tree. In Figure 12.4, these adjustments are indicated by the feedback arrows leading into Steps 1 and 2. Even if the Strategic IO Map doesn't change, the conditions in the external environment might evolve enough to generate a new mismatch against the original IO Map. This definitely defines a macro-level OODA loop. The company that cycles through this seven step constraint management model faster than its competitors is undoubtedly more agile than they are.

SUSTAINING THE PROCESS

As we discussed in chapter 4, sustaining the cycle of strategy development, execution, evaluation, and adjustment is perhaps a more difficult challenge than merely creating a strategy in the first place. Unlike a combat operation, which has a well-defined beginning and end, "strategic navigation" is a continuous process. Boyd's OODA loop prescribes how the process should work:

- Observe the environment and the effects of changes (CM model Steps 1 and 2).

- Orient the decision maker with respect to the multitude of factors that comprise the environment, especially the uncertainty and ambiguity (also CM model Steps 1 and 2).

- Decide what to do to improve the advantage, or eliminate/minimize the gap between what *is* and what *should be* (CM model Steps 3, 4, and 5).

- Act quickly and decisively (CM model Step 6).

And repeat that cycle over and over (CM model Step 6 to Steps 3 or 5, and Step 7 to Steps 1 or 2) until each step leads implicitly—without having to consciously think about it—to the next. Speed through the process is certainly important, as it enables the organization to "get inside the decision cycle" of the competition. But equally (or more) important is effective *orientation*—the act of creating a mental picture (perception) of the situation that is as close as possible to reality as a basis for decision and action.

MEASURING SYSTEM SUCCESS

How do we evaluate the progress of strategy deployment (Step 6), or the strategy as a whole (Step 7)? The answer to the first is relatively easy. Strategy execution is embodied in the Prerequisite Trees, which are essentially multiple projects. The global measures of project success are performance, schedule, and cost. By establishing some performance criteria, a schedule of some kind, and a budget for each Prerequisite Tree, we have the success measures in place to evaluate the success of execution.

The answer to the second is a little more challenging. The strategy as a whole is successful if it satisfies the necessary conditions for achieving the system's goal, and realizes the goal itself. Typically, there are several necessary conditions, usually no more than three to five at the highest level, but possibly including others that support those few in a hierarchy.

Goldratt has suggested that the goal of for-profit companies is usually to make more money, both now and in the future, and that in doing so two supporting necessary conditions are satisfied customers and secure, satisfied employees.[2] These two necessary conditions are certainly common to all kinds of organizational systems, whether they're commercial for-profit companies or not. There are inevitably other necessary conditions as well, relating to the specific business that the organization is in and the environment in which it operates. Whatever the set of necessary conditions might be, some surrogate measurement is essential to effectively evaluate progress in satisfying them.

THROUGHPUT, INVESTMENT, AND OPERATING EXPENSE

In *The Haystack Syndrome*, Goldratt introduced three measures of systemic success: throughput, inventory (later extended to include capital investment), and operating expense.[3]* Throughput is a measure of progress toward the system's goal. Investment and operating expense measure the cost of reaching that goal. Though these are primarily financial measures of success, there are situations in which throughput is not measured financially.

Goldratt defines throughput (T) in a commercial organization as the rate at which a system generates money through sales.[4] Investment (I) is all the money a system invests in purchasing things it intends to sell.[5] This includes real property, capital assets, equipment, and similar things subject to depreciation. Operating expense (OE) is all the money a system spends turning I into T.[6] OE includes all fixed expenses, general and

---

* For the purposes of this book, we'll use the term *investment* to connote both capital investment and inventory intended for conversion into salable product or service.

administrative, including all labor, both direct and indirect. In other words, OE is the price we pay to open the doors of the organization for business each day.

These three measures are useful in assessing system success because they are measurable in units (financial) that are commonly accepted and understood throughout human society. Consequently, they are relatively easy to use as measures of a system's success in attaining its goal. How much progress did we make toward our goal this quarter? Let's see how much throughput we generated. How quickly are we "burning through" the money we have to make that progress? Let's see whether we're above or below the budgeted consumption rate for investment and operating expense for the same period. Any variance from expectations can be treated as a system-level deviation from our strategic plan. A gap analysis (Current Reality Tree) can be constructed to identify the root causes, and corrective action can be applied in the places where it will do the most good in the shortest possible time.

T, I, and OE (sometimes referred to as *throughput accounting,* or *constraints accounting*) have been explained by others in more detail than is possible here. In addition to *The Haystack Syndrome,* several other exceptional sources are available.[7-10]

NOT-FOR-PROFIT ORGANIZATIONS AND GOVERNMENT AGENCIES

By now, some of you are thinking, "This constraint management model for strategy development may work for commercial for-profit companies in a competitive environment, but what about not-for-profit organizations and government agencies?"

The short answer is that the constraint management model will work for such organizations, too. The adjustments needed to translate it to these environments are minimal. How can this be? Let's review the model from the beginning, with two examples of not-for-profit groups in mind: the U.S. Department of State and a large medical center.

The Department of State is a government agency, which, by definition makes it not-for-profit. It certainly *consumes* money, but it doesn't produce any, so it doesn't have a quarterly "bottom line" requirement. Neither does it really compete with similar departments of state, or foreign ministries.

A medical center might be for-profit or not-for-profit. In this example, we'll say it's not-for-profit, meaning that it generates money, but that money is used to defray the expenses of the medical center or to invest in new or improved medical treatment capability, not for distribution to shareholders.

The first step in the constraint management model is to determine the system boundary, its goal, and the necessary conditions for its success. Can these tasks be done for the U.S. State Department and our medical center? Undoubtedly so. Each one has a potential Strategic Intermediate Objectives Map, waiting to be constructed.

The second step is to analyze the gap between the Strategic IO Map and the current condition of either the State Department or the medical center. Is this possible? Certainly! If either the State Department or the medical center isn't achieving the level of success its sponsors (the president of the United States and the medical center's board of governors) believe it should, a Strategic Current Reality Tree, complete with unde-sirable effects and root causes, can be constructed. Given that both the international sit-uation and the healthcare industry have undergone almost cataclysmic changes over the past 20 years—and are still changing at an accelerating rate—I think it would be safe to say that there's no danger of a "zero gap" anytime soon.

The first part of the third step is identifying and resolving strategic conflict. Does the Department of State experience conflict? I hope to tell you! Both internal and exter-nal, as it happens. There are the differences of opinion on what course U.S. foreign pol-icy should take (internal), and there are disputes with both allies and potential adversaries (external). Does the medical center experience conflict? Undoubtedly so. If it's not responding to patient complaints (sometimes tort lawsuits), it's at loggerheads with insurance companies, or government or professional oversight bodies. These would qualify as external conflicts. And anytime resource allocation decisions must be made, there's potential for internal conflict. Can both the State Department and the medical center use Strategic Evaporating Clouds to resolve these conflicts? No question about it.

The second part of the third step calls for constructing a strategy for the future. Can the Department of State and the medical center each benefit from having a clear state-ment of ultimate objectives and an unequivocal depiction—in other words, a Strategic Future Reality Tree—of the cause and effect to achieve them? What do you think the answer to that question is?

The fourth step is verifying the new strategy and anticipating where and how "the wheels might come off the wagon." Do you think that either the State Department or the medical center might be more confident of their ability to reach their long-term goals if they knew that their future strategy had been thoroughly evaluated and "bulletproofed" *before* they embarked on it? Wouldn't *you* be?

The fifth step is deployment of the strategy. Could the medical center, or the State Department, benefit from structuring execution of policy as an arrangement of interre-lated Prerequisite Trees, converted to projects with time schedules and accountabilities assigned? How about that new wing for the hospital, or that new, cooperative initiative with a former international adversary?* I submit that they could.

Finally, could the State Department and the medical center benefit from a structured effort to monitor and adjust, as necessary, the deployment of their new policies? Who could argue otherwise? It's at this point, however, that some adjustments to the con-straint management model are necessary, particularly the measurements.

Not-for-profit organizations like the medical center are still in the business of mak-ing money. Their working capital comes from revenue receipts. The same is true of char-ities, such as the United Way or the Red Cross. These revenue receipts may come from different sources—insurance and patient payments, in the case of the medical center—but they constitute the lifeblood of the organization. The goal of the medical center might

---

* Okay, I admit it—some government agencies wallow in lack of accountability. And maybe some not-for-profit non-governmental agencies, do, too (the U.S. Olympic Committee, for example). But does it *have* to be that way?

not be to make more money, now and in the future, but that would certainly be a necessary condition to achieving its larger goal, which might be an increased level of wellness in society.

The State Department, on the other hand, doesn't sell services to customers the way the medical center does, nor does it accept charitable contributions as the United Way does. Rather, it operates on a fixed budget appropriated from tax revenues by the Congress of the United States. Investment and operating expense are thus fixed, determined ahead of time, and provided to the Department of State—not sustained through revenues generated by selling services.

So, how is progress toward the goal measured if throughput can't be expressed in financial terms for a government agency? This raises the question of the ultimate goal of a not-for-profit organization and how to measure it when it's not financial. The answer is *deviation reduction.* The organization's strategy calls for closing the gaps between the current situation and the desired future, as expressed in the goal and critical success factors of the Strategic IO Map. When few or none of those critical success factors are financial, the measure of progress is reducing the number and size of the deviations between what's happening now and what the Strategic IO Map says *should* be happening. Even if the deviations can't be expressed in financial terms, they can be approximated by some surrogate measure. For example, a few years ago the American Society for Quality created the American Customer Satisfaction Index (ACSI), a surrogate for measuring customer satisfaction (a highly subjective thing!) in a variety of industries.* Some similar measure could be customized for not-for-profits or government agencies.** Ultimately, however, the measure of progress toward nonfinancial goals, such as the State Department or medical center might have, is the reduction or elimination of undesirable effects—those statements of deviation between the current situation and the desired future state.

In summary, the constraint management model isn't just for commercial for-profit organizations, nor is it applicable only to competitive environments. Just as many of the precepts of Sun Tzu can apply to nonmilitary organizations, the same kind of translation of the constraint management model is possible to noncommercial environments.

CONCLUSION

We're finally at the point you probably wondered whether you'd ever see: the end of this book. Well, perhaps not quite the end. There are several useful appendixes that follow this chapter. These appendixes are intended to help deepen your understanding of the constraint management model for strategy development and the tools for applying it.

---

 * Visit www.asq.org/info/acsi/index.html for more on the ACSI.

** Wouldn't you just *love* to see something like the ACSI applied to the Internal Revenue Service, for example?

The renowned science fiction writer, Robert A. Heinlein, once postulated what he called the *curve of human achievement*.[11] Figure 12.5 is an adaptation of Heinlein's curve. The 21st century is here, and it's carrying us into the future at a breathtaking rate. Who, 20 or 30 years ago, could have predicted the extent to which computers, communications, biotechnology, and their benefits and liabilities, would impact our lives today? The slope of Heinlein's curve was almost linear for hundreds of years, and relatively flat. Sometime in the mid-1800s, it started turning geometric. The acceleration of progress in the 20th century was almost mind-boggling. Now we find ourselves on the cusp of the 21st century. Is there any rational reason to believe that Heinlein's curve will flatten out and become linear again? In 1885, the head of the U.S. Patent Office was quoted as saying that they should soon be out of business, because at that point in time, just about everything had already been invented. Surely we're not so dumb as to draw the same conclusion!

As technology leaps ahead, it influences the social, societal, economic, and political aspects of our world as well. The world becomes "smaller," and as national economies become increasingly more international (or supranational), it becomes more and more difficult to contemplate doing anything without considering the complex interactions of cause and effect that might result. The importance of systems thinking increases. This is true whether your business is commercial, governmental, charitable, or just personal. If you continue to operate in the ways you always have, you'll continue to realize the results you've always had—while the rest of the world passes you by.

On the other hand, if this book prompts you to begin thinking a little more holistically, and a little less suboptimally, then my objective will have been realized. The environmental movement used to display signs and bumper stickers that said, "Think

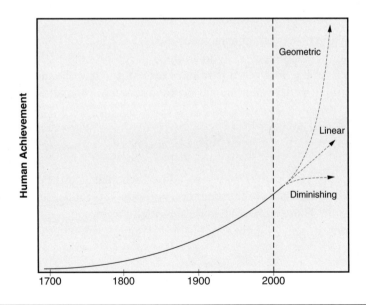

Figure 12.5 The human achievement curve. Where are we going from here?
Source: Adapted from R. A. Heinlein, *Expanded Universe.* Used with permission.

globally, act locally." Nice sentiment, but without the tools to think globally and connect that global thinking to local action, it'll never happen. Maybe the constraint management model can help.

> *So when the front is prepared, the rear is lacking, and when the rear is prepared, the front is lacking. Preparedness on the left means lack on the right, preparedness on the right means lack on the left. Preparedness everywhere means lack everywhere. When troops are on guard in many places, they are perforce scattered into small bands.*
>
> —Master Sun
> *Sun Tzu and the Art of War*

ENDNOTES

1. R. Coram, *Boyd: The Fighter Pilot Who Changed the Art of War* (New York: Little, Brown and Co., 2002): 334–35.
2. E. M. Goldratt, *Goldratt Satellite Program*, tape #8, "Strategy and Tactics" (The Netherlands: A.Y.G.I. Limited, 1999), www.eligoldratt.com.
3. E. M. Goldratt, *The Haystack Syndrome: Sifting Information Out of the Data Ocean* (Croton-on-Hudson, NY: The North River Press, 1990).
4. Goldratt, *Haystack Syndrome*, 19.
5. Ibid, 23.
6. Ibid, 29.
7. J. A. Caspari, *Constraint Management: Using Constraints Accounting Measurement to Lock in a Process of Ongoing Improvement* (unpublished as of July 2002, but available by individual arrangement with John Caspari at jacaspari@aol.com).
8. T. Corbett, *Throughput Accounting* (Great Barrington, MA: The North River Press, 1998).
9. E. Noreen, D. Smith, and J. Mackey, *The Theory of Constraints and Its Implications for Management Accounting* (Great Barrington, MA: The North River Press, 1995).
10. D. Smith, *The Measurement Nightmare: How the Theory of Constraints Can Resolve Conflicting Strategies, Policies, and Measures* (Boca Raton, FL: St. Lucie Press, 2000).
11. R. A. Heinlein, *Expanded Universe* (New York: The Berkeley Publishing Group, 1980): 322.

Appendix A

The Crawford Slip Method

BACKGROUND

In 1925, Dr. C. C. Crawford, professor of education at the University of Southern California, found himself in need of a way to capture and arrange large volumes of facts and data gathered from many different sources in the course of his research.

Like any other researcher, Crawford was faced with the challenge of arranging disparate bits of information in a coherent sequence. It seemed to be an insurmountable task. The most frustrating aspect of his challenge was capturing his data in small enough "chunks" to allow rearranging easily. Longhand text on standard-sized pages, the widely accepted format, wasn't the answer.

Crawford found that if he wrote his data, as he collected it, on small slips of paper, it made for easier rearranging later. He also discovered that if he wrote his ideas one per slip, his papers, articles and books almost edited themselves. As he refined his method, he found that writing sentences along the widest dimension of the slips and crowding the edges permitted him to overlay them, like shingles or roof tiles. (See Figure A.1.) It was thus possible to have complete paragraphs—even whole pages—develop in "loose-leaf" fashion in front of his eyes. Editing and rearranging drafts became infinitely easier. Eventually, Crawford went on to write many books using this method.[*]

Later, in the 1940s, Crawford took the method forward by a huge leap. He began asking others to write their thoughts down on "Crawford slips." He found that he could collect ideas, impressions, facts, knowledge, and the creativity of large numbers of people simultaneously and very quickly. Much like brainstorming, originated in 1941 by Alex Osborn, at the world-renowned advertising agency Batten, Barton, Durston, and Osborn, writing Crawford slips became a tool to unlock people's creativity.

---

[*] I personally saw 14 linear feet of bookshelf space in Crawford's office taken up with books he'd written this way over the course of his nearly 70-year career.

215

- Write the *long* way
- Crowd the *top edge* (don't write in the middle)
- Write in *complete* sentences, but make them *short* and *simple*
- Write *legibly*
- Write *only one* thought or sentence per slip
- If you need to write more than one sentence to express your idea, write additional sentences on *separate slips*
- Don't use the pronouns "it" or "this," or their variations
- Don't use *acronyms* unless you've spelled out the term first

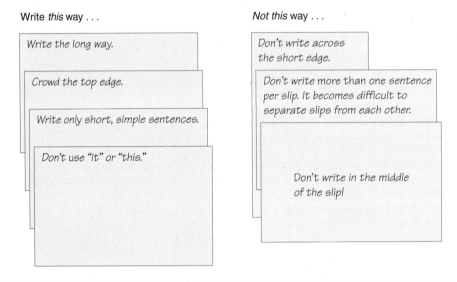

Write *this* way . . .

Not *this* way . . .

Write the long way.

Crowd the top edge.

Write only short, simple sentences.

Don't use "it" or "this."

Don't write across the short edge.

Don't write more than one sentence per slip. It becomes difficult to separate slips from each other.

Don't write in the middle of the slip!

Figure A.1 Directions for writing Crawford slips.

Crawford envisioned it as a way of capturing the knowledge of people who *know*—those closest to the problem or issue at hand. Yet the Crawford slip method offered significant benefits that brainstorming didn't.

- *Focus.* Because Crawford carefully constructed focused questions, or "targets," to direct people's creative energies, digressions, extraneous data, and "fishing expeditions" were virtually eliminated.

- *Speed.* Brainstorming, by its verbal nature, is sequential, meaning that only one person can express an idea at a time. Writing Crawford slips is like parallel processing—everyone writes simultaneously and silently. Ideas come out at a much greater speed from a group.

- *Volume.* There are practical limits to the size of a brainstorming group, and this number is usually no more than six to 10. The size of a Crawford slip session is limited only by logistics: how many people can you fit into a room?*

---

* I personally conducted a Crawford slip session for more than 600 people in a single room, collecting in excess of 1,800 improvement ideas on a focused topic in less than 15 minutes.

- *Level playing field.* The success of brainstorming depends on the group dynamic. Strong, assertive personalities can overwhelm more passive members. Ideas may be "ramrodded" by forceful people, motivating others to just keep quiet and not share ideas. Crawford slip writing "levels the playing field." Since ideas are not discussed as they are written, no idea gets preferential consideration because of the personality who offered it. Ideas can be more objectively evaluated on their own merit.

- *Anonymity.* Because Crawford slips aren't signed or otherwise distinguished by who wrote them, nobody knows who wrote each idea. This anonymity encourages frankness that might otherwise be stifled in an open group discussion.

- *Data capture.* Unlike brainstorming, the speed of the recorder or note-taker doesn't constrain the productivity of the Crawford slip method. Data are captured immediately, by the very act of writing slips, by each participant and as fast as ideas can be written down.

- *Easy sorting.* Crawford slips are easily sorted, since each idea is written on a separate slip. Similar ideas can be grouped by content topic.

APPLICATION: DOUGLAS AIRCRAFT, 1944

Crawford spent his university break during the summer of 1944 contributing to the war effort as an "expediter" at the Douglas Aircraft plant in Long Beach, California. At the time, the plant, producing B-26 bombers for the Army Air Corps, was hopelessly backlogged with work, more than four months behind the planned delivery schedule, even though it operated three shifts a day, seven days a week.

Crawford persuaded production managers to allow him to enlist the creativity of the workforce in resolving the production delays. Crawford brought the entire first shift of employees, no more than half a dozen at a time, into a small meeting room for 15 minutes per group. He posed the questions, "Why are we behind schedule, and how do we fix it?" Each group wrote as many ideas as they could on slips in the few minutes they were spared from their production work. By the end of the first shift, every worker on the plant floor and all supervisors, right up through plant management, had written slips. And there were thousands of slips.

On the second shift, Crawford rotated in production supervisors and managers for an hour or so in groups of five or six. Under his direction, they sorted and classified all the thousands of slips by function. Then they sorted each of these classification categories.

On the third shift, Crawford directed a single team of production managers and supervisors in writing new production procedures and policies, based on the data sorted by the second shift. By 7:00 AM the next morning, the whole production process had been modified on paper.

When the first shift reported back for work that morning, they were briefly instructed in the new procedures, which were based on the slips they themselves had written the day before. They set about instituting the new procedures on their shift. By the time the second shift reported for work, the entire production process had been transformed—a mere 32 hours after the first steps were taken to identify the problems. By the time the summer was over and Crawford headed back to his "day job" at the university, the production backlog was gone, and the rate had actually increased.

THE CRAWFORD SLIP METHOD AND THE LOGICAL THINKING PROCESS

The Crawford slip method naturally "fits" with the logical *thinking process* created by Goldratt. The thinking process is a logical tool designed to structure the answers to the three central questions any manager faces:

- What to change?

- What to change to?

- How to cause the change?

In some respects, the thinking process can be likened to a radar-controlled air defense system. It's an instrument that identifies a system's major problem and focuses attention on it through visible indicators. Then it aims the appropriate countermeasures at the problem and "pulls the trigger." But like any effective weapon system, the thinking process has to have *something* to shoot. A gun without bullets isn't very useful.

In the case of the thinking process, the "bullets" are the collective knowledge of people involved in the system—knowledge about how the system works (or doesn't work), and what the problems are. So, much as an effective air defense system has missiles to shoot, the thinking process needs knowledge—otherwise it might as well be shooting blanks. The Crawford slip method can provide the "ammunition" for the thinking process to fire.

Think back to the Douglas Aircraft example. What did Crawford do, except ask the plant workers the same three questions the thinking process asks: *What* to change, what to change *to,* and *how to cause* the change to happen? In this appendix, I'll show you how to use the Crawford slip method to gather the bullets to fire with the thinking process.

A FIVE-STEP PROCESS

Using the Crawford slip method to energize creativity is a five-step process. A very stratified form is presented here, designed for the express purpose of collecting people's expertise, intuition, knowledge, and creativity to provide the building blocks, or content, of strategic logic trees, which are the core of this book. These five steps, in sequence, are:

1. *Create the "target" questions.* You don't need to do that in this application of the Crawford slip method. I've provided a complete set of targets in the pages that follow. Each target is designed to elicit the ideas that will comprise the content of a different tree.

2. *Motivate the audience.* You *do* have to do this. The people you convene to write their ideas on slips need to have some idea of what you're trying to achieve, and why their inputs are so important. They also need to know *how* you expect them to write their ideas down. A typical "motivational orientation" is also provided here in bullet form. Feel free to modify it to suit your unique needs, but *keep it short.* The less time spent on talk and the more on writing, the better. Note that a significant part of the orientation includes specific directions on how the slips are to be written. Be a "bulldog" about insisting on adherence to the format, or you'll pay a price in lost time (and frustration) during the sorting process.

3. *Write the slips.* A section below provides directions on how the facilitator should conduct the slip-writing session. Slip writers don't need to see this page.

4. *Sorting and classifying.* Several of the targets are constructed so that slips will "coalesce" into clusters for easier conversion into logic trees. Other targets will produce functional groupings alone. Sorting and classifying is an intuitive exercise, but I've provided some general guidance in a section entitled "Sorting and Classifying Slips," below.

5. *Conversion of slips into logic trees.* Refer to the section entitled "Converting Sorted Slips into Logic Trees" for guidance on structuring the clusters formed in the sorting-and-classifying stage into a completed tree.

1. CRAWFORD SLIP TARGET QUESTIONS FOR STRATEGY DEVELOPMENT

To construct an effective Strategic Intermediate Objectives (IO) Map, have your audience write for five minutes on Target A and 10 minutes each on Targets B and C. Put each of your target questions on separate pages, so that your can show only one target at a time. The slips written and sorted on these targets will be uses to construct the S-IO Map.

Target A: The Goal of the Organization: What is our purpose for being in business?

- Think about the reasons your organization exists.

- What is the *one* overriding *goal* of your organization?

- What do *you* think the goal is?

- What do you think the *owner's* goal is?

- Write the goal in a short, simple sentence.

- Write it as many different ways as you can think of, each way on a *separate slip.*

- *One short, simple* sentence per slip.

- Write across the *long* dimension, crowd the *top edge* (use more than one line, if necessary).

Target B: The Organization's Critical Success Factors: What necessary conditions must be satisfied to achieve the goal?

- Think about the things that must be done to achieve the organization's goal.

- What is absolutely indispensable to achieving it?

- Name the three to five nonnegotiable conditions that must be satisfied to realize the organization's goal.

- Think "high level" as well as "nuts and bolts."

- Think *external* (market, competitive environment) as well as *internal.*

- Write these necessary conditions in short, simple sentences.

- Write them as many different ways as you can think of, each way on a *separate slip.*

- *One short, simple* sentence per slip.

- Write across the *long* dimension, crowd the *top edge* (use more than one line, if necessary).

Target C: The Organization's Values: What principles are important in conducting business?

- Think about the things that must be done to achieve the organization's goal and necessary conditions.

- What are the "rules of engagement?"

- What important principles or *"rules of the road"* should be followed in pursuing the goal and necessary conditions?

- Write these principles *(values)* in short, simple sentences.

- Write them as many different ways as you can think of, each way on a *separate slip.*

- *One short, simple* sentence per slip.

- Write across the *long* dimension, crowd the *top edge* (use more than one line, if necessary).

Once the Strategic Intermediate Objectives Map is constructed, you're ready to begin identifying the size and scope of the gap between where your organization is (current reality) and where you want it to be (the S-IO Map). Use Target D, below, to develop the building blocks for a Strategic Current Reality Tree.

Target D: The Organization's Current Reality: The deviation between what *is* and what *should be*

- Consider the IO Map we built earlier.
- Now think about the "real company world," as you know it.
- Why are the two *not* the same?
- Where do the differences lie?
- What is the nature of the deviation between the IO Map and existing reality?
- What are the *indications* that the company is *not* achieving the IO Map objectives?
- In what ways is the system less than perfect?
- How is the organization not achieving the objectives in the IO Map?
- Why are these deviations *bad* for the system?
- What failures to achieve the necessary conditions/critical success factors do they cause?
- Why do these deviations exist?
- What causes the deviations?
- Write as many ideas as you can on Post-It notes.
- *Short, simple, complete* sentences.
- *One* sentence per Post-It note.
- Write *separate notes* for more than one sentence.
- Don't use impersonal pronouns ("it" or "this").
- Write across the *long* dimension, crowd the *top* (non-sticky) *edge* (use more than one line, if necessary).

The product of the S-CRT is a set of clearly identified root causes of the aforementioned gap. These are the policies, issues, situations, or factors that must be changed if the gap between the S-CRT and the S-IO Map is to be eliminated. Often, however, there are persuasive reasons to leave the existing situation alone—in other words, not to change it. This kind of "push back," whether personal or organizational in nature, is an indication of conflict, either overt or hidden. In order to address and resolve such conflict effectively, it must first be laid out in the open for everyone to see, along with the assumptions underlying each side of it. The Strategic Evaporating Cloud (S-EC) must be constructed by someone who knows how to do it before the Crawford slip can be used. Once this is done, use Targets E and F below to identify all the assumptions underlying each side of the conflict.

Target E: Conflict Resolution: Identifying underlying assumptions behind the *status quo*

- Consider each of the root causes identified in the Strategic CRT.
- All policies or practices were put in place originally for some valid reason.
- Identify the ones that seem to serve some useful purpose.
- What are the compelling reasons to leave them alone (that is, not change)?
- Write on Post-It notes as many reasons as you can for leaving root causes alone.
- Write one reason per slip.
- Annotate each slip with the root cause to which it applies (for example, "P1," "P3," "P5," and so on).
- Short, simple, complete sentences.
- One sentence per Post-It note.
- Write separate notes for more than one sentence.
- Don't use impersonal pronouns ("it" or "this").
- Write across the *long* dimension, crowd the *top edge* (non-sticky), use more than one line only if necessary.

Target F: Conflict Resolution: Identifying underlying assumptions behind the *change*

- Consider each of the *changes* you're motivated to make to eliminate each root cause.
- All changes have reasons behind them.
- What are the compelling reasons for changing existing policies or ways of doing things?
- Write on Post-It notes as many reasons as you can for changing root causes.
- Also write all the reasons you can think of to make the specific change you believe should be done.
- Write one reason per slip.

- Annotate each slip with the change to which it applies (for example, "P2," "P4," "P6," and so on).

- Short, simple, complete sentences.

- One sentence per Post-It note.

- Write separate notes for more than one sentence.

- Don't use impersonal pronouns ("it" or "this").

- Write across the *long* dimension, crowd the *top edge* (non-sticky), use more than one line only if necessary.

Execution of an injection (policy change or new initiative) requires identifying and eliminating obstacles first. The following Crawford slip target is designed to elicit the obstacles that stand in the way of successful change. Ask your "brain trust" to identify the obstacles using Target G.

Target G: Implementation Obstacles: What keeps us from executing our injections?

- Think, in turn, about each of the injections needed to make the Strategic FRT unfold.

- Many injections have obstacles to their execution.

- Many have several supporting actions that must take place first.

- List all the obstacles you can think of for each injection.

- What stands in the way of putting them into effect?

- Write each obstacle on a Post-It note.

- Write the number of the injection it obstructs in the upper right corner.

- Write *short, simple, complete* sentences.

- One sentence per Post-It note.

- Write separate notes for more than one sentence.

- Don't use impersonal pronouns ("it" or "this").

- Write across the *long* dimension, crowd the *top* (non-sticky) edge (use more than one line, if necessary).

Obstacles to implementing policy changes or new initiatives must be overcome if change is to succeed. Intermediate Objectives (IO) are the discrete actions taken to overcome obstacles. You might call these solutions to the implementation problems. Use Target H to stimulate people's creativity on how to overcome obstacles.

Target H. Intermediate Objectives (IO): How to overcome obstacles

- Consider each obstacle identified for each injection in turn.
- Obstacles are overcome by intermediate objectives.
- Each IO is a way to overcome an obstacle.
- What ways can you think of to overcome each obstacle?
- If you were "king for a day," how would you deal with each obstacle?
- "Bypass" the obstacles, don't necessarily "obliterate."
- Some obstacles might require more than one IO.
- Some IOs might overcome more than one obstacle.
- Write as many ideas (IOs) as you can for each obstacle on Post-It notes.
- Stick the related IOs onto the obstacle they are intended to overcome.
- Write *short, simple, complete* sentences.
- One sentence per Post-It note.
- Write separate notes for more than one sentence.
- Don't use impersonal pronouns ("it" or "this").
- Write across the *long* dimension, crowd the *top* (non-sticky) edge (use more than one line, if necessary).

Overcoming obstacles is only part of implementation. There are key tasks that must be accomplished for which there are no particular obstacles. Target-I is designed to help elicit those tasks from those who have the expertise to advise on implementation.

Target I. Ensuring Completeness: How to avoid missing something critical

- Overcoming obstacles alone is not enough.
- Some critical implementation tasks have no obstacles.
- But they must not be overlooked, nonetheless.
- Consider the injections you're trying to execute.
- Besides the IOs to overcome obstacles, what *other* critical tasks must be completed to ensure success?
- What are the necessary actions or activities without which implementation will fail?

- Think of as many *key tasks* as you can.

- Write them on Post-It notes.

- Write *short, simple, complete* sentences.

- One sentence per Post-It note.

- Write separate notes for more than one sentence.

- Don't use impersonal pronouns ("it" or "this").

- Write across the *long* dimension, crowd the *top* (non-sticky) edge (use more than one line, if necessary).

Once you have all the intermediate objectives needed to overcome obstacles to each injection and all the key tasks for each injection that have no associated obstacles, fold them together in the sequence they must occur to complete a Prerequisite Tree. You should have a different Prerequisite Tree for each injection complex enough to require one.

2. MOTIVATING THE AUDIENCE

Begin the Crawford slip writing session with a brief (one to two minute) motivational orientation. You can brief your slip writers from the outline provided below, or you can create your own. If you create your own, be sure that it covers the following topics (in no more than a sentence or two):

- Overview/objective

- Why you were selected

- What we want you to do

- How your inputs will be used

- Directions for writing slips (show example)

Here's an example of a motivational orientation for your audience:

Developing Company Strategy

Why we're soliciting your help:

- We need your help to make [organization] more successful.

- The ways to overcome the challenges [organization] faces in the next five years are "locked up" in your brain.

- Help us liberate those answers.

- Nobody understands [organization], its competitive environment, its capabilities, and its deficiencies as completely as you do.

- Help us to paint a complete, accurate picture of what [organization] current situation is, and what should be done about it.

- To collect this information from you, we'll ask you to write ideas on slips of paper (Post-It notes) in response to specifically focused target questions.

- Treat these questions as *open-ended;* in other words, *no one-word* answers.

- There may be more than one way to solve a particular problem—tell us *all* of the ways.

- Your answers to these questions will be *anonymous*—no names will be associated with them—so feel free to say exactly what you think.

- Be as thorough as you can.

- Write your ideas in more than one way, if you think it will help.

- Please follow some simple directions for writing your slips (refer to Figure A.1; show this to the audience).

3. WRITING THE SLIPS (LOGISTICS)

Facilities. What do you need to conduct a Crawford slip session? First, you need a room big enough to hold the participants. For strategy-building, that should probably not exceed 10 to 12 people, and maybe fewer. The number of participants is up to you. Just remember: "garbage in, garbage out." Not just anybody who might want to participate, or who might be available to participate, has the real insight needed to provide useful input. For your slip writers, you should enlist people who really *know* what's going on in the organization or its external environment, otherwise all you'll get is speculation, not ideas of value.

Make sure every participant has a comfortable chair to sit in, with adequate lighting and table space to lay slips out overlapped after they write them. You'll need enough slips to write on so that you don't run out. Crawford used standard bond paper, cut into eight identical parts. For building strategy trees, however, you'll probably find 3 × 5 inch Post-It notes[*] more effective. Each slip writer should have his or her own pad of Post-It notes. Make sure participants have bold felt-tip pens to write with. You'll want them to be able to read these slips when they're posted on walls six to 10 feet away.

The ideal place to post completed slips is on a wall-mounted or large free-standing whiteboard. Have a set of dry-erase marking pens and an eraser available to draw logical arrows and sufficiency ellipses to connect the Post-It note slips.

With a conference table and chairs, the wall or whiteboard, Post-It notes, CSM targeting notes, and bold felt-tipped pens, you're ready to start.

---

[*] Post-It notes are a trademark of the 3M Corporation.

Time. How long should you allow for writing slips? Normally, 10 minutes per target. You can expect an average of about one idea per minute from each person. You should be able to cover all the targets related to the Strategic IO Map in about 30 minutes or less. The same is true of the conflict assumptions and the obstacles and intermediate objectives for the Prerequisite Tree. Writing the slips for the Strategic Current Reality Tree, however, should take considerably less time, since there's only one target.

Distributing materials. Display each target individually on a screen (use an overhead or digital projector). Also hand out individual sheets of paper with the targets printed on them, one per page. Don't let the audience see any targets except the one they will be working on next. Collect any target sheets you distribute before you distribute subsequent ones, so they never see more than one at a time.

What to say (and not say) when giving instructions. Don't prejudice your audience's thinking by giving too many instructions on what to write. Read the motivational orientation verbatim. Show the illustration (Figure A.1) on how slips should (and should not) be written. Read the targets verbatim, but don't add any amplifying remarks. Then say, "Go!" and start timing. Give them a one-minute warning to wrap up their last slip, and call "Stop writing" when time expires.

What to do while they're writing slips. While the audience is writing, walk around the table or room and glance over their shoulders. Make sure they're following the slip-writing instructions. If you find someone who isn't (for example, incomplete sentences, more than one sentence per slip, illegible writing, and so on), stop the audience from writing, hold up the offending slip, and remind them of the format. (You shouldn't have to do this more than once, and if you do a good job briefing the audience to begin with, perhaps not at all.)

What to do with the slips when time expires. After you call for the audience to stop writing on a particular target, tell them to overlay their slips on one another like shingles, so that a column of individual sentences can be read without having to shuffle slips. (It's particularly annoying to have to rearrange slips when you're using Post-It® notes, which stick together.)

Collect the slips after writing on each target is completed, sort them according to the guidance provided below.

4. SORTING AND CLASSIFYING SLIPS

Once your "brain trust" has written slips on a particular Crawford slip target, you're ready to start sorting. Try having the slip writers do this for you. Divide the group into pairs. If you have an odd number, put three in one group. Then divide the pile of slips approximately equally among the groups, and give them the following instructions:

- Spread the slips out on the table in front of you, so that each slip is individually readable.

- Read each slip silently, and decide whether there are duplicate statements (slips that say essentially the same thing). Stack these on top of one another.

- Consolidate the content of duplicate slips and write a new slip that captures the meaning of all similar slips in a single statement. After this step, you should have fewer slips, each one conveying a different idea.

- Look for slips that seem to be related to one another. (This is an intuitive judgment.) Separate these related slips from the rest and arrange them so that the one that seems to precede is below the one that seems to follow. Use the sticky part of the Post-It notes to affix them to their related slips. These related slips represent layers of cause and effect in the logic tree that will follow.

- Transfer the cluster of related slips intact to the wall or whiteboard. These clusters will form the branches of the logic tree you'll construct and verify using the categories of legitimate reservation.*

5. CONVERTING SORTED SLIPS INTO LOGIC TREES

The slips that people write to define the goal and necessary conditions (Crawford slip Targets A, B, and C) become the content of the Strategic Intermediate Objectives Map (S-IO Map). Chapter 5 provides guidance on how to construct an S-IO Map. Just put it together like a jigsaw puzzle, using the Crawford slips as the content. Refine the logical connections using the categories of legitimate reservation.

Other chapters provide similar guidance for the other logic trees (chapter 7: Strategic Current Reality Tree; chapter 8: Strategic Evaporating Clouds; chapter 10: Future Reality Tree; chapter 11 Prerequisite Trees).[1]**

ENDNOTES

1. For more on the Crawford slip method, see: H. W. Dettmer, *Brainpower Networking with the Crawford Slip Method* (Victoria, British Columbia: Trafford, 2003, www.trafford.com).

---

* Refer to Dettmer (1997 or 1998), or Scheinkopf (1999) for a complete description of the categories of legitimate reservation and how to use them to prepare sound logic trees.

** Dettmer (1997 and 1998) and Scheinkopf (1999) provide detailed instructions on constructing Current Reality Trees.

Appendix B

U.S. Transportation Command

BACKGROUND

The U.S. Transportation Command is a unified command, with global responsibility, composed of major individual service commands (Army, Navy, and Air Force). It was an outcome of the Goldwater-Nichols Act of 1987, which prompted the first major reorganization of the Department of Defense in 40 years.

The Goldwater-Nichols Act of 1987 created the U.S. Transportation Command (USTRANSCOM) as a "paper command." This means it was to be a joint service headquarters that had no operational forces assigned to it in peacetime. However, in wartime, operational command of all the transportation assets in the Department of Defense—Army, Navy, and Air Force—would be consolidated under this headquarters.

Three organizations comprise the military transportation infrastructure:

- Military Traffic Management Command (MTMC), an Army organization headquartered near Washington, D.C., and responsible for all surface (ground) transportation for deploying military forces.

- Military Sealift Command (MSC), a Navy organization also headquartered near Washington, D.C., and responsible for all military cargo shipping and naval ports.

- Air Mobility Command (AMC), an Air Force organization headquartered in Illinois responsible for all military cargo planes and military aerial ports.

Since none of these commands alone has enough ground, sea, or air transportation vehicles to do the whole deployment job in wartime, each of them also manages the contracting of commercial ground, sea, and air carriers in supporting the Department of Defense mission.

So in peacetime, MTMC, MSC, and AMC all function largely independently, as they traditionally have. And in peacetime, USTRANSCOM has no real authority over Department of Defense transportation assets. Its function is limited to unified transportation planning for times of war.

But in times of national emergency or war, MTMC, MSC, and AMC all cede their control to the commander-in-chief (CinC) of USTRANSCOM. To avoid unnecessary duplication of staff and effort, the Air Force's AMC commander also serves as CinCTRANSCOM, and the USTRANSCOM staff is populated by members of each of the individual services' component transportation staffs. The headquarters for USTRANSCOM was also collocated with USAF AMC headquarters at Scott AFB, Illinois.

Organizations such as USTRANSCOM—those with real authority only in time of war—experience a significant problem with the dual authority arrangement: they don't practice in peacetime working as a unified whole, the way they would be expected to work in wartime. Yet they're expected to "get it right the first time" when a war actually breaks out.

DESERT SHIELD/DESERT STORM

Desert Shield, the operational deployment of forces in defense of Saudi Arabia in 1990, and Desert Storm, the subsequent combat offensive to liberate Kuwait from Iraqi occupation in 1991, exposed some problems with the peacetime–wartime dichotomy in managing military transportation.

Ultimately, these large-scale operations succeeded, but much of that success came in spite of military transportation "glitches," not because of sterling performance by the new unified command. The transportation system moved millions of tons of military equipment and supplies from North America and Europe to Saudi Arabia and the Indian Ocean in record time. But much of it ended up in ports or storage areas in containers without anyone knowing what was inside them or where key pieces of equipment or supplies were.

The reason that this disorganization didn't deteriorate into a complete debacle was that the enemy—the Iraqi military in Kuwait—was considerate enough to sit passively by and just watch the allied coalition take a "leisurely" five months to bring its forces and equipment into the combat theater and get them ready for "the party."*

LESSONS LEARNED

In the postwar analysis, CinCTRANSCOM realized that there were probably better ways to operate the military transportation system in the future. In other words, if they

---

* There was a time, shortly after Iraq occupied Kuwait in August 1990, when Iraqi forces could have continued rolling into—and over—Saudi Arabia, and there would have been little or nothing the United States could have done to stop them.

could have done it over, there were many things they would have done differently. Moreover, it was unlikely that future wars would offer an enemy so accommodating as to sit still for months while the United States moved the bulk of its war fighting capability into place. Neither was it certain that a good transportation infrastructure—seaports, airfields, and roads—would be available in the next engagement, as it was in Saudi Arabia.[*]

In summary, a lot of good fortune smiled on the coalition forces logistically in the Persian Gulf War. There was no assurance that this would be so in the future. USTRANSCOM's challenge was to find the best way to manage the equivalent of a company operating throughout the world with $5.6 billion in assets spread across the entire continental United States.

CinCTRANSCOM'S CHARTER

In July 1992, General Ronald C. Fogleman, USAF (CinCTRANSCOM), formed a special initiative team to address the challenges in supporting future combat operations anywhere in the world. Three people made up this team: Lieutenant Colonel Randal Fullhart, USAF; Commander Kevin Quinn, USN; and a U.S. Army officer from the MTMC.[1]

General Fogleman charged this team, composed of just three people, with creating a "blueprint" for the entire defense transportation system over the next 18 years. In other words, what should the defense transportation system look like in the year 2010, and how should this $5.6 billion company be reengineered to accomplish that vision?

A major influence on what this blueprint would look like was the so-called "peace dividend." With the collapse of the Soviet Union and communism throughout most of the world, the chief reason for the United States to maintain a huge defense establishment seemed to be evaporating. Significant political pressure led to the downsizing of U.S. military forces. Most of the forces maintained in Europe to deter Soviet "adventurism" were recalled to the United States and either deactivated or reassigned to the reserves. Bases were closed, numbers of active duty personnel were reduced, and military equipment was disposed of or mothballed.

But in concept, the mission remained the same: transport forces to respond militarily on short notice anywhere in the world—and "do it right the first time." Only now the military transporters had fewer assets and people available to do the job, and fewer forward operating bases overseas to work from. So in addition to supporting the same mission, USTRANSCOM was faced with doing so with fewer resources.[**] In other words, maintain the same level of effectiveness with greater efficiency. And without the forward-deployed bases of the cold war era, most of the responding forces would have

---

[*] As luck would have it, this proved to be the case in Afghanistan in 2001.

[**] There's a saying in the military that "we've been doing so much with so little for so long, that pretty soon we'll be able to do everything with nothing!"

to be transported from the distant end of a long transportation chain, making success all the more dependent on effective, efficient military transportation management.

WHERE TO START?

To begin this overwhelming task, the initiatives team had to learn more about how the components of the military transportation system did their jobs.[*]

For several months, they interviewed transporters from each of the military services—the people who actually did the work of moving things. In the process of finding out how the job was done, they also "got an earful" about what wasn't working well inside and between transportation components.

Lt. Col. Fullhart and Commander Quinn returned to headquarters with reams of information about the military transportation structure, including about 170 serious indications that things weren't going as well as they should.[**] As they sat in Illinois looking at this pile of problems, they tried to figure out how to organize it. Another headquarters staff officer, Captain Mark Fowler, USAF, provided the answer.

Captain Fowler was knowledgeable in the logical thinking process created by Goldratt. In a relatively short time, he helped the initiatives team structure the information gathered during its research into a Current Reality Tree.[‡†] At the bottom of the tree was a relatively small number of critical root causes that needed changing to eliminate the undesirable effects.

At this point, the initiatives team made an important decision. Before proceeding any further, they decided to show their Current Reality Tree to General Fogleman. Normally in the military this isn't done. Staff officers are trained "from infancy" not to take problems to the commander. Instead, they're instructed to present the problem, followed immediately by a recommended course of action. But this situation was different. The scope of the problems was so immense and diverse that they didn't have any idea how to attack them. And they were concerned about trying to develop solutions before the CinC had completely "bought into" the statement of the problem. So they scheduled an informal meeting with the CinC and presented the Current Reality Tree. Afterward, they were glad they did. Because the general concurred with their definition of the problem, they were able to proceed to develop solutions for the critical root causes, confident in the knowledge that, from the CinC's perspective, they were solving

---

[*] One of the drawbacks in building a systemwide strategic plan for an organization as complex as USTRANSCOM is that few people, if any, have a complete appreciation for "the big picture." And a system perspective is absolutely essential for effective strategy development.

[**] Based on what we know now, we'd refer to these indicators as *undesirable effects*—UDEs. But at the time, Lt. Col. Fullhart and Commander Quinn weren't familiar with that term.

[‡] As nearly as I can determine, this was the first Current Reality Tree that might be considered truly strategic (S-CRT).

[†] Regretfully, the logic trees constructed by Lt. Col. Fullhart and Commander Quinn are not available for publication, or I would have provided examples of them.

the right problem and not going down the wrong track. In other words, they were "doing it right the first time."

THE FUTURE REALITY TREE

The initiatives team quickly realized that solving most of these problems was well beyond their depth of knowledge and expertise. They needed the assistance of people who really knew how the system operated "where the rubber meets the road." In December 1993, the initiatives team convened a conference that they called "DTS-2010" (Defense Transportation System, 2010). They invited representatives from each of the units within MTMC, MSC, and AMC. These were many of the same people they had originally interviewed when they were gathering the inputs that became the Current Reality Tree.

The team began the conference by explaining their charter—to create a DTS-2010 strategic plan for the CinC—and soliciting the attendees' help in doing so. Then they presented the Current Reality Tree and solicited ideas on how to overcome the critical root causes. For most of the conference, they took notes rather than doing much of the talking themselves. They asked pertinent questions (the Socratic approach) and helped surface underlying conflicts for resolution, using Evaporating Clouds. By the conclusion of the conference, they had enough information to begin building a Strategic Future Reality Tree (S-FRT).

When the S-FRT was completed, they prepared to present it to the CinC. But as in any hierarchical organization, middle-level staff can't usually just march into the chief executive's office and start briefing. Before that could happen, the team had to coordinate their findings with all of the functional directors who reported directly to the CinC, and whose responsibilities were affected in the S-FRT. These functional directors were all brigadier and major generals, and the initiatives team had to review the S-FRT with many of them individually. In most cases, the functional directors supported their findings as presented. In at least one case, a director found a significant deficiency in their S-FRT, which they were able to correct before their final presentation to the CinC.

THE FINAL PRESENTATION

After the functional reviews of the S-FRT were completed, it was time to show the results to General Fogleman. The initiatives team made this presentation in the headquarters conference room, with the CinC, the deputy CinC, and all the brigadier and major generals in attendance.

At the conclusion of the presentation, the CinC said that the team had exceeded his most liberal expectations of what they would provide. He approved the plan embodied in the S-FRT, and he offered the opinion that most of the injections in it were within his span of control, meaning that there were few authority obstacles to implementation.

After the conclusion of the meeting, the CinC directed the initiatives team to deliver the same S-FRT presentation to the chairman of the Joint Chiefs of Staff. He also formed an execution team, composed of staff officers from the various functional areas, under the leadership of a senior civilian government service executive, to begin creating the Prerequisite Trees needed to implement the DTS-2010 plan. Captain Fowler assisted this team with the creation of those trees in mid-1994.

CONCLUSION

The USTRANSCOM application of the thinking process in developing its DTS-2010 plan is probably the first large-scale strategic application of what has become the constraint management model for strategy development. Since that time, other organizations have used essentially the same process, but the USTRANSCOM case remains the most prominent, high-level strategic example.

ENDNOTE

1. R. Fulhart and K. Quinn, "TOC Application: U.S. Transportation Command," videotape SJC-4 (Avram Y. Goldratt Institute, 1994).

Appendix C

Wurtzberg Corporation

BACKGROUND

The Wurtzberg Corporation is a small, family-owned metal stamping plant in the Midwest. Wurtzberg's annual revenues were $21 million last year. This was the third straight year that revenues had remained level. However, Wurtzberg's profits were going in the opposite direction. The first year they reported $2.2 million in profits on its revenues. In the second year, profits dropped to $1.2 million. By the third year, profits were down to $500,000.

Wurtzberg's general manager was in a quandary. It was no secret that costs were rising and the company had to do something to bring them under control. But what to attack first? Wurtzberg decided to apply the constraint management model to solve their problem. The problem analysis ended up pointing toward the need for a new strategy.

THE PROCESS

The company's "brain trust"* met for three days at an off-site location.

The problem analysis began with the development of a Strategic Intermediate Objectives (S-IO) map, followed by a Strategic Current Reality Tree (S-CRT) to establish the size and scope of the gap between where Wurtzberg was and where they wanted to be. Figure C.1 shows Wurtzberg's S-IO map.

---

* The general manager, production manager, sales manager, tool and die manager, chief financial officer, and personnel manager.

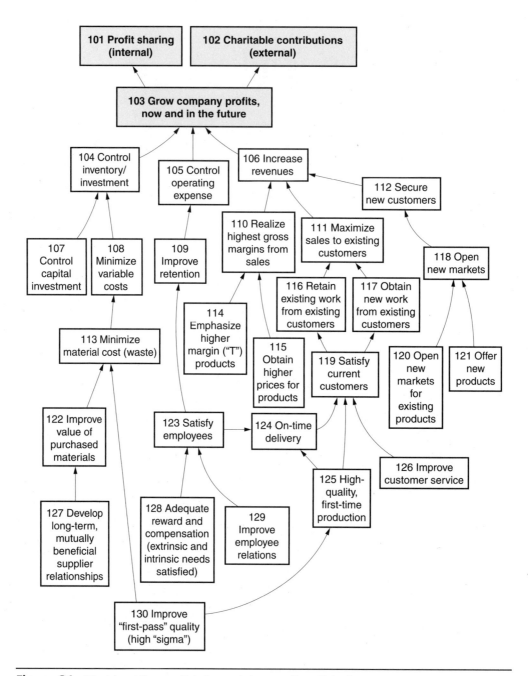

Figure C.1   Wurtzberg Corporation Strategic Intermediate Objectives.

The S-IO Map was completed in about three hours. Because the inputs came from the senior management team, and because they constructed the S-IO Map with guidance from the facilitator, there was complete agreement that it accurately reflected what the company should be striving for.

The group commenced constructing the S-CRT immediately. This consumed the rest of the first day and part of the morning of the second day. The critical success factors from the S-IO map provided the standards from which the undesirable effects were identified and the gap analysis was created. Figure C.2a through C.2e show a large part of Wurtzberg's S-CRT.

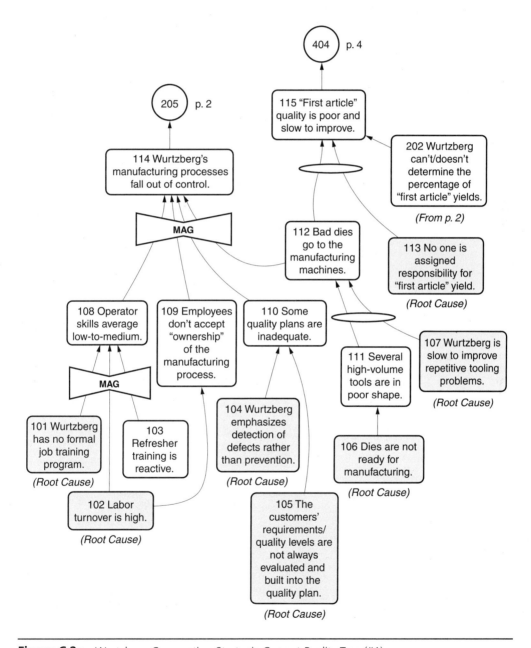

Figure C.2a Wurtzberg Corporation Strategic Current Reality Tree (#1).

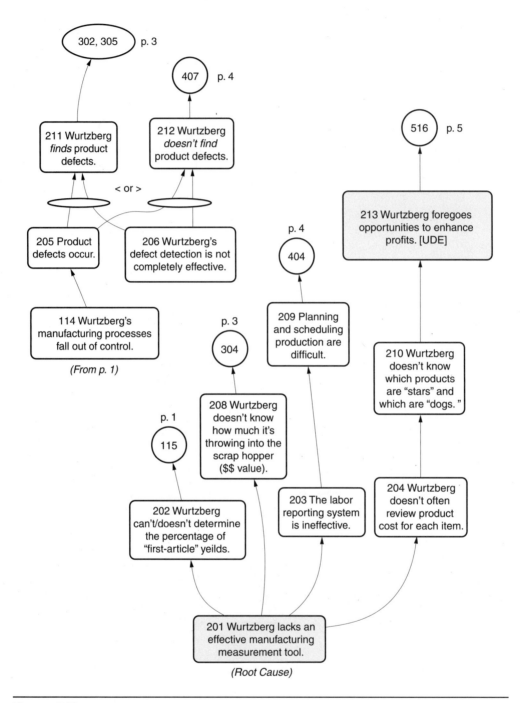

Figure C.2b Wurtzberg Corporation Strategic Current Reality Tree (#2).

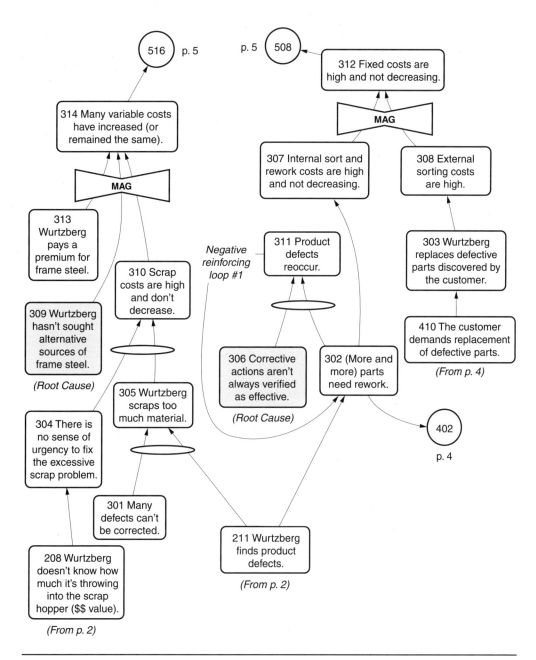

Figure C.2c Wurtzberg Corporation Strategic Current Reality Tree (#3).

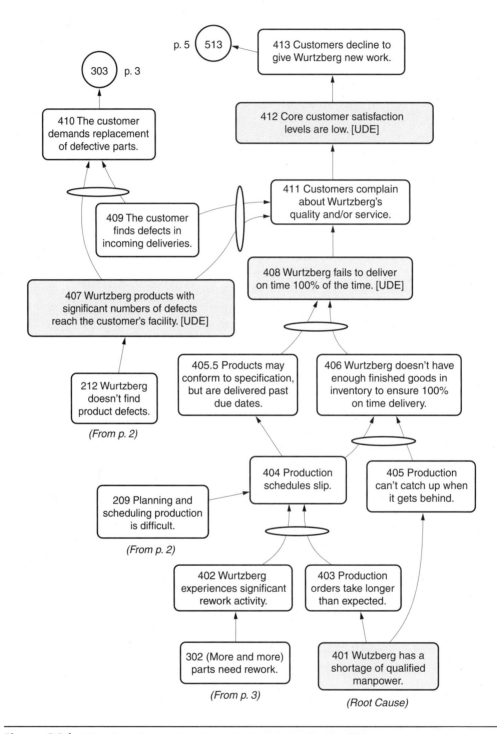

Figure C.2d Wurtzberg Corporation Strategic Current Reality Tree (#4).

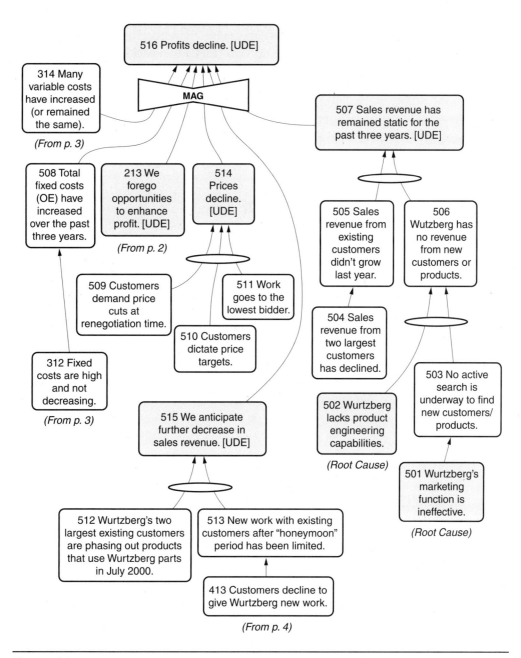

Figure C.2e Wurtzberg Corporation Strategic Current Reality Tree (#5).

As you read the S-CRT, bear in mind that the cause-and-effect depiction begins with root causes in Figure C.2a and progresses upward (logically speaking) to the undesirable effects in Figure C.2e. Normally, you begin reading each connection starting with Figure C.2a following the direction of the arrows through each successive page to Figure C.2e. However, before you begin doing so, I suggest that you first take a quick look at Figure C.2e. Read the undesirable effects. This is where the causality eventually leads. It's usually easier to read through the preceding four pages with patience when you have some idea where the journey is going to end.

THE NATURE OF THE GAP

On the face of it, this would appear to be just a routine thinking process problem-solving analysis. However, on closer examination of the S-CRT, a few key strategic factors should be apparent. Wurtzberg's technical capability is centered on an obsolescent, low-technology business: metal stamping. As original equipment manufacturers—Wurtzberg's primary customers—increasingly designed products with integrated circuits, miniaturization, molded plastic components, and more precise specifications, stamped metal parts became less and less satisfactory. Moreover, the creation of acceptable dies for stamping is a time-consuming process—six months or more from initial order until the dies are ready for manufacturing processes to begin. This effectively limits both the potential customer base and the types of products that Wurtzberg can produce.

Wurtzberg needed to rethink its entire line of business, with an eye toward eventually replacing its core competency (stamping) with new capabilities such as precision metal-cutting, machining, and forming.

OMISSIONS IN THE WURTZBERG EXAMPLE

For Wurtzburg, this was a paradigm shift of major proportions. This is a painful thing for the management of any traditional, family-owned business to contemplate. Normally, the prospect of changing root causes as elemental as the ones in Figure C.2 would produce resistance of some kind. Wurtzberg was no exception. Naturally, opinions were divided on what should be done—or not done. But the conflicts and their resolution are sensitive issues to the company. Consequently, the Strategic Evaporating Clouds, one major branch of the Strategic Future Reality Tree, and all but one Prerequisite Tree have been omitted in this appendix. The omissions directly concern product and market diversification issues, and the capacities and capabilities required to support them, for the same reason. Figure C.3f of the S-FRT indicates where the omitted branches connect to the larger tree.

However, while Wurtzberg contemplated the reinvention of their business (certainly a major strategic effort), they needed to "keep the store operating for business." This meant fixing problems with their existing operations while they laid the foundation for the future. So, what *is* reflected in these trees is the part of Wurtzberg's strategy that doesn't address their new direction, but which was nevertheless necessary to sustain the company while they executed their new market strategy.

WURTZBERG'S NEW INTERNAL STRATEGY

While there was disagreement among Wurtzberg's managers on the external (market) strategy, there was none on repairing the internal operations problems. The executive management team, guided by the facilitator, created injections to remedy each of the internal operational problems. A summary of these injections—less the sensitive ones— can be found in Table C.1.

Over the rest of the second day and the first two hours of the third day, the executive team created the Strategic Future Reality Tree (S-FRT) shown in Figure C.3. The rest of the morning and the afternoon of the third day was devoted to constructing Prerequisite Trees for all the injections that required them. In the interest of brevity, only one Prerequisite Tree (Figure C.4) is provided for illustration.

Table C.1 Summary of injections—Wurtzberg Corporation.

INJECTIONS

No.	Page	Injection	PRT Required?
1.	1	Labor turnover is no longer a problem.	Yes
2.	1	A formal training program is established.	Yes
3.	1	Customer requirements are converted to and incorporated into an engineering/quality plan (new jobs).	Yes
4.	1	Operators accept responsibility for their own quality control.	Yes
5.	1	Customers' requirements are clearly identified, verified, and confirmed (new jobs).	Yes
6.	1	Final inspection is eliminated.	No
7.	2	Dies are ready for production on time.	Yes
8.	2	Engineering accepts responsibility for "first article" yield.	Yes
9.	2	Quality determines who is responsible for process corrective action.	Yes
10.	2	Quality verifies that process corrective action is effective.	Yes
11.	3	Wurtzberg has an effective manufacturing measurement system.	Yes
12.	3	Wurtzberg fills manpower gaps/shortages.	Yes
13.	4	Wurtzberg "buffers" its production schedule to allow for variation and uncertainty.	Yes
14.	4	Wurtzberg uses a "finite loading" algorithm to schedule its work centers.	Yes
15.	5	Wurtzberg acts on the knowledge about improvement opportunities.	Yes
16.	6	Wurtzberg has an effective marketing/sales program (high "hit" rate).	Yes
17.	6	Wurtzberg knows who the desirable customers are (industry segment).	No
18.	6	Wurtzberg chooses the best options for capital expansion "ΔT–ΔOE"	Yes

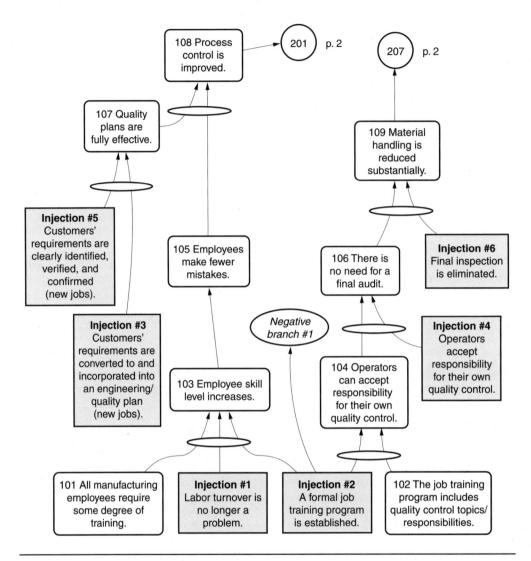

Figure C.3a   Wurtzberg Corporation Strategic Future Reality Tree (#1).

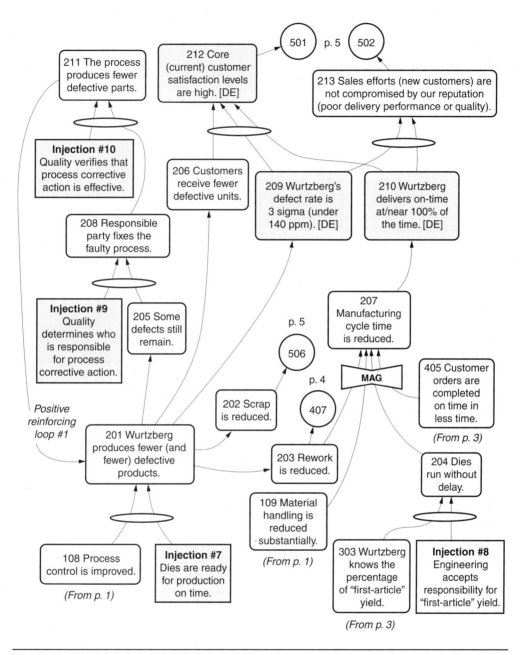

Figure C.3b Wurtzberg Corporation Strategic Future Reality Tree (#2).

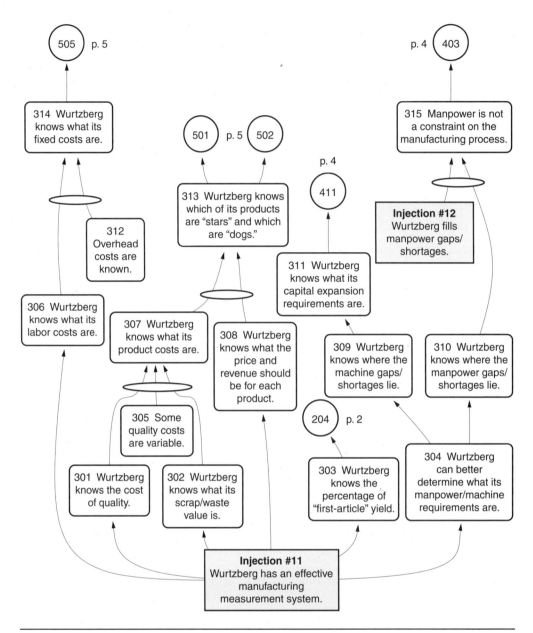

Figure C.3c   Wurtzberg Corporation Strategic Future Reality Tree (#3).

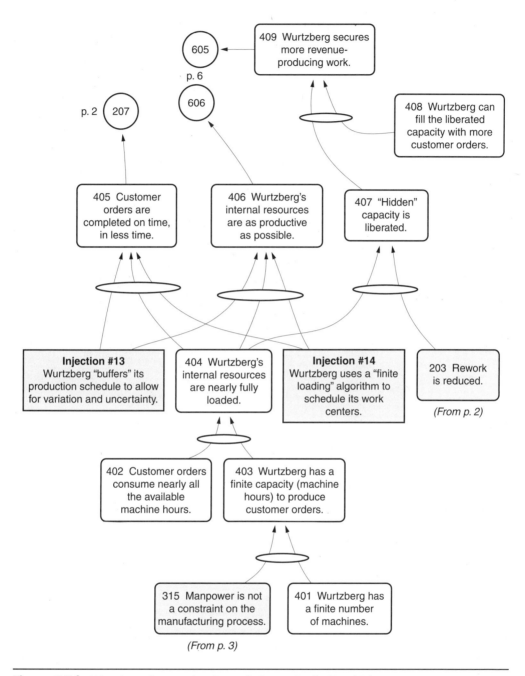

Figure C.3d Wurtzberg Corporation Strategic Future Reality Tree (#4).

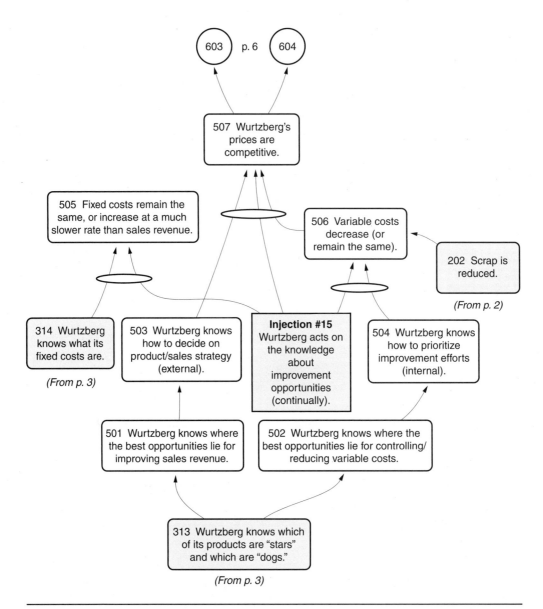

Figure C.3e Wurtzberg Corporation Strategic Future Reality Tree (#5).

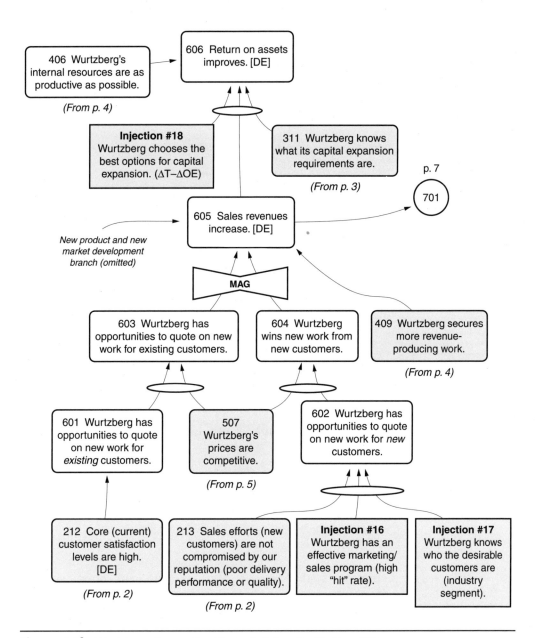

Figure C.3f Wurtzberg Corporation Strategic Future Reality Tree (#6).

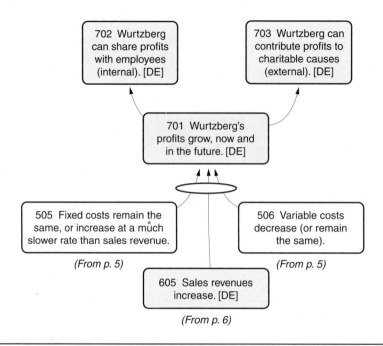

Figure C.3g Wurtzberg Corporation Strategic Future Reality Tree (#7).

SUMMARY AND CONCLUSION

Wurtzberg may not be a typical company,* but it's a useful example from a number of standpoints. It has both production operations and marketing and sales functions. The three often don't talk to one another. Problems from one inevitably have some impact on one or more of the others, and on the success of the company as a whole.

The picture these trees present is not the complete strategic picture, just the operations part. Which brings up two questions:

1. Is it possible to use the thinking process exclusively internally, in production operations for example, to solve problems?

2. Is a strategic analysis really complete without the whole picture?

The answer to the first is "yes," and the second is "no." As long as you acknowledge that you might be working on the most visible problems, but not necessarily the most important ones, you can use the thinking process to solve internal problems. Had Wurtzberg not addressed the marketing and sales problem (excluded from this example for competitive reasons), they would have risked winning the production battle but losing the war.

---

* Of course, no company will admit to being "typical." Everybody's different, you know. No matter how many similarities there might be between situations, the common refrain I always hear is, "Yeah, but we're different."

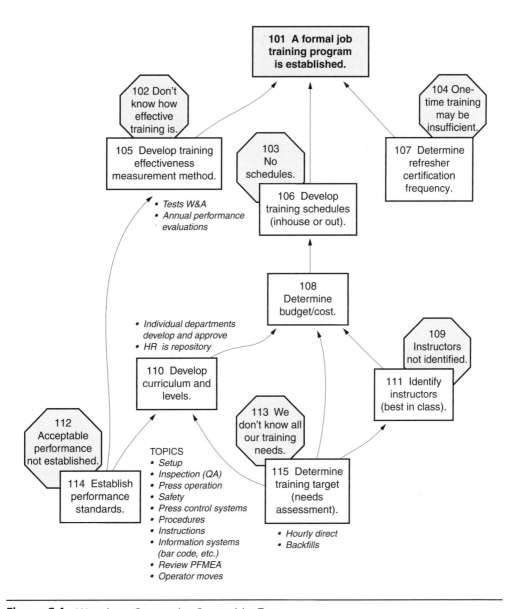

Figure C.4 Wurtzberg Corporation Prerequisite Tree.

Appendix D

Olympic AquaVentures

A START-UP COMPANY

In Appendix C, we saw how the constraint management model was applied to an existing company having a need to change its course. The constraint management model can be applied to start-up organizations, too, though there are some differences.

Remember that in an existing organization, we started with a Strategic Intermediate Objectives (S-IO) Map to define the ultimate destination, then we compared the existing situation to that S-IO Map to come up with the size and scope of the gap, which was reflected in the Strategic Current Reality Tree (S-CRT).

But there are two key differences between existing organizations and new ones. The most obvious is that in a start-up there is no real gap to analyze in an S-CRT. Consequently, a start-up organization won't have a S-CRT of its own. There *will* be an S-CRT, but it won't be the start-up organization's tree.

The second difference is that the start-up organizations—at least the ones with any potential to succeed—don't just spring from nowhere without some kind of motivation. In most cases, they're formed to fill a verifiable need. That need could be expressed as a root cause in a higher-level depiction of current reality. Let's call this the strategic current reality of the external environment. It's the presence of this tree that demonstrates an unfulfilled need, which the formation of the start-up organization is intended to satisfy.

So, in the case of a start-up organization, the logical place to begin is the S-CRT of the external environment, not the new organization's S-IO Map. The external S-CRT essentially says, "Here's an opportunity to fill a significant need." Those who would then propose to fill that need would create their start-up organization's S-IO Map. And that map would culminate at the top with a successful organization that embodies the external need satisfaction. Since that organization has no prior history from which to establish a gap analysis, no S-CRT is created for the start-up.

The net effect is that the sequence of trees looks a little different for a start-up organization. The first would be an S-CRT that really represents the current reality of the external environment. Second comes the proposed start-up organization's S-IO Map to address the external needs. Then come the Strategic Evaporating Clouds (S-EC), the Strategic Future Reality Tree (S-FRT), and finally the Prerequisite Trees for executing the S-FRT. Let's see an example of how this new sequence might look.

MARINE AQUACULTURE

We begin with the external environment. An oceanographer in the Pacific northwest of the United States was the technical director of a small family-owned shellfish-growing operation. In the process of keeping up with the state of the market environment in the industry, he observed a number of verifiable facts:

• Demand for seafood, especially finfish, was high throughout the world, and especially in Europe and Asia. In fact, demand had been increasing geometrically for the past 50 years, not coincidentally at a rate that closely parallels the increase in world population. In the latter half of the 20th century, the demand for seafood in the industrialized world, in particular, has increased as people have become more health-conscious and aware of the benefits of having more fish in their diets.

• The world's fisheries were either producing at maximum capacity or declining in production as they were fished out, or as restrictions on catches were levied. Fishing, once a "mom-and-pop" kind of enterprise, had become big business, as large companies applied modern industrial techniques to an age-old profession. Traditional small fishing boats were replaced by "factory" ships that caught, processed, and froze huge volumes of fish right out on the ocean. Huge drift nets, some as long as 30 miles in length, seined hundreds of miles of oceans, bringing in millions of fish in short periods of time. The fishing industry worldwide became "efficient." Maybe too efficient.

Wild fisheries became depleted and were closed for long periods of time while natural stocks recovered. Some stocks never have recovered, and those that have are now monitored very closely by national and multinational regulatory agencies. Second-generation harvests have been carefully controlled and restricted to prevent depletion in the future.

• The demand for seafood has been increasing while, one by one, wild fisheries have reached maximum production limits. The situation reached a point in 1999 where the worldwide demand for seafood exceeded the available supply, and it will continue to do so for the foreseeable future. In other words, the increasing geometric demand curve intersected a flat (or slightly declining) supply curve.

• Marine aquaculture—the raising of fish for commercial sale—had been practiced extensively in Europe for many years, but the countries of the European Union still had to import 40 percent of their seafood.

• Industrialized Asia (Japan, South Korea, Hong Kong, and Singapore) began increasing its imports of seafood as the output of its own fisheries began to decline.

• The world's population was not decreasing.

In early 2002, our visionary oceanographer saw in this situation a viable commercial business opportunity. Together with a business consultant well versed in continuous improvement and leading-edge project and production management methodologies, the oceanographer formed Olympic AquaVentures, LLC for the purpose of creating a marine aquaculture business capable of capitalizing on the worldwide unfulfilled need identified above.

This was no small undertaking. Besides the usual competitive business pressures, marine aquaculture is, by its very nature, different from land-based farming in a number of ways. For one thing, it's in or underwater, which poses logistical challenges that a Kansas wheat farmer never faces.

For another, it uses non-owned resources—coastal and offshore waters are a resource held in common by the people of a country. Consequently, commercial aquaculture is subject to environmental and other regulatory requirements not experienced by most land-based farming businesses. (For example, not many apple orchards constitute a potential hazard to navigation.)

Then there is the issue of aesthetics. People with water views are often not pleased with the prospect of floating aquaculture facilities being visible from their windows. So, besides the technical challenges, there are social, political, and environmental hurdles to overcome as well.

And there are unique logistical constraints posed by the nature of the product: seafood is inherently more perishable, more quickly, than just about any other kind of agricultural product. Moreover, the technology associated with successful aquaculture, while not in the realm of "rocket science," is still heavily dependent on the state of the art in marine biology, and much of the research needed for aquaculture to succeed on a large scale is still underway.

All of the bulleted observations above pointed toward the potential to fill a virtually bottomless need. And all of the challenges described in the preceding paragraphs would have to be overcome in order to fill that need.

THE EXTERNAL ENVIRONMENT

The situation in the external environment is reflected in Figure D.1. Notice that the S-CRT for the worldwide seafood environment contains two critical root causes:

1. There is a high and increasing demand for fish throughout the world (101).

2. Existing aquaculture operations don't come close to filling the gap in the supply of wild-capture fish (108).

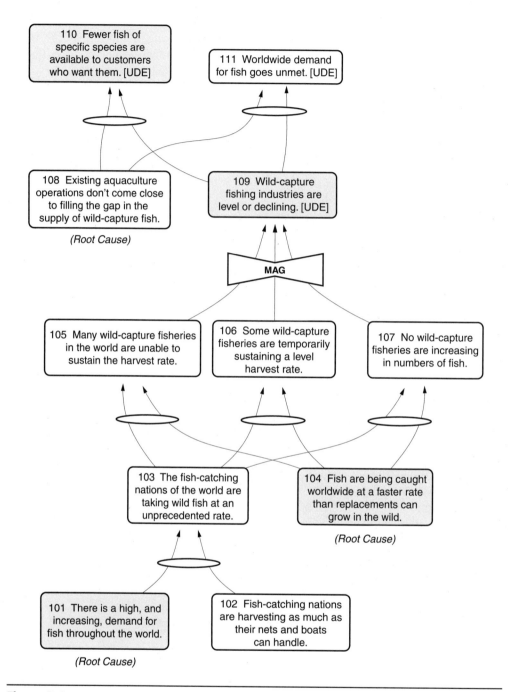

Figure D.1   Wild-capture fisheries Current Reality Tree.

On a world scale, it's virtually impossible for one organization, or even one country, to satisfy the needs implied in these root causes. But the direct and unavoidable implication is that there's excellent potential to create a highly profitable marine aquaculture operation that would enjoy the enviable situation of a never-ending worldwide demand for its products.

The oceanographer decided to explore the possibilities inherent in filling this unmet need through the creation of a significant finfish-growing operation.

CONTRIBUTING FACTORS

Beyond the worldwide supply and demand for seafood, several national and local factors combined to make the commencement of Olympic AquaVentures an opportune undertaking.

First, the United States was experiencing a $10 billion annual trade deficit in seafood, its second largest trade deficit in a natural resource behind oil. The U.S. Department of Commerce was favorably inclined to supporting any efforts to reverse that trade deficit.

Second, the marine conditions at certain locations in the Pacific northwest were ideal for establishing an aquaculture operation. The water is among the cleanest and purest in the world, and high quality, unpolluted water for growing fish is a rare treasure. Moreover, large stocks of native fish species prized throughout the industrialized world once grew there naturally, though they are largely fished out now. Farmed fish of these species made excellent candidates for grow-out, yet posed no danger to wild stocks.

The third factor was economic. The economy of the target county for the location of Olympic AquaVentures was deteriorating badly, as industries, driven by a perceived need for better efficiency, began to close and move out of the area and consolidate in larger metropolitan centers. This county had a pressing need to improve its economic condition through an increase in full-time family-wage jobs with medical benefits. The county's economic development council needed to attract existing businesses to locate there, and new business ventures to choose the county as the place to start.[*]

It's worth noting that even in places where the economy is thriving, new businesses founded on the idea of finding a need and filling it start up all the time. Many succeed, but most fail. One reason is that the founders fail to recognize all the requirements for success and to see all the pitfalls in the road ahead.

---

[*] Now, an S-CRT for the county could be constructed that would express these economic needs concisely, but that's a completely different set of strategy trees. The strategy discussed in this appendix is *not* the county's—it's Olympic AquaVentures' strategy. So I've provided the discussion of the factors above merely as a way of characterizing the local environment in which Olympic AquaVentures must operate.

Besides advantages, the contributing factors above also posed conflicts and obstacles for Olympic AquaVentures, some of which will be identified shortly. However, all of these opportunities and challenges are tailor-made for the constraint management model for strategy development, which can improve the odds of success the first time and instill confidence in the founders that they're doing the right things at the right times.

ORGANIZING A COMPLEX SITUATION

It was clear to the founders of Olympic AquaVentures that a systematic approach to developing and executing its strategy would be required. The interdependent relationship between a budding marine aquaculture business and the economic, social, political, environmental, and regulatory context almost demanded the kind of systems approach inherent in the constraint management model. Consequently, it was only natural that the founders should apply it.

They developed a complete set of strategic thinking process trees to shape the future of their creation. Some of those actual trees* are provided in this appendix as a way of illustrating what can be done with the constraint management model.

The first is a Strategic Intermediate Objectives Map (Figure D.2). Notice that this S-IO Map differs slightly from the ones illustrated in chapter 5. Technically, the S-IO Map culminates with block 100: Olympic AquaVentures' (OAV) profitability. But remember, if you look lower in the tree (block 122), you'll notice that one of the intermediate objectives is public and political support. In order to achieve that IO, at some point the public and the politicians must see the connection between OAV's success and the satisfaction of their own necessary conditions. Those conditions are reflected in the external IOs (B, C, and D) at the top of Figure D.2.

In examining the IOs in OAV's S-IO Map, three potential conflicts became obvious to the founders. These conflicts had to do with environmental concerns, aesthetics, and the treaty rights of Native American tribes. Figures D.3a through D.3c show these conflicts, their underlying assumptions, and the injections designed to resolve them.

The OAV Strategic Future Reality Tree (Figures D.4a through D.4h) outlines the strategy the company will follow to achieve the IOs in the S-IO Map. In the interest of simplifying the illustration, the references to the IOs in Figure D.2 are omitted, but an observant reader will be able to see easily the IOs in the S-FRT. There are 27 injections in this S-FRT (refer to Table D.1 for a consolidated list.) These injections are all things that must be done because they're not happening now—and won't without concerted effort.

---

* It's not possible to include all of the OAV trees here. There are too many of them, and some of them are proprietary (mostly the Prerequisite Trees).

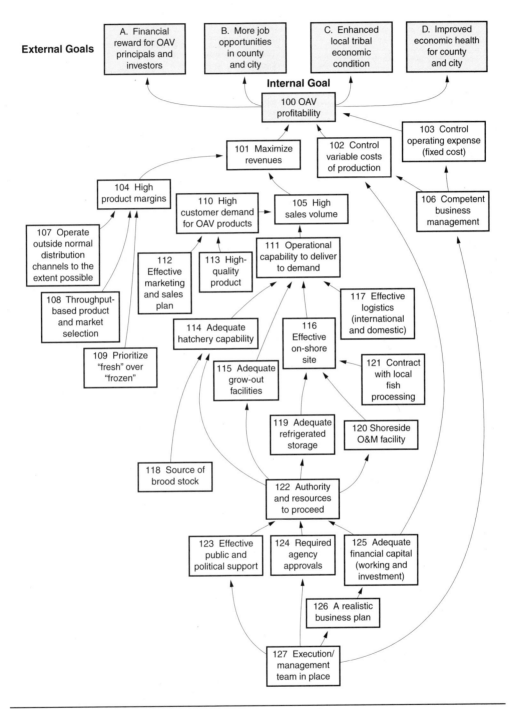

Figure D.2 Strategic IO Map—Olympic AquaVentures LLC.

Assumptions:
5. The conditions for raising fish locally are optimal.
6. There are suitable locations for siting.
7. Regulatory approvals can be obtained.
8. Sufficient funding can be obtained.
9. There are no insurmountable technological obstacles.
10. Effective shipping to customers worldwide is possible.
11. Worldwide markets will buy the fish we raise.

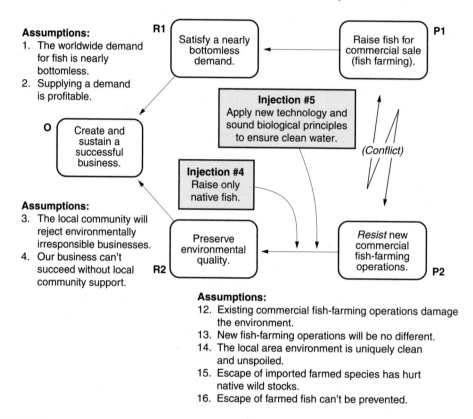

Assumptions:
1. The worldwide demand for fish is nearly bottomless.
2. Supplying a demand is profitable.

R1 Satisfy a nearly bottomless demand.

P1 Raise fish for commercial sale (fish farming).

O Create and sustain a successful business.

Injection #5
Apply new technology and sound biological principles to ensure clean water.

(Conflict)

Injection #4
Raise only native fish.

Assumptions:
3. The local community will reject environmentally irresponsible businesses.
4. Our business can't succeed without local community support.

R2 Preserve environmental quality.

P2 *Resist* new commercial fish-farming operations.

Assumptions:
12. Existing commercial fish-farming operations damage the environment.
13. New fish-farming operations will be no different.
14. The local area environment is uniquely clean and unspoiled.
15. Escape of imported farmed species has hurt native wild stocks.
16. Escape of farmed fish can't be prevented.

Figure D.3a   Strategic Conflict #1—Aquaculture industry and the environment.

Assumptions:
5. The conditions for raising fish locally are optimal.
6. There are suitable locations for siting.
7. Regulatory approvals can be obtained.
8. Sufficient funding can be obtained.
9. There are no insurmountable technological obstacles.
10. Effective shipping to customers worldwide is possible.
11. Worldwide markets will buy the fish we raise.

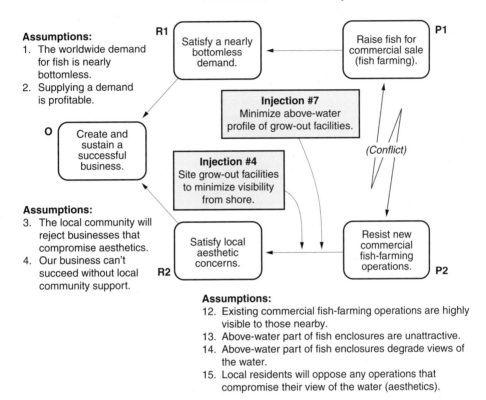

Assumptions:
1. The worldwide demand for fish is nearly bottomless.
2. Supplying a demand is profitable.

R1 Satisfy a nearly bottomless demand.

P1 Raise fish for commercial sale (fish farming).

O Create and sustain a successful business.

Injection #7
Minimize above-water profile of grow-out facilities.

Injection #4
Site grow-out facilities to minimize visibility from shore.

(Conflict)

Assumptions:
3. The local community will reject businesses that compromise aesthetics.
4. Our business can't succeed without local community support.

R2 Satisfy local aesthetic concerns.

P2 Resist new commercial fish-farming operations.

Assumptions:
12. Existing commercial fish-farming operations are highly visible to those nearby.
13. Above-water part of fish enclosures are unattractive.
14. Above-water part of fish enclosures degrade views of the water.
15. Local residents will oppose any operations that compromise their view of the water (aesthetics).

Figure D.3b Strategic Conflict #2—Aquaculture industry and aesthetics.

Assumptions:
7. The conditions for raising fish locally are optimal.
8. There are suitable locations for siting.
9. Regulatory approvals can be obtained.
10. Sufficient funding can be obtained.
11. There are no insurmountable technological obstacles.
12. Effective shipping to customers worldwide is possible.
13. Worldwide markets will buy the fish we raise.

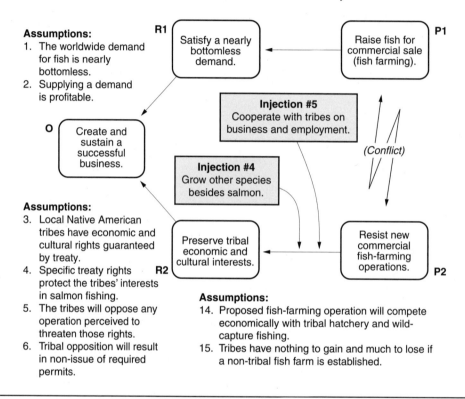

Assumptions:
1. The worldwide demand for fish is nearly bottomless.
2. Supplying a demand is profitable.

R1 — Satisfy a nearly bottomless demand.

P1 — Raise fish for commercial sale (fish farming).

O — Create and sustain a successful business.

Injection #5 Cooperate with tribes on business and employment.

Injection #4 Grow other species besides salmon.

(Conflict)

Assumptions:
3. Local Native American tribes have economic and cultural rights guaranteed by treaty.
4. Specific treaty rights protect the tribes' interests in salmon fishing.
5. The tribes will oppose any operation perceived to threaten those rights.
6. Tribal opposition will result in non-issue of required permits.

R2 — Preserve tribal economic and cultural interests.

P2 — Resist new commercial fish-farming operations.

Assumptions:
14. Proposed fish-farming operation will compete economically with tribal hatchery and wild-capture fishing.
15. Tribes have nothing to gain and much to lose if a non-tribal fish farm is established.

Figure D.3c   Strategic Conflict #3—Aquaculture industry and Native American tribes.

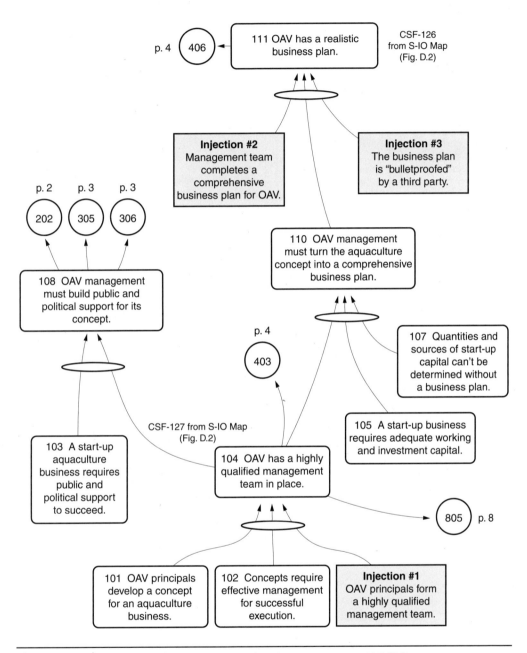

Figure D.4a Strategic Future Reality Tree—Olympic AquaVentures, LLC (#1).

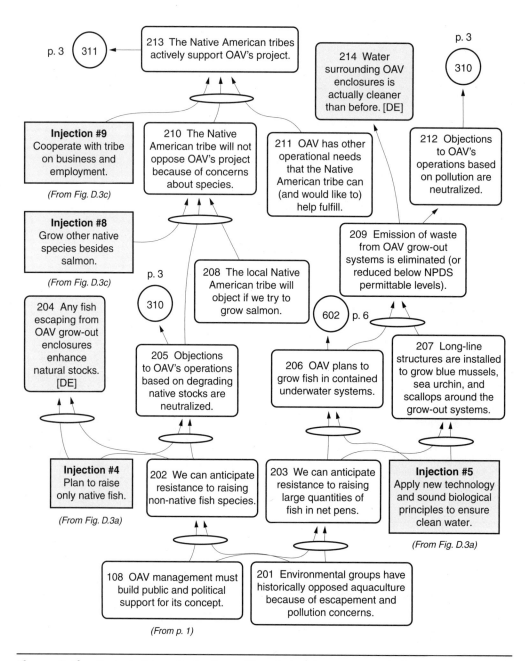

Figure D.4b Strategic Future Reality Tree—Olympic AquaVentures, LLC (#2).

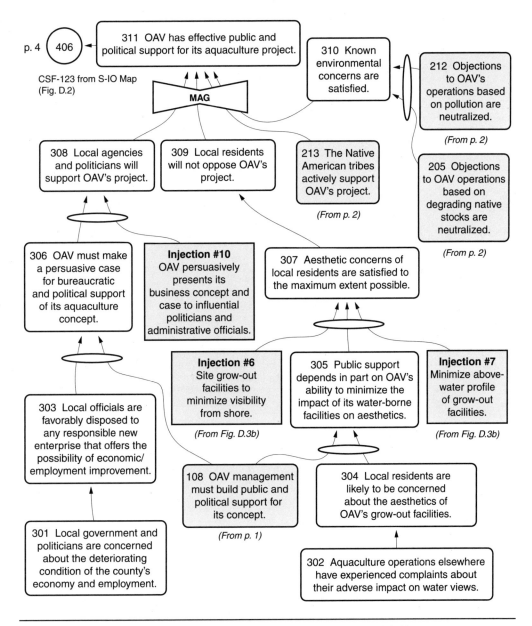

Figure D.4c   Strategic Future Reality Tree—Olympic AquaVentures, LLC (#3).

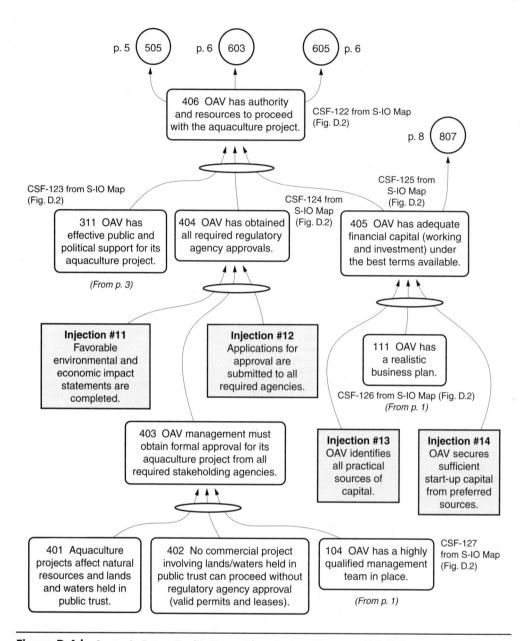

Figure D.4d   Strategic Future Reality Tree—Olympic AquaVentures, LLC (#4).

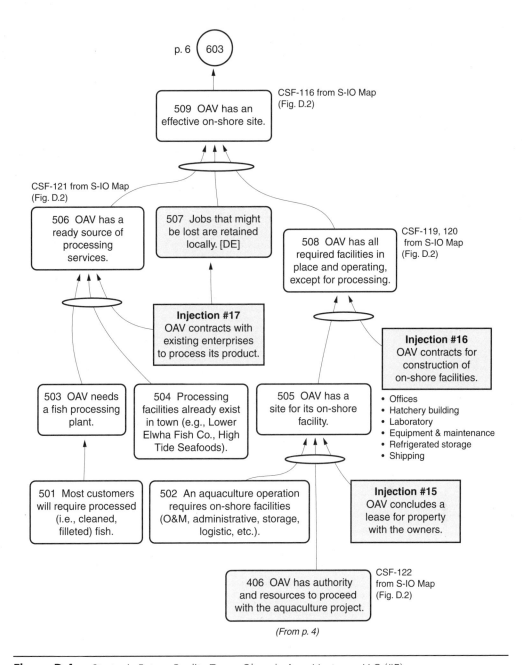

Figure D.4e Strategic Future Reality Tree—Olympic AquaVentures, LLC (#5).

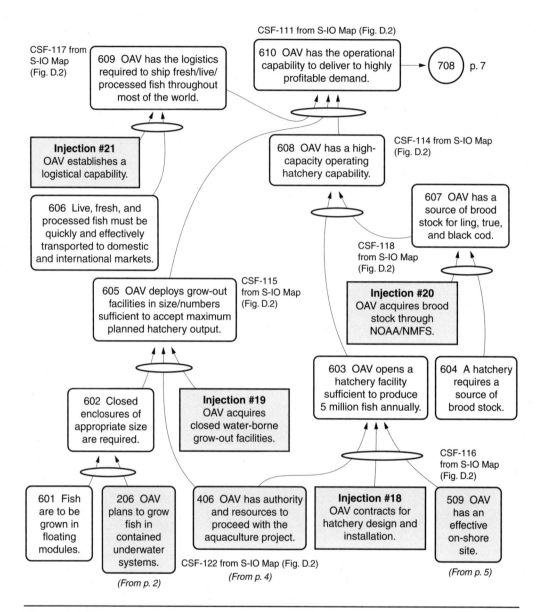

Figure D.4f   Strategic Future Reality Tree—Olympic AquaVentures, LLC (#6).

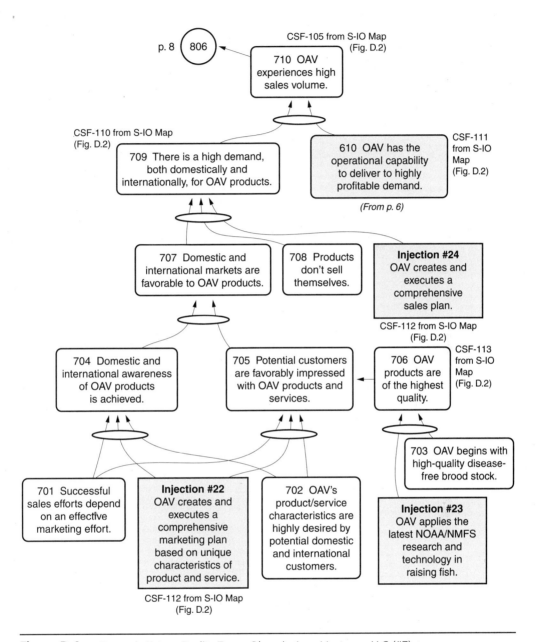

CSF-105 from S-IO Map
(Fig. D.2)

p. 8   806

710 OAV experiences high sales volume.

CSF-110 from S-IO Map
(Fig. D.2)

709 There is a high demand, both domestically and internationally, for OAV products.

610 OAV has the operational capability to deliver to highly profitable demand.

CSF-111 from S-IO Map (Fig. D.2)

(From p. 6)

707 Domestic and international markets are favorable to OAV products.

708 Products don't sell themselves.

Injection #24
OAV creates and executes a comprehensive sales plan.

CSF-112 from S-IO Map (Fig. D.2)

704 Domestic and international awareness of OAV products is achieved.

705 Potential customers are favorably impressed with OAV products and services.

706 OAV products are of the highest quality.

CSF-113 from S-IO Map (Fig. D.2)

703 OAV begins with high-quality disease-free brood stock.

701 Successful sales efforts depend on an effective marketing effort.

Injection #22
OAV creates and executes a comprehensive marketing plan based on unique characteristics of product and service.

702 OAV's product/service characteristics are highly desired by potential domestic and international customers.

Injection #23
OAV applies the latest NOAA/NMFS research and technology in raising fish.

CSF-112 from S-IO Map
(Fig. D.2)

Figure D.4g   Strategic Future Reality Tree—Olympic AquaVentures, LLC (#7).

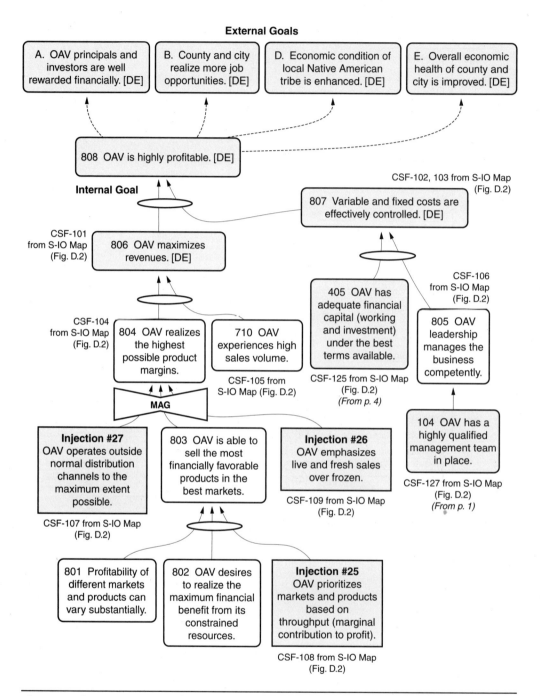

Figure D.4h   Strategic Future Reality Tree—Olympic AquaVentures, LLC (#8).

Table D.1 Summary of injections—Olympic AquaVentures, LLC.

No.	Page	Injection	PRT required?
1.	1	OAV principals form a highly qualified management team.	No
2.	1	Management team completes a comprehensive business plan for OAV.	Yes
3.	1	The business plan is "bulletproofed" by a third party.	No
4.	2	Plan to raise only native fish.	No
5.	2	Apply new technology and sound biological principles to ensure clean water.	Yes
6.	3	Site grow-out facilities to minimize visibility from shore.	Yes
7.	3	Minimize above-water profile of grow-out facilities.	Yes
8.	2	Grow other native species besides salmon.	No
9.	2	Cooperate with tribe on business and employment.	Yes
10.	3	OAV persuasively presents its business concept and case to influential politicians and administrative officials.	Yes
11.	4	Favorable environmental and economic impact statements are completed.	Yes
12.	4	Applications for approval are submitted to all required agencies.	Yes
13.	4	OAV identifies all practical sources of capital.	Yes
14.	4	OAV secures sufficient start-up capital from preferred sources.	Yes
15.	5	OAV concludes a lease for property with the owners.	Yes
16.	5	OAV contracts for construction of on-shore facilities.	Yes
17.	5	OAV contracts with existing enterprises to process its product.	Yes
18.	6	OAV contracts for hatchery design and installation.	Yes
19.	6	OAV acquires closed water-borne grow-out facilities.	Yes
20.	6	OAV acquires brood stock through NOAA/NMFS.	Yes
21.	6	OAV establishes a logistical capability.	Yes
22.	7	OAV creates and executes a comprehensive marketing plan based on unique characteristics of product and service.	Yes
23.	7	OAV applies the latest NOAA/NMFS research and technology in raising fish.	No
24.	7	OAV creates and executes a comprehensive sales plan.	Yes
25.	8	OAV prioritizes markets and products based on throughput (marginal contribution to profit).	No
26.	8	OAV emphasizes live and fresh sales over frozen.	No
27.	8	OAV operates outside normal distribution channels to the maximum extent possible.	Yes

A few of the injections are relatively straightforward. Because they pose no great difficulty, Prerequisite Trees for these injections aren't required. Most injections, however, *do* need Prerequisite Trees. Figure D.5 is offered as one example of the many Prerequisite Trees that will be required. These injections and the associated Prerequisite Trees have been converted into a meta-level critical chain project network, as explained in chapter 11 ("Projectizing" Prerequisite Trees).

All that's left now is for you to visualize how OAV's approach might be translated to *your* start-up organization.

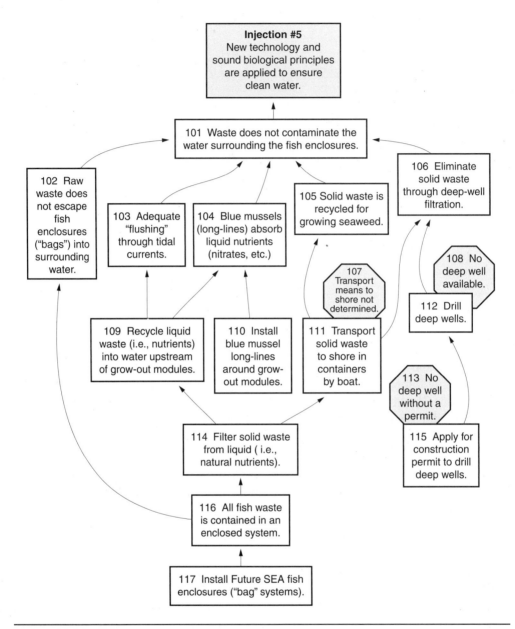

Figure D.5   Prerequisite Tree—Injection #5 Olympic AquaVentures, LLC.

Appendix E

Strategic Conflicts (Examples)

Inability to make progress is often an indication of hidden conflict between the forces of change and the forces trying to preserve the status quo. Sometimes these forces are internal to a specific individual.* Other times, they're different factions within an organization. Conflict may be obvious or recognized, or it might be subtle. When conflict poses a direct impediment to achieving the goal of an organization, it can be considered a strategic conflict.

To demonstrate the broad applicability of the Strategic Evaporating Cloud (S-EC), three examples of strategic conflict follow. One is from commercial business, one is military, and the third is from a governmental agency.**

A COMMERCIAL BUSINESS CONFLICT

Let's revisit the problem of airline profitability. There is ample evidence that the airlines were already self-destructing before the terrorist attacks. Beyond the issues related to security (baggage and passenger screening), convenience is particularly important. One reason that passengers have cited for not flying, especially since September 11, 2001, is inconvenience—too many changes of planes, too many missed connections, too many times that baggage didn't follow on the connecting flight. One of the principal culprits behind this "connection" problem is the hub-and-spoke system: all the major airlines

---

* "To be, or not to be . . . that is the question." William Shakespeare, *Hamlet,* Act II, Scene 1.

** In point of fact, *all* the logic trees in the thinking process are applicable to commercial, governmental, and military systems alike. The Strategic Evaporating Cloud offers the most concise way to demonstrate this by example.

route all flights through a few key airports, called "hubs." The routes to the outlying airports they serve are "spokes" radiating from those hubs.*

Thus, passengers wanting to fly from Philadelphia to Colorado Springs, for example, have no option to fly direct. They must fly first to the hub of some airline (Pittsburgh for U.S. Airways, Chicago or Denver for United Airlines, or Dallas-Fort Worth for Delta and American). There they must change planes, often with either too much waiting time, or too little margin for delayed arrivals, before they can fly on to Denver. Besides adding time to the overall trip, it adds stress and often inconvenience to the passenger. (For example, try getting off an inbound United flight at gate 16 in Denver, and making it to the outbound flight at gate 66 in 26 minutes without running most of the way!)

Airlines used to fly point-to-point. Why do they fly hub-and-spoke now? The short answer is cost reduction. They made a conscious decision to inconvenience the passenger in favor of reduced costs. But now passengers are deciding that inconvenience is a good reason to eliminate discretionary travel. The airlines all want to increase revenues again, and restoring point-to-point would go a long way toward eliminating passenger perception of inconvenience. But the airlines don't make any substantive strategic changes (and, for sure, the decision whether to fly point-to-point or hub-and-spoke is a strategic decision). So they find themselves in a conflict situation that looks much like Figure E.1.

To improve profitability (their objective), they must increase revenues and control costs (both nonnegotiable necessary conditions). To increase revenues, they should fly point-to-point (one prerequisite). But to keep costs under control, they should fly through hubs-and-spokes (the conflicting prerequisite).

Figure E.1 shows the assumptions associated with each side of the conflict. These assumptions may be obvious to everyone, but maybe not. They may be consciously known, or unconsciously assumed. But not all of them are valid assumptions, and these invalid assumptions prevent resolution of the conflict. By finding out which assumptions are invalid, the door opens to alternatives, which we call "injections." The basic characteristic of an injection is that it offers an option to replace one of the conflicting prerequisites without compromising either of the nonnegotiable necessary conditions.

In Figure E.1, three injections are shown. Injection #1 is something of a compromise— flying some percentage of the schedule point-to-point, perhaps at slightly increased prices for those passengers willing to pay a little more for the convenience, while the rest of the schedule is flown through the hub-and-spoke to satisfy those for whom low price is the ultimate discriminator.

Injections #2 and #3 go together. They permit the replacement completely of P2 (fly through hubs-and-spokes). Is it practical to do this? I offer for your consideration Southwest Airlines, which not only flies point-to-point exclusively, but also does so at lower fares than the other major airlines can match—and is the most profitable airline in America while doing so, too. Why is Southwest able to do this, and the other airlines don't think they can? *It's because the other airlines are operating under erroneous*

---

* One passenger at Atlanta's Hartsfield Airport was heard to remark with disgust, "When I die, I'll probably have to change in Atlanta on my way to hell!"

Assumptions:
1. There is no room to increase revenues by competing on the basis of price.
2. All major airlines fly hub-and-spoke routes.
3. Hub-and-spoke is inconvenient for passengers.
4. Many passengers value convenience enough to pay more for it (especially business flyers).

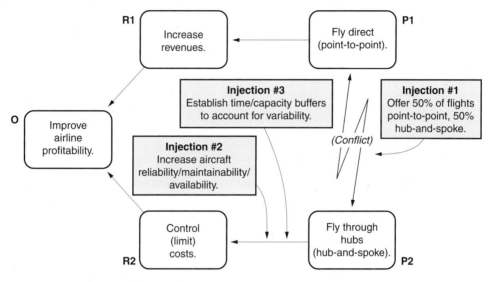

Assumptions:
5. Point-to-point requires extensive maintenance support at every stop.
6. Full maintenance support at every stop is cost-prohibitive.
7. Airplanes break down frequently, so maintenance coverage is essential at each stop.
8. Hub-and-spoke is cost-efficient for all airlines.
9. Most customers are willing to put up with the inconvenience of hub-and-spoke for lower ticket prices.
10. There is no way to fly point-to-point and keep prices low.
11. Nobody else flies anything except hub-and-spoke (i.e., no alternative for passengers).

Figure E.1   Strategic Conflict—passenger convenience and airline routes.

assumptions that they haven't yet identified! Identifying these assumptions is the first step to a breakthrough solution to their profitability problem.

A MILITARY CONFLICT

Here's a "hot" conflict pertaining to a military situation. And, boy, is it ever strategic! In the summer of 2002, the major international news issue was whether or not the United States would, or should, stage a preemptive attack on Iraq. The primary motivation for doing so was the president's concern about Iraq's evolving capability to produce nuclear weapons. This is no irrational concern. As far back as 1982, Israel took unilateral action to destroy a nuclear reactor Iraq was using to produce nuclear material for weapons. Even limited U.N. arms inspections after the Persian Gulf War revealed that Iraq was actively pursuing a nuclear weapons program. Unspecified intelligence reports since Saddam Hussein threw out the U.N. arms inspectors indicated that Iraq had been proceeding with diligence to build nuclear weapons.

Given Iraq's known support for terrorist organizations, Hussein's willingness to use poison gas on his own people as well as opponents, and unreleased intelligence reports,[*] the U.S. administration concluded that some direct action was warranted to remove Saddam Hussein from power and replace the existing Iraqi government with another one more agreeable to eliminating the nuclear threat. Through various press leaks—almost unavoidable in Washington, D.C.—the world became aware that the Bush administration intended to forcibly remove Hussein from power and remove the threat of nuclear weapons from Iraq.

The U.S. military, of course, would bear the primary responsibility for prosecuting such an attack. This prospect did not elicit much joy within the U.S. Department of Defense. You might say that the professional warriors were conflicted. On one hand, they recognized the need to achieve the objective. On the other hand, doing so posed some severe problems for them. Take a look at Figure E.2a. While it might not paint a completely accurate picture of the strategic conflict the military commanders faced, it's probably not too far wrong.[**]

The assumptions on each side of the conflict are self-explanatory. They may not be complete, and some important ones may be missing. But this conflict clearly represents the prevailing thinking within the President's inner circle.

The injections shown in Figure E.2a are not really new, breakthrough ideas. Both have been discussed in the press and in television news programs. They're offered here only as examples of possible ways to break the conflict. The accompanying sidebar on Operation Iraqi Freedom, page 279, provides some insight on the relationship between the Evaporating Cloud and the way events actually played out.

A GEOPOLITICAL CONFLICT

There's another facet to the Iraqi nuclear weapons situation, one that poses a somewhat higher-level, broader conflict. We might call this the geopolitical conflict. The military conflict embodied in Figure E.2a affected primarily the Department of Defense. The larger conflict, illustrated in Figure E.2b, might be called the State Department's conflict.

---

 [*] You *know* they're not telling everything they know.

 [**] Bear in mind that I had to construct this Evaporating Cloud from information available in the public media. (The Department of Defense must have forgotten to invite me to their planning meetings!)

Assumptions:
1. On-site search-and-destroy operations by U.S. military forces are the only way to guarantee that Iraq's nuclear weapons are eliminated.
2. On-site search-and-destroy operations by U.S. forces will be resisted violently by the Iraqi military.
3. Iraq's military is a shell of its former self, after the Persian Gulf War.
4. The Iraqi Army will be unable to mount an effective resistance to an American attack.
5. The people of Iraq will not actively support Saddam Hussein or the Iraqi military in resisting an American invasion.
6. An American invasion can be effectively executed without allied logistical support and without excessive casualties.

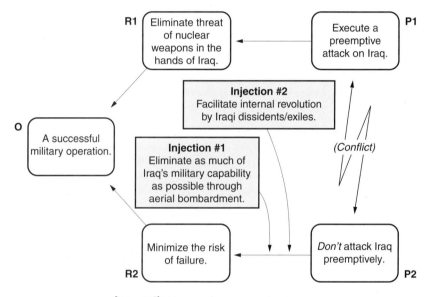

Assumptions:
7. An invasion of Iraq can't be successfully executed without regional forward deployment bases.
8. No nation in the region is willing to give the U.S. access to forward deployment bases voluntarily.
9. Iraq is prepared to put its citizens in harm's way (between its military forces/ nuclear weapons and invading American forces).
10. Many people in Iraq will help Saddam Hussein resist an American invasion.
11. An invasion is likely to incur heavy Iraqi civilian casualties.
12. A resisted invasion quickly becomes a war of attrition.

Figure E.2a   Strategic Conflict—Iraq and weapons of mass destruction (the military situation).

This is the situation that affects America's standing in the international community of nations. It develops from the same two conflicting prerequisites (to attack Iraq, or not to attack). But it leads to necessary conditions and an overall objective with considerably broader implications. Notice in this representation of the conflict, there are also assumptions shown supporting the "necessity" of the requirements (R1 and R2). The

Assumptions:
1. If Saddam Hussein has nuclear weapons available, he will use them on someone, somewhere.
2. Saddam Hussein would not hesitate to provide nuclear weapons to terrorists.

Assumptions:
5. Saddam Hussein can't be trusted to tell the truth about his nuclear weapons.
6. Hussein will not voluntarily give up nuclear weapons (or stop trying to develop them).
7. Replacement of Hussein with a more cooperative government is the only realistic way to eliminate Iraq's nuclear threat.
8. A preemptive attack on Iraq is the only way to change the government in Iraq.

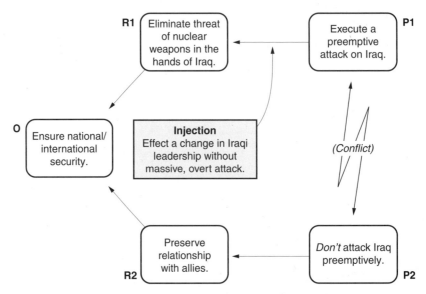

Assumptions:
3. Even as the world's only superpower, the U.S. requires favorable relations among the nations of the world.
4. The U.S. hasn't the resources to be the world's policeman alone.

Assumptions:
9. Our relationship with allies will be irreparably damaged if we attack Iraq unilaterally.
10. Allies will not support an attack on Iraq without persuasive evidence of a clear and present danger of nuclear weapons.
11. It would be logistically impossible to attack Iraq effectively without active assistance of allies in the region.
12. Some Islamic U.S. allies whose assistance is critical can't be seen to support the United States in an attack on another Islamic nation that is perceived to be unjustified.

Figure E.2b Strategic Conflict—Iraq and weapons of mass destruction (the geopolitical situation).

only reason these assumptions might need to be articulated is if there were some prospect that one or the other of the necessary conditions might be challenged.

Notice that the injection in this conflict is somewhat vague: *Effect a change in Iraqi leadership without massive, overt attack.* The instinctive reaction of most readers might be, "Yeah, right. We'll be able to do that—when pigs fly!" But the essence of the Evaporating Cloud is that it offers the opportunity—it opens the door a crack—

Operation *Iraqi Freedom*—The Military and Geopolitical Situations

It's worth noting that the conflict addressed in the second example (Figure E.2a) was resolved in a win–win manner, but the third one (Figure E.2b) was not.

Military. Even though it's highly unlikely that an Evaporating Cloud was used, the risk of heavy casualties was almost completely eliminated through a combination of psychological warfare efforts in advance of the conflict, special operations, aerial bombardment, and maneuver warfare, all of which sowed confusion in the ranks of the Iraqi military and almost completely destroyed its will to fight. (Boyd would have been proud!) Thus, both requirements (R1 and R2) in the military Evaporating Cloud were essentially satisfied. And the hostilities were favorably (for the U.S.) concluded with fewer casualties than occurred in Operation Desert Storm—in spite of the fact that the scope of the task and the operating theater were much larger, and the military force used was less than half that used 12 years earlier.

Geopolitical. After several months of diplomatic efforts, the U.S. opted to cease further efforts to enlist the cooperation of France and Germany, two traditional allies, and proceed with "forcible disarmament" of Iraq, supported by a "coalition of the willing." This was clearly a decision with strategic implications. The win–lose outcome imposed on France and Germany has strained relations between those countries and the U.S. However this situation plays out in the future, it could have been projected through the use of a negative branch (see chapter 10).

Ultimately, there may be situations in which a win–win solution—an effectively broken conflict using an Evaporating Cloud—might be technically and economically feasible (a negotiated diplomatic settlement in Iraq might have been). But it might not be politically feasible. In essence, this is what happened to precipitate Operation Iraqi Freedom. This is not to imply that win–lose solutions can't be effective. The war in Iraq clearly demonstrated that they can. In the short term, the U.S. "won" the geopolitical conflict, while France and Germany "lost." In some cases, win–lose outcomes might even be preferable, provided that you can live with the consequences!

It's possible that no diplomatically negotiated settlement between the U.S. and France and Germany would have proven effective (by U.S. standards) in the end. It's equally likely that no solution involving the use of force at *any* time, even after diplomacy was given a chance to work, would have been acceptable to France and Germany. The Evaporating Cloud isn't always a feasible way to resolve disputes. Generally, it requires that both sides are interested in resolving differences in a way that provides a win for both sides. Neither the U.S. nor France and Germany were able to reach that common ground. In any kind of strategic situation, geopolitical or business, this can be expected to happen periodically. In such cases, contrary to the opinion of some, overwhelming force (even violence) *can* resolve the situation. But both sides must fully understand the consequences and be prepared to live with them.

for a breakthrough solution: a truly creative new idea that nobody might ever have thought about otherwise. By allowing that the injection is a condition of future reality that we want to achieve, it reduces the challenge to a creative exercise in "how to make it happen," not what to do.

A LOCAL GOVERNMENT CONFLICT

In 2002 the politicians in a small seaside city were faced with a conflict: whether or not to approve a waterfront development project. The rural city, less than 20,000 in population, had been suffering economic decline for more than 10 years, as commercial fishing and logging businesses closed down because of overharvesting. Unemployment soared, crime inched upward, and the county in which the city was located ranked 29th economically out of 29 counties in the state. The city fathers were desperate to reverse this unfavorable trend.

One bright spot in the city's situation over the past 10 years had been tourism. A place of exceptional natural beauty and ecological resources (with a national park nearby), the city had attracted a healthy tourist trade during the summer months. But winters were economically bleak, and recreational tourism alone was insufficient—and too inconsistent—to sustain the city's economy year-round.

A developer approached the city with the idea of building a 140-room waterfront hotel and conference center to attract convention and meeting trade to the area. While the city would never be another Las Vegas, the town fathers believed that enough additional convention and conference trade could be attracted to offset the off-season loss of tourism. Initial steps were taken to obtain the required approvals to commence the project. The project became known publicly—and opposition was swift.

Other hotel and motel owners, already strapped for business, saw their livelihoods disappearing as a new, large hotel drew its occupancy from them. Environmentalists opposed it on the usual grounds. Many residents decried the aesthetic impact that a big hotel would have on the waterfront, and others protested the hotel's obstruction of their water view. The city fathers were faced with the conflict in Figure E.3.

Two injections could break this conflict, and they could do so by replacing either one of the conflicting prerequisites. The first injection would be for the city to contract with a market research firm to determine whether demand for a conference center actually exists, and what sort of market niche it would fill. This would be done before the final decision is made to approve the development. The second injection, exploration of alternative development opportunities, could be done simultaneously. In the event that executing the first injection reveals insufficient demand for a new conference center, a search for alternatives could already be underway. Even if there is sufficient demand to justify going ahead with the conference center, the alternative options could supplement the conference center development.

In reading the assumptions underlying R2–P2, it's clear that number 10 doesn't pertain to the economics of the hotel business. In fact, since the aesthetic/environmental complaints represent a totally different argument, it would probably be wise to separate that issue from the hotel economics dilemma. This can easily be done by constructing a different Evaporating Cloud that replaces "Maintain community harmony" in R2 with a different requirement: "Preserve aesthetics and the environment." There would be an entirely new set of assumptions under the R2–P2 part of this new conflict, and any injections would have to address aesthetics and the environment exclusively.

Assumptions:
1. The new hotel/conference center is indispensable to economic development.
2. There are no other economic development options on the horizon.
3. A new hotel/conference center is the best option for encouraging economic development.
4. The economy will actually improve with the addition of a new hotel/conference center.
5. Any adverse effects from building a new hotel/conference center are minimal or acceptable.

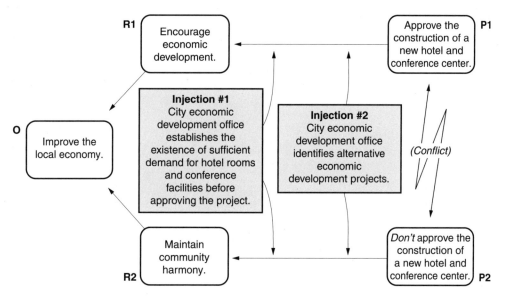

Assumptions:
6. The new hotel/conference center will degrade or kill existing motels/hotels.
7. Building a new hotel/conference center doesn't address the real local economic problems.
8. Building a new hotel/conference center will only add to existing low occupancy problems.
9. Opponents will sue to stop the project.
10. Environment/aesthetics will be degraded by adding two new large buildings to the waterfront.

Figure E.3 Strategic Conflict—local government.

SUMMARY

It's not likely that any strategy can be completely defined or executed without resolving strategic-level conflicts. This is true whether the organization in question is a commercial company, a government agency, or a not-for-profit organization. Fortunately, the Strategic Evaporating Cloud is flexible enough to accommodate different situations. For that matter, Strategic Current Reality Trees, Future Reality Trees, and Prerequisite Trees are, too.

Appendix F
Strategic "Wisdom"

People are keen observers of organizational policy and behavior. Often they can be exceptionally creative in expressing their observations. Over a period of years, I have encountered some of these expressions. Most were meant to be humorous. A few are sad commentaries on the way business is typically done today.

I've included below three such expressions that I believe are pertinent to the discussion of strategy: *Murphy's Laws of Combat, The Book of Douglas,* and *Dead Horse Strategies.* Each in its own way offers some words of wisdom about the formation or execution of strategy. Perhaps you'll find a few "nuggets of gold" in these.

MURPHY'S LAWS OF COMBAT

1. You are not a superman.

2. If it's stupid but works, it ain't stupid.

3. Cluster bombing from B-52s is very, very accurate. (The bombs always hit the ground.)

4. It is generally inadvisable to eject directly over the area you just bombed.

5. Don't look conspicuous; it draws fire. (This is why aircraft carriers are called "bomb magnets.")

6. Any ship can be a minesweeper—once.

7. Don't draw fire; it irritates the people around you.

8. Whoever said the pen is mightier than the sword obviously never encountered automatic weapons.

9. Don't ever be the first, don't ever be the last, and don't ever volunteer to do anything.

10. Never tell the platoon sergeant you have nothing to do.

11. "Aim towards the enemy." (Instruction printed on U.S. rocket launcher)

12. When in doubt, empty your magazine.

13. When the pin is pulled, Mr. Grenade is not our friend.

14. Never share a foxhole with anyone braver than you are.

15. Never forget that your weapon was made by the lowest bidder.

16. If your attack is going well, it's an ambush.

17. No plan survives first contact with the enemy intact.

18. All five-second grenade fuzes will burn down in three seconds.

19. If you are forward of your unit position, the artillery will fall short.

20. The enemy diversion you are ignoring is the main attack.

21. The most important things are always simple.

22. The simple things are always hard.

23. The easy way is always mined.

24. If you are short of everything except enemy, you are in combat.

25. When you have secured an area, don't forget to tell the enemy.

26. Incoming fire has the right-of-way.

27. Friendly fire isn't.

28. Mines are equal opportunity weapons.

29. If the enemy is in range, so are *you*.

30. No combat-ready unit has ever passed inspection.

31. Beer math: Two beers times 37 men equals 49 cases.

32. Body count: Two guerrillas plus one portable plus two pigs equals 37 enemy killed in action.

33. Things that must be together to work usually can't be shipped together.

34. Radios will fail as soon as you need fire support desperately.

35. Anything you do can get you shot, including doing nothing.

36. Tracers work both ways.

37. The only thing more accurate than incoming enemy fire is friendly fire.

38. Make it tough for the enemy to get in, and you won't be able to get out.

39. If you take more than your fair share of objectives, you will have more than your fair share of objectives to take.

40. When both sides are convinced that they are about to lose, they are both right.

41. Professional soldiers are predictable, but the world is full of amateurs.

42. Murphy was a grunt (foot soldier).

43. If you find yourself in a fair fight, you didn't plan your mission properly.

THE BOOK OF DOUGLAS

In the late 1980s, the Douglas Aircraft Division of the McDonnell-Douglas Corporation (now a part of Boeing), attempted to grasp total quality management with a vengeance. Though it was touted as a corporate strategy, there was little or no connection between the execution (implementation) and any real consideration of strategy at the corporate level. It became little more than an exercise in cost-cutting to make the Division's product lines more competitive with those of Boeing and Airbus. The effort, dubbed total quality management systems (TQMS) had a disastrous impact on the Douglas Aircraft Division and its people. Around 1990, the TQMS story, as seen from the perspective of the workforce and rendered into a biblical verse style, began circulating anonymously through the company's e-mail system as "The Book of Douglas." This long verse is presented here in its entirety, poetic but tragic testimony to the disconnect between strategy and implementation.

In the beginning was the plan and the assumptions.
And the assumptions were without form, and full of voids.
For the plan was completely without substance;
And darkness was upon the face of the workers.

And the workers went unto their section managers,
And said:
"The plan is a crock of shit, and it stinks."

And the section managers went unto their branch Managers and said: "It is a pail of dung, and none may abide the odor thereof."

And the branch managers went unto their managers and said:
"It is a container of excretion, and it is very strong,
Such that none here may abide by it."

And the managers went unto their Director and said:
"It is a vessel of fertilizer, and none may abide its strength."

And the Director went unto the Vice President Deputy General Manager and said:
"It contains that which aids plant growth and it is very strong."

*And the Vice President Deputy General Manager
   went unto the Vice President and said:*
"It promotes growth and is very powerful."

*And the Vice President went unto the President
   and said:*
*"This powerful new plan will actively promote the
   growth and efficiency*
*Of the departments and their area's productivity
   and quality of product,*
*Yea, unto all their customers, both internal and
   external."*
And the President looked upon the plan
*And believing all that was said to him, saw that it
   was good.*
For he sought not the council of those who knew.

And, lo, the plan became TQMS.
Darkness was upon the face of the workers
*And a great wailing and gnashing of teeth were
   heard throughout the land.*

Rumors, and rumors of rumors, filled the air;
*Lines both horizontal and vertical divided the
   leaders from their followers.*

And the President heard the rumors,
*And the lamentations of the workers filled his
   dreams.*

So the President came before the workers,
*At least the workers of the Tribe called "Salaried,"
   and spoke unto them, saying:*

*"Let me share with you my vision of what we
   can do*
And where we can go together."

*"We can starve the Giant to the North by stealing
   his substance;*
*And we can trample the frogs to the East with feet
   shod with protectionism."*

"But only if we go forth together because
Now Everything Depends On Everyone;
*And we must Satisfy Your Customers with first time
   Quality;*
And work Exactly To The Requirements,
*Or Cause the Requirements To Be Officially
   Changed.*

*For have I not gone unto those who form the minds
   of the masses*
And said unto them, 'Walk like you talk'?
*And have they not spread this about the land on
   paper both white and yellow?*

We must now show that we are not infirmed
*And that the corridors of our city are not filled
   with those despised members*
Of the tribe Walkers of the Halls."

*And the President said: "I have pulled down the
   House of Douglas,*
And laid bare the skeletons in the closet.
*I have cast down the Hordes of those called
   Directors,*
But with compassion will I not cast them out."

*"I will take those who are cast down and join them
   to the Family of the Staff,*
*So that they may bring Wisdom and Knowledge
   among you."*

*As he spoke, the other members of Family of
   the Staff*
Muttered and murmured among themselves, saying:
*"He steals our future, and our way is blocked by
   falling bodies.*
*He sends among us the fallen clad in rich clothing
   and heavy with coin.*
*Who will we be now? Fetchers of water and
   keepers of notes?"*

*But the President heard not their discontent and
   continued.*
"I have stirred the pot and pruned the tree,
*So where once there were many branches now
   there are but five.*

*"You will all come before my chosen and be
   appraised by them,*
*For I seek among you diamonds and rubies from
   among the common stones."*
But his words fell on deaf ears among those
*Who had seen members of the House of
   Management*
*And the Family of the Staff receive the summons to
   appear before the chosen.*
*For they formed a mighty pool from which few
   could be picked,*
*Leaving those not of the House of Management or
   Family of the Staff*
With future closed, chosen not.

*So the President spoke into the night, and he
   began to see heads*
*Moving in agreement, seeing not that the eyes of
   the Workers were closed,*
Like their ears.
And they saw nor heard naught.

The Workers saw not the vision, for the makers of
   the vision
Spoke not with the workers but hid themselves
   away
In caves both big and small.
The City of Aircraft teemed with teams, but the
   team spirit
Found not its way to the workers.
Those who knew spoke not, while those who knew
   not spoke loudly.

The leaders came not among the people; neither
   the President, nor the Vice President,
Nor the Vice President General Manager,
Nor the Vice President Deputy General Manager
   were seen by the workers.

Neither were they seen by those of the Tribe called
   "Salaried"
Nor those of the Tribe called "Hourly."

And darkness was on the face of the land.

DEAD HORSE STRATEGIES

Dakota tribal wisdom says that when you discover you're riding a dead horse, the best strategy is to dismount. However, in business we often try other strategies with dead horses, including the following:

1. Buy a stronger whip.

2. Change riders.

3. Threaten the horse with termination.

4. Say things like, "This is the way we have always ridden this horse."

5. Appoint a committee to study the horse.

6. Arrange to visit other sites to see how they ride dead horses.

7. Lower the standards so that dead horses can be included.

8. Appoint a tiger team to revive the dead horse.

9. Ride the dead horse "outside the box."

10. Buy a commercial off-the-shelf dead horse.

11. Create a training session to increase our riding ability.

12. Reclassify the dead horse as "living-impaired."

13. Donate the dead horse to a recognized charity, thereby deducting its full original cost, which can be applied against a new dying horse.

14. Compare the state of dead horses in today's environment.

15. Change the autopsy report to declare that "This horse is not dead."

16. Kill all the other horses, so this one will look the same.

17. Name the dead horse "Paradigm Shift" and keep riding it.

18. Ride the dead horse "smarter," not harder.

19. Hire outside contractors to ride the dead horse.

20. Harness several dead horses together for increased speed.

21. Do a time management study to see if the lighter riders would improve productivity.

22. Declare that "No horse is too dead to beat."

23. Call the dead horse a "joint venture" and let others ride it.

24. Provide additional funding to increase the horse's performance.

25. Do a cost analysis study to see if contractors can ride it cheaper.

26. Purchase an aftermarket product to make dead horses run faster.

27. Declare the horse is "better, faster, and cheaper" dead.

28. Form a quality circle to find uses for dead horses.

29. Rewrite the expected performance requirements for horses.

30. Declare that "This horse was procured with cost as an independent variable."

31. Get the horse a Web site.

32. Promote the dead horse to a supervisory position.

Glossary

categories of legitimate reservation (CLR): A set of eight rules of logic used to verify the validity of logical connections in a current reality tree or future reality tree.

core problem (CP): A root cause that connects to a substantial majority of the undesirable effects in a current reality tree, including the worst one(s). Always a system constraint.

critical success factor (CSF): One of a very few nonnegotiable necessary conditions that must be satisfied in order for the goal to be achieved; discrete elements whose presence is required for success. Having them alone is not a guarantee of success, but not having them is a guarantee of failure. See "Necessary Condition."

Current Reality Tree (CRT): A logic tree that shows an unbroken chain of cause and effect between undesirable effects and the root causes that produce them; it also depicts lateral dependencies among elements of a system.

desirable effect (DE): A favorable outcome, as measured against a standard established by the system's goal or necessary conditions. An indication (positive) that the goal or a necessary condition is being achieved. The ultimate outcome of an injection.

Evaporating Cloud (EC): A five-element diagram used to express inherent or hidden conflict that exists within a system or situation. Designed to facilitate resolution of conflict. Sometimes referred to as a *conflict resolution diagram.* Composed of an objective, two requirements, and two conflicting prerequisites. Supported by assumptions concerning each logical connection in the diagram.

Future Reality Tree (FRT): A logic tree that shows an unbroken chain of cause and effect between a contemplated action (injection) and the ultimate desired effects of that action. A means to test the logical validity of a proposed change before actually committing resources to the change.

goal: The ultimate or long-term end or reason for doing something or participating in an activity; the expected ultimate outcome.

injection: An action or condition that does not currently exist in reality, and which must be initiated by someone in order to ultimately produce desired effects that don't exist now. An entry point into a future reality tree or negative branch.

intermediate objective (IO): One of several elements in a Prerequisite Tree or Intermediate Objective Map; a discrete intermediate action or condition that must be performed or achieved in order for another intermediate objective, or the ultimate injection, to be achieved. Sometimes intended to overcome an obstacle. Sometimes merely a necessary condition without an obstacle.

Intermediate Objective (IO) Map: A hierarchical structure of necessary conditions, in the sequence they must be achieved, leading to attainment of a goal or overall objective. A type of Prerequisite Tree, but without obstacles and including intermediate objectives for which there is no particular paired obstacle. At a strategic level, an IO map represents the system goal and the hierarchy of necessary conditions (critical success factors) without which the goal cannot be achieved.

investment, or inventory (I): All the money a system invests in the physical capacity (plant, facilities, equipments, and other illiquid assets) or the raw material needed for conversion into salable product; money tied up within the system.

Johari window: A conceptual model of knowledge; a two-by-two matrix that characterizes what we know and don't know about ourselves, and what others know and don't know about us. (In this book we adapt the concept to classify our own knowledge about our environment into: (a) that which we *know,* and *know* that we know; (b) that which we *know* and *don't know* that we know; (c) that which we *don't know,* and *know* that we don't know it; and (d) that which we *don't know,* and *don't know* that we don't know it.)

Joint Operation Planning and Execution System (JOPES): The process used by the U.S. Department of Defense and the unified commands to plan large-scale integrated combat operations in specific geographic theaters; integrated with and fully supports the policies and objectives of the JSPS.

Joint Strategic Planning System (JSPS): The process used by the U.S. Department of Defense to create a fully integrated (land, sea, and air) global military strategy that achieves national military objectives.

objective: A shorter-term outcome; the expected result of a limited operation or tactical effort.

OODA loop. A prescriptive repeating cycle of four actions (observe, orient, decide, act) than enable a person or an organization to adapt to a changing environment. Created by John R. Boyd to characterize dynamic systems from individuals all the way up through complex organizations. Cycling through your own OODA loop faster than opponents can cycle through theirs produces victory in competition.

operating expense (OE): All the money a system pays out in recurring expenses to open the doors for business each day; all categories of fixed expenses (excluding investment/inventory items), including direct and indirect labor; money flowing out of the system.

magnitudinal "and": A bowtie-shaped symbol used in a current reality tree or future reality tree to represent an additive effect among several independent causes. Each cause alone is capable of producing some degree of the indicated effect, but in combination the effect is magnified.

mission: The chosen activity or business an organization elects to engage in, or is assigned; equivalent to a purpose; "the business we're in."

mission, enemy, terrain and weather, troops and support available, time, and civil considerations (METT-TC): Factors a military commander considers when developing the commander's intent for subordinate units. Elements of intelligence needed to formulate an effective combat operation strategy.

necessary condition (NC): A condition essential to the attainment of a goal. Failure to satisfy the necessary condition precludes or seriously degrades goal attainment.

negative branch (NB): A special kind of Future Reality Tree designed to identify unintended, undesirable consequences of an action (injection). May be part of a larger Future Reality Tree that shows desirable effects, or may stand alone. Intended to permit action to be planned to prevent the emergence of the new undesirable effect.

policy constraint: A policy, originating either within a system or without, that constitutes a core problem or root cause of failure to achieve the system's goal or a necessary condition (undesirable effect).

Prerequisite Tree (PRT): A logic tree that depicts the obstacles to executing a chosen course of action (injection), the intermediate objectives required to overcome the obstacles, and the sequence in which they must be completed for the injection to occur.

purpose: See "mission."

root cause (RC): The lowest level of cause in a current reality tree over which a decision maker has some latitude to influence or change. Often a system constraint.

sufficiency ellipse: A symbol used in a current reality tree or future reality tree to indicate dependency among multiple causes. "Dependency" in a logic tree (represented by an ellipse) means that the removal or absence of any one cause precludes the indicated effect from occurring (that is, all causes represented must be present).

throughput (T): All the new money, over and above variable costs, a for-profit system generates from the sale (to outside customers) of product or services; in a not-for-profit company, throughput is some other nonfinancial measure of goal attainment.

undesirable effect (UDE): An unfavorable outcome, as measured against a standard established by the system's goal or necessary conditions. An indication (negative) of a breakdown in a system, or the failure to achieve the system's goal or a necessary condition. Results from a root cause or core problem.

vision: An image, mental or documented, of what the future will look like when the mission is successfully accomplished and the goal is achieved.

value: A principle or guideline, voluntarily assumed, that is considered crucial for the organization to adhere to in the pursuit of its goal.

Bibliography

Ackoff, R. L. *A Concept of Corporate Planning.* New York: John Wiley & Sons, 1970.

Adams, M. "Airport gridlock." *USA Today* (14 August 2000).

———. "Frequent Fliers Not So Frequent after Sept. 11 Attacks." *USA Today* (27 November 2001).

Alderfer, C. P. *Existence, Relatedness, and Growth: Human Needs in Organizational Settings.* New York: The Free Press, 1972.

Altshuller, G., trans. by L. Shulyak. *And Suddenly the Inventor Appeared* (Worcester, MA: Technical Innovation Center, 1992).

Andrews, K. R. *The Concept of Corporate Strategy.* Homewood, IL: Richard D. Irwin, 1971.

Ansoff, H. I. "The State of Practice in Planning Systems." *Sloan Management Review* (winter 1977): 1–24.

———. *Implanting Strategic Management.* Englewood Cliffs, NJ: Prentice Hall, 1984.

Ansoff, H. I., et al. "Does Planning Pay? The Effect of Planning on Success of Acquisitions in American Firms." *Long Range Planning* III, no. 2 (December 1970): 2–7.

Athey, T. H. *Systematic Systems Approach: An Integrated Method for Solving Systems Problems.* Englewood Cliffs, NJ: Prentice Hall, 1982.

Boyd, J. R. *A Discourse on Winning and Losing,* an unpublished overhead slide presentation (1987).

Bulkeley, W. M. "Travel Fears, Economy Trims Turnout at Corporate Conventions, Meetings." *Wall Street Journal,* (11 January 2002).

Burton, J. G. *The Pentagon Wars: Reformers Challenge the Old Guard.* Annapolis, MD: Naval Institute Press, 1993.

"The New Breed of Strategic Planner." *Business Week.* (September 17, 1984): 62–66, 68.

Burns, T., and G. M. Stalker. *The Management of Innovation.* London: Tavistock Publications, 1961.

Caspari, J. A. *Constraint Management: Using Constraints Accounting Measurement to Lock in a Process of Ongoing Improvement.* Unpublished as of July 2002, but available by individual arrangement with John Caspari (JACaspari@aol.com).

Christensen, C. R., et al. *Business Policy: Text and Cases,* 5th ed. Homewood, IL: Richard D. Irwin, 1982.

Clancy, T. and F. Franks, Jr. *Into the Storm: A Study in Command.* New York: G.P. Putnam's Sons, 1997.

Clark, C. *Brainstorming: How to Create Successful Ideas.* North Hollywood, CA: Melvin Powers Wilshire, 1958.

Coram, R. *Boyd: The Fighter Pilot Who Changed the Art of War.* New York: Little, Brown, and Co., 2002.

Corbett, T. *Throughput Accounting.* Great Barrington, MA: The North River Press, 1998.

Costello, J. "Alaska Airlines Is Publicly Offering Elite Status to United Frequent Fliers." *Wall Street Journal* (8 January 2002).

Cowley, M., and E. Domb. *Beyond Strategic Vision: Effective Corporate Action with Hoshin Planning.* Boston, MA: Butterworth-Heineman, 1997.

Delbecq, A., A. Van de Ven, and D. Gustafson. *Group Techniques for Program Planning: A Guide to Nominal Group and Delphi Processes.* Middleton, WI: Green Briar Press, 1986.

Deming, W. E. *The New Economics for Industry, Government, Education.* Cambridge, MA: MIT Center for Advanced Engineering, 1993.

Dettmer, H. W. *Goldratt's Theory of Constraints: A Systems Approach to Continuous Improvement.* Milwaukee: ASQ Quality Press, 1996.

———. *Breaking the Constraints to World-Class Performance.* Milwaukee: ASQ Quality Press, 1998.

French, J. R. P., and B. Raven. "The Basis of Social Power." in *Studies in Social Power,* ed. D. Cartwright. University of Michigan: Ann Arbor Institute for Social Research, 1959.

Fullhart, R., and K. Quinn. "TOC Application: U.S. Transportation Command." Videotape SJC-4. Avraham Y. Goldratt Institute, 1994.

Gibson, J. L., J. M. Ivancevich, and J. H. Donnelly, Jr. *Organizations: Behavior, Structure, and Processes,* 7th ed. Homewood, IL: Richard D. Irwin, 1991.

Goldratt, E. M. *Critical Chain.* Great Barrington, MA: The North River Press, 1997.

———. *The Goal: A Process of Ongoing Improvement,* 2nd rev. ed. Croton-on-Hudson, NY: The North River Press, 1992.

———. *Goldratt Satellite Program.* Tape #8, "Strategy and Tactics." The Netherlands: A.Y.G.I. Limited. (www.eligoldratt.com), 1999.

———. *The Haystack Syndrome: Sifting Information Out of the Data Ocean.* Croton-on-Hudson, NY: The North River Press, 1990.

Gray, D. H. "Uses and Misuses of Strategic Planning." *Harvard Business Review* (January–February 1986): 89–97.

Hammond, G. T. *The Mind of War: John Boyd and American Security.* Washington, D.C.: Smithsonian Institution Press, 2001.

Hamza, K. Interview on PBS-TV, *Frontline,* PBS and WGBH, 1999. (Transcript: http://www.pbs.org/wgbh/pages/frontline/shows/unscom/interviews/hamza.html.)

Heinlein, R. A. *Expanded Universe.* New York: The Berkeley Publishing Group, 1980.

Hekhuis, D. J., "Commentary." In D. E. Schendel and C.W. Hofer, eds., *Strategic Management: A New View of Business Policy and Planning.* Boston, MA: Little, Brown, 1979.

Herzberg, F., B. Mausner, and B. Snyderman. *The Motivation to Work.* New York: John Wiley and Sons, 1959.

Holley, D. "Toyota Heads Down a New Road." *Los Angeles Times* (16 March 1997).

Joint Staff Officers College, JSOC Publication 1, *Joint Staff Officers Guide,* 2000.

Kanter, R. M. "Power Failures in Management Circuits." *Harvard Business Review* (July–August 1979): 65–75.

Krone, R. M. *Systems Analysis and Policy Sciences.* New York: John Wiley and Sons, 1980.

Leach, L. P. *Critical Chain Project Management.* Boston: Artech House, 2000.

Lepore, D., and O. Cohen. *Deming and Goldratt: The Theory of Constraints and the System of Profound Knowledge.* Great Barrington, MA: The North River Press, 1999.

Lilly, R. T., with F. O. Smith. *The Road to Manufacturing Success: Common Sense Throughput Solutions for Small Business.* Boca Raton, FL: St. Lucie Press, 2001.

Lind, W. S., et al. "Changing the Face of War: Into the Fourth Generation." *Marine Corps Gazette* (October 1989): 22–26.

Luft, J. *Group Processes: An Introduction to Group Dynamics,* 2nd ed. Palo Alto, CA: National Press Books, 1970.

Maslow, A. H. *Motivation and Personality.* New York: Harper and Row, 1954.

McClelland, D. C. "Business Drive and National Achievement." *Harvard Business Review* (July–August 1962): 99–112.

McNeilly, M. *Sun Tzu and the Art of Business: Six Strategic Principles for Managers.* New York: Oxford University Press, 1996.

Mintzberg, H. *The Rise and Fall of Strategic Planning.* New York: The Free Press, 1994.

Mintzberg, H., B. Ahlstrand, and J. Lampel. *Strategy Safari: A Guided Tour through the Wilds of Strategic Management.* New York: The Free Press, 1998.

Newbold, R. C. *Project Management in the Fast Lane: Applying the Theory of Constraints.* Boca Raton, FL: CRC/St. Lucie Press, 1998.

Noreen, E., D. Smith, and J. Mackey. *The Theory of Constraints and Its Implications for Management Accounting.* Great Barrington, MA: The North River Press, 1995.

Porter, M. E. *Competitive Strategy.* New York: The Free Press, 1980.

———. "Corporate Strategy: The State of Strategic Thinking." *The Economist* 303, no. 7499 (23 May 1987):17–22.

Pyzdek, T. *The Handbook for Quality Management.* Tucson, AZ: Quality Publishing, 2000.

Reuters News Service (CNN Financial Network). "Lucent Ousts Hopkins as CFO." (6 May 2001).

Ringbakk, K. A. "The Corporate Planning Life Cycle—An International Point of View." *Long Range Planning* (September 1972): 10–20.

Royko, M. *Boss: Richard J. Daley of Chicago.* New York: E. P. Dutton, 1971.

Rumelt, R. P. "Evaluation of Strategy: Theory and Models." In D. E. Schendel and C. W. Hofer, eds., *Strategic Management.* Boston, MA: Little, Brown, 1979.

Scheinkopf, L. J. *Thinking for a Change: Putting the TOC Thinking Processes to Work.* Boca Raton, FL: CRC/St. Lucie Press, 1999.

Schragenheim, E., and H. W. Dettmer. *Manufacturing at Warp Speed: Optimizing Supply Chain Financial Performance.* Boca Raton, FL: St. Lucie Press, 2000.

Seattle Times, "Postal Service May End Saturday Delivery." (3 April 2001).

Selden, P. H. *Sales Process Engineering.* Milwaukee: ASQ Quality Press, 1997.

Siegel, G. B., and R. Clayton. *Mass Interviewing and Marshalling of Ideas to Improve Performance.* Lanham, MD: University Press of America (Rowan and Littlefield Publishing), 2001.

Soto, O. R. "Rohr Reports Big Increase in Earnings; Riverside Plant Said Safe from Being Closed Down." *The Press-Enterprise* (Riverside, CA), (22 May 1996).

Smith, D. *The Measurement Nightmare: How the Theory of Constraints Can Resolve Conflicting Strategies, Policies, and Measures.* Boca Raton, FL: The St. Lucie Press. 2000.

Starbuck, W. H. "Acting First and Thinking Later: Theory versus Reality in Strategic Change." In J. M. Pennings et al., *Organizational Strategy and Change.* (San Francisco: Jossey-Bass, 1985): 336–72.

Strauss, G. "Airlines' Finances Shaken Again." *USA Today* (13 November 2001).

Sun Tzu. *The Art of War.* Translated by Thomas Cleary. Boston, MA: Shambhala Publications, 1988.

Terninko, J., A. Zusman, and B. Zlotin. *Systematic Innovation: An Introduction to TRIZ.* Boca Raton, FL: St. Lucie Press, 1997.

Trottman, M. "Antidotes to Airport Rage." *Wall Street Journal* (14 August 2000).

USA Today, "Post Office Considering E-Mail Services." (8 August 2000).

U.S. Air Force Handbook (1999). http://www.af.mil/ lib/congress/1999/106handbk.pdf

U.S. Army Field Manual 3-0, *Operations,* June 2001.

Webster's New Universal Unabridged Dictionary. New York: Barnes and Noble Co., 1989.

Weihrich, H., and H. Koontz. *Management: A Global Perspective,* 10th ed. New York: McGraw-Hill, 1993.

Index